# DID
# MUHAMMAD
# EXIST?

# DID MUHAMMAD EXIST?

An Inquiry into
Islam's Obscure Origins

**ROBERT SPENCER**

Wilmington, Delaware

The images on pages 43 and 46 are © Dumbarton Oaks, Byzantine Collection, Washington, DC, and are reprinted with permission from Dumbarton Oaks. The images on page 44 originally appeared in Karl-Heinz Ohlig and Gerd-R. Puin, eds., *Die dunklen Anfänge* (Berlin: Verlag Hans Schiler, 2005), and are reprinted with permission from Verlag Hans Schiler and Volker Popp.

Library of Congress Cataloging-in-Publication Data

Spencer, Robert, 1962–
  Did Muhammad exist? : an inquiry into Islam's obscure origins / by Robert Spencer.
     p. cm.
  Includes bibliographical references (p. 239) and index.
  ISBN 978-1-61017-061-1
  1. Muhammad, Prophet, d. 632. 2. Islam—Controversial literature. 3. Koran—Controversial literature. 4. Koran—Criticism, interpretation, etc. I. Title.
  BT1170.S645 2012
  297.6'3—dc23
                        2011052576

Published in the United States by:

ISI Books
Intercollegiate Studies Institute
3901 Centerville Road
Wilmington, Delaware 19807-1938
www.isibooks.org

Manufactured in the United States of America

Dedicated to all those who do not fear to go
wherever the truth may lead them

*Note:* No system of transliteration for Arabic words and names is entirely satisfactory. English simply is not equipped to render the subtleties of the Arabic alphabet. I have systematized the spelling in the quotations for the ease of the reader and have generally eliminated the apostrophes that stand in English texts for various elements of the Arabic alphabet, except where words are in common use, such as *Qur'an*, and where the result of the removal of such marks is unfortunate in English, such as *Sad* rather than *Sa'd*.

# Contents

Foreword *by Johannes J. G. Jansen*                                    ix
Chronology of Key Events                                               xiii
Muhammad and His Family, according to Islamic Tradition                xvi

Introduction      The Full Light of History?                           1
Chapter 1         The Man Who Wasn't There                            17
Chapter 2         Jesus, the Muhammad                                 41
Chapter 3         Inventing Muhammad                                  63
Chapter 4         Switching On the Full Light of History              87
Chapter 5         The Embarrassment of Muhammad                      107
Chapter 6         The Unchanging Qur'an Changes                      125
Chapter 7         The Non-Arabic Arabic Qur'an                       143
Chapter 8         What the Qur'an May Have Been                      161
Chapter 9         Who Collected the Qur'an?                          187
Chapter 10        Making Sense of It All                             203

Notes                                                                 219
Further Reading                                                       239
Acknowledgments                                                       241
Index                                                                 243

# Foreword

*by Johannes J. G. Jansen*

**M**uhammad, the prophet of Islam, is strongly present in the minds of millions of Muslims. This makes it difficult to imagine that he may not have been an actual person—as real as Richard Nixon.

Muslims have a strong and vivid memory of the founder of the religious movement we now know as Islam. This memory appears to be so strong and so vivid that even academic professionals whose daily duties include weighing the evidence for and against Muhammad's historicity must have days in which they think that their intellectual pursuits make no sense.

It is indeed tempting to believe that Muhammad existed in the same way our forefathers did, if only because he is fully alive in the mind of his followers. But a closer look at the historical evidence may soon make the skeptic envious of all those who believe Muhammad really existed. It must be a blessing indeed to be able to believe there are no problems with Muhammad's historicity.

Logicians have repeatedly argued that nonexistence cannot be proved. When the British philosopher Bertrand Russell once suggested that there was no rhinoceros in the lecture room, his young Austrian pupil Ludwig Wittgenstein started to look under the desks, chairs, and tables. He was not convinced. The lesson of the story is a simple one: To offer proof of existence may sometimes be difficult, but to prove nonexistence is simply impossible.

Nevertheless, it is reasonable to have doubts about Muhammad's historicity. To begin, there are no convincing archaeological traces that confirm the traditional story of Muhammad and early Islam. The scholars and scribes of Islam know an awful lot about the religion's early decades—but what they recount finds no confirmation in physical remains of any kind from the period and places concerned. What they know is limited to stories, and to the same stories retold.

Like the stories themselves, the background against which the stories of Muhammad's career are set lack outside confirmation. We do not know much about the general circumstances in seventh-century Arabia, but the picture that the Islamic tradition offers is not confirmed by what we do know. In fact, archaeological findings occasionally contradict the traditional Islamic picture. Inscriptions, for example, suggest that the ancient Arabs were not pagans, as Islam teaches, but rather monotheists who believed in one God, the Creator of heaven and earth.

Only more archaeological work in present-day Arabia and Greater Syria can possibly solve the dilemmas that have arisen concerning the historicity of Muhammad, but the rulers of these territories probably will not permit scholarly research that might eventually contradict what those in power see as religious truth. And if the outcome of the research is determined beforehand by religious necessities, scholars will not be interested in the results.

An Iraqi scholar, Ibn Ishaq (c. 760), wrote a book that is the basis of all biographies of Muhammad. No biographical sketches of Muhammad exist that do not depend on Ibn Ishaq. If an analysis of Ibn Ishaq's book establishes that for whatever reason it cannot be seen as a historical source, all knowledge we possess about Muhammad evaporates. When Ibn Ishaq's much-quoted and popular book turns out to be nothing but pious fiction, we will have to accept that it is not likely we will ever discover the truth about Muhammad.

Next to Ibn Ishaq, the Qur'an itself looks like reasonably reliable testimony about Muhammad and his career. But we run into trouble when we want to reconstruct Muhammad's life and teachings from the Qur'an, for the book as we know it today may not be an authentic reproduction of an Arabic text dictated to Muhammad in the early seventh century. There are reasons to believe that the Qur'an took its present shape not in the seventh century but later or even much later. The Arabic alphabet in which the Qur'an is written did not yet exist in the early seventh century, so it is improbable that Muhammad's secretaries, if brought back to life, would be able to recognize a modern edition of the Qur'an as part of the holy text that was dictated to them in fragments during Muhammad's lifetime—that is, if such dictation occurred.

The collections of Islamic traditions known as the Hadith form the third source from which Muhammad's life may be reconstructed. The Hadith are actually not one source but rather a group of sources, of unequal quality. Some of the traditions are unreliable even according to Muslim scholarly opinion. Muslim scribes and scholars accuse some of the transmitters of this material of fabricating their stories. It is perfectly possible to fabricate stories about real persons (see any newspaper, or Facebook), but to form a picture of the life of someone as eminent as Muhammad, one would rather not make use of stories that may have been fabricated.

To find out the truth about Richard Nixon was difficult, and it would have been impossible without the tapes. In the case of Muhammad, there are no tapes. There is not much at all. There actually is so little that the gravest suspicions are justified.

*Johannes J. G. Jansen served as Houtsma Professor for Contemporary Islamic Thought at the University of Utrecht (Netherlands) until his retirement in 2008. He is the author of several books, including* The Dual Nature of Islamic Fundamentalism *and* The Interpretation of the Koran in Modern Egypt, *and he has translated the Qur'an into Dutch.*

# Chronology of Key Events

In this chronology, incidents that rest on less than firm historical ground than is ordinarily assumed are marked in italics.

610      *Muhammad receives his first revelation of the Qur'an from Allah, through the angel Gabriel*

610–632      *Muhammad periodically receives revelations of the Qur'an*

632      *Muhammad dies*

632–634      *Caliphate of Abu Bakr*

632–633      *Wars of Apostasy*

632      *December: Battle of Yamama, death of many who had memorized portions of the Qur'an; according to Islamic tradition, this was the impetus for the first collection of the Qur'an*

633      Arabian invasion of Iraq

634–644      *Caliphate of Umar*

636–637      Arabian conquest of Syria and Palestine

Late 630s      Christian document is published that mentions an unnamed and still-living Arabian prophet "armed with a sword"

639      Arabian conquest of Armenia and Egypt

Early 640s      Thomas, a Christian priest, mentions a battle between the Byzantines and the "*tayyaye d-Mhmt*" east of Gaza in 634

644          Arabian conquest of Persia

644–656      *Caliphate of Uthman*

640s–650s    Coin in Palestine bears the inscription "Muhammad" but depicts
             a figure holding a cross

650s–660s    Arabian conquest of North Africa

651          Muawiya, governor of Syria, writes to the Byzantine emperor
             Constantine calling on him to renounce Jesus and worship the
             God of Abraham

653          *Uthman collects the Qur'an, standardizes its text, has variants
             burned, and distributes his version to all the Islamic provinces*

654          Arabian conquest of Cyprus and Rhodes

656–661      *Caliphate of Ali*

661–680      Caliphate of Muawiya

660s/670s    Coin depicts Muawiya holding a cross topped with a crescent

660s/670s    Armenian bishop Sebeos writes a semihistorical, semilegendary
             account of Mahmet, an Arab preacher who taught his people
             to worship the God of Abraham and who led twelve thousand
             Jews, along with Arabs, to invade Palestine

662          Bathhouse in Palestine is dedicated with an official inscription
             that mentions Muawiya and bears a cross

674          First Arabian siege of Constantinople

680          Anonymous chronicler identifies Muhammad as leader of the
             "sons of Ishmael," whom God sent against the Persians "like the
             sand of the sea-shores"

680–683      Caliphate of Yazid I

Early 680s   Coins apparently depicting Yazid feature a cross

685          Abdullah ibn Az-Zubair, rebel ruler of Arabia, Iraq, and Iran,
             mints coins proclaiming Muhammad as prophet of Allah

685–705      Caliphate of Abd al-Malik

| | |
|---|---|
| 690 | Nestorian Christian chronicler John bar Penkaye writes of Muhammad's authority and the Arabians' brutality |
| 690s | Coptic Christian bishop John of Nikiou makes first extant mention of "Muslims" (although the earliest available edition of his work dates from 1602 and may have been altered in translation) |
| 691 | Dome of the Rock inscription declares that "Muhammad is the servant of God and His messenger" and that "the Messiah, Jesus son of Mary, was only a messenger of God," and features an amalgamation of Qur'an quotes |
| 696 | First coins appear that do not feature an image of the sovereign and do feature the Islamic confession of faith (*shahada*) |
| 690s | According to a variant Islamic tradition, Hajjaj ibn Yusuf, governor of Iraq, collects the Qur'an, standardizes its text, has variants burned, and distributes his version to all the Islamic provinces |
| 690s | Hajjaj ibn Yusuf introduces into mosque worship the practice of reading from the Qur'an, according to a later Islamic tradition |
| 690s | Hajjaj ibn Yusuf adds diacritical marks to text of the Qur'an, enabling the reader to distinguish between various Arabic consonants and thereby make sense of the text |
| 711–718 | Muslim conquest of Spain |
| 730 | Christian writer John of Damascus refers to Islamic theology in detail, and to suras of the Qur'an, although not to the Qur'an by name |
| 732 | Muslim advance into western Europe is stopped at the Battle of Tours |
| 750s–760s | Malik ibn Anas compiles the first Hadith collection |
| circa 760 | Ibn Ishaq collects biographical material and publishes first biography of Muhammad |
| 830s–860s | The six major Hadith collections are compiled and published, providing voluminous detail about Muhammad's words and deeds |

# Muhammad and His Family,
## According to Islamic Tradition

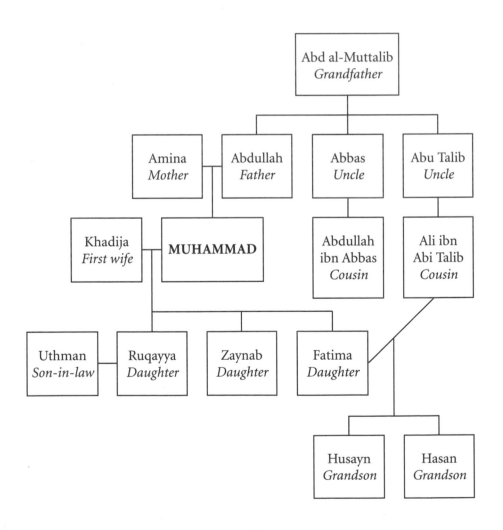

Abd al-Muttalib
*Grandfather*

Amina
*Mother*

Abdullah
*Father*

Abbas
*Uncle*

Abu Talib
*Uncle*

Khadija
*First wife*

**MUHAMMAD**

Abdullah
ibn Abbas
*Cousin*

Ali ibn
Abi Talib
*Cousin*

Uthman
*Son-in-law*

Ruqayya
*Daughter*

Zaynab
*Daughter*

Fatima
*Daughter*

Husayn
*Grandson*

Hasan
*Grandson*

Muhammad was the son of Abdullah and Amina.

Muhammad's paternal grandfather, Abd al-Muttalib, had a son, Abbas. His son, Abdullah ibn Abbas, was Muhammad's cousin. Many hadiths are attributed to Abdullah ibn Abbas as the ultimate source: The chain of transmitters begins with him as the witness of the event recounted.

Abdullah's brother Abu Talib was Muhammad's guardian after the deaths of Abdullah and Amina. He was also the father of Ali ibn Abi Talib, who was Muhammad's cousin and the founding figure of Shiite Islam.

Muhammad and his first wife, Khadija, had three daughters: Fatima, Zaynab, and Ruqayya.

Fatima married Ali ibn Abi Talib and had five children, including the Shiite heroes Hasan and Husayn. The latter was killed in the Battle of Karbala in 680, which sealed the split between the Sunnis and the Shiites.

Ruqayya married Uthman, who became the third caliph after Abu Bakr and Umar.

Ali succeeded to the caliphate when Uthman was murdered. When Ali was murdered, Muawiya, Uthman's cousin, became caliph.

# Introduction

# The Full Light of History?

In place of the mystery under which the other religions have covered their origins, [Islam] was born in the full light of history; its roots are on the surface. The life of its founder is as well known to us as that of any sixteenth-century reformer. We can follow year by year the fluctuations of his thought, his contradictions, his weaknesses.

—*Ernest Renan, "Muhammad and the Origins of Islam" (1851)*

## Shadows and Light

Did Muhammad exist?

It is a question that few have thought to ask, or dared to ask.

For most of the fourteen hundred years since the prophet of Islam is thought to have walked the earth, almost everyone has taken his existence for granted. After all, his imprint on human history is enormous.

The *Encyclopedia Britannica* dubbed him "the most successful of all Prophets and religious personalities." In his 1978 book *The 100: A Ranking of the Most Influential Persons in History*, historian Michael H. Hart put Muhammad in the top spot, explaining: "My choice of Muhammad to lead the list of the world's most influential persons may surprise some readers and may be questioned by others, but he was the only man in history who was supremely successful on both the religious and secular level."[1]

Other historians have noted the extraordinarily rapid growth of the Arabian Empire in the period immediately following Muhammad's death. The Arabian conquerors, evidently inspired by his teaching, created an empire that in fewer than one hundred years stretched from the Iberian Peninsula to India. Not only was that empire immense, but its cultural influence—also founded on Muhammad's teaching—has been enduring as well.

Moreover, Islamic literature contains an astounding proliferation of biographical material about Muhammad. In his definitive two-volume English-language biography of Muhammad, *Muhammad at Mecca* (1953) and *Muhammad at Medina* (1956), the English historian W. Montgomery Watt argues that the sheer detail contained in the Islamic records of Muhammad, plus the negative features of his biography, make his story plausible.[2]

However sharply people may differ on the virtues and vices of Muhammad, and on the value of his prophetic claims, virtually no one doubts that he was an actual person who lived in a particular time and a particular place and who, more to the point, founded one of the world's major religions.

Could such a man have never existed at all?

There is, in fact, considerable reason to question the historicity of Muhammad. Although the story of Muhammad, the Qur'an, and early Islam is widely accepted, on close examination the particulars of the story prove elusive. The more one looks at the origins of Islam, the less one sees.

This book explores the questions that a small group of pioneering scholars has raised about the historical authenticity of the standard account of Muhammad's life and prophetic career. A thorough review of the historical records provides startling indications that much, if not all, of what we know about Muhammad is legend, not historical fact. A careful investigation similarly suggests that the Qur'an is not a collection of what Muhammad presented as revelations from the one true God but was actually constructed from already existing material, mostly from the Jewish and Christian traditions.

The nineteenth-century scholar Ernest Renan confidently claimed that Islam emerged in the "full light of history." But in truth, the real story of Muhammad, the Qur'an, and early Islam lies deep in the shadows. It is time to bring it into the light.

## Historical Scrutiny

Why embark on such an inquiry?

Religious faith, any religious faith, is something that people hold very deeply. In this case, many Muslims would regard the very idea of applying historical scrutiny to the traditional account of Islam's origins as an affront. Such an inquiry raises questions about the foundational assumptions of a belief system that guides more than a billion people worldwide.

But the questions in this book are not intended as any kind of attack on Muslims. Rather, they are presented as an attempt to make sense of the available data, comparing the traditional account of Islam's origins against what can be known from the historical record.

Islam is a faith rooted in history. It makes historical claims. Muhammad is supposed to have lived at a certain time and preached certain doctrines that he said God had delivered to him. The veracity of those claims is open, to a certain extent, to historical analysis. Whether Muhammad really received messages from the angel Gabriel may be a faith judgment, but whether he lived at all is a historical one.

Islam is not unique in staking out its claims as a historical faith or in inviting historical investigation. But it is unique in *not* having undergone searching historical criticism on any significant scale. Both Judaism and Christianity have been the subject of widespread scholarly investigation for more than two centuries.

The nineteenth-century biblical scholar Julius Wellhausen's *Prolegomena zur Geschichte Israels* (*Prolegomena to the History of Israel*), a textual and historical analysis of the Torah, revolutionized the way many Jews and Christians looked at the origins of their scriptures and religious traditions. By the time Wellhausen published his study in 1882, historical criticism, or higher criticism, of Judaism and Christianity had been going on for more than a hundred years.

The scholarly "quest for the historical Jesus" had begun in the eighteenth century, but it was in the nineteenth century that this higher criticism took off. The German theologian David Friedrich Strauss (1808–1874) posited in his *Das Leben Jesu, kritisch bearbeitet* (*The Life of Jesus, Critically Examined*) (1835) that the miracles in the Gospels were actually natural events that those anxious to believe had seen as miracles. Ernest Renan (1823–1892) in his *Vie de Jésus* (*The Life of Jesus*) (1863) argued that the life of Jesus, like that of any other man, ought to be open to historical and critical scrutiny. Later scholars such as Rudolf Bultmann (1884–1976) cast strong doubt on the historical value of the Gospels. Some scholars asserted that the canonical Gospels of the New Testament were products of the second Christian century and therefore of scant historical value. Others suggested that Jesus of Nazareth had never even existed.[3]

Eventually, higher critics who dated the Gospels to the second century became a minority of scholars. The consensus that emerged dated the Gospels to within forty to sixty years of the death of Jesus Christ. From that gap between the life of their protagonist and their publication, many scholars concluded that the Gospels were overgrown with legendary material. They began trying to sift through the available evidence in order to determine who Jesus was and what he really said and did.

The reaction within the Christian world was mixed. Many Christians dismissed the higher criticism as an attempt to undermine their faith. Some criticized it for excessive skepticism and one-sidedness, regarding historical-critical investigations of the Gospels and the historicity of Christ as the critics' effort to justify their own unbelief. But others were more receptive. Large Protestant churches such as the Episcopalians, Presbyterians, and Methodists ultimately abandoned Christian dogma as it had hitherto been understood, espousing a vague, nondogmatic Christianity that concentrated on charitable work rather than doctrinal rigor and spirituality. Other Protestant denominations (including splinters of the three named above) retreated into fundamentalism, which in its original formulation was a defiant assertion, in the face of the higher critical challenge, of the historicity of the Virgin Birth of Christ, his Resurrection, and more.

Pope Leo XIII condemned the higher criticism in his 1893 encyclical *Providentissimus Deus*, but nine years later he established the Pontifical Biblical Commission, which was to use the tools of higher criticism to explore the scriptures within a context respectful to Catholic faith. In 1943 Pope Pius XII encouraged higher critical study in his encyclical *Divino Afflante Spiritu*. The Catholic Church ultimately determined that because its faith was historical, historical study could not be an enemy of faith, provided that such investigations did not simply provide a cover for radical skepticism.

The higher criticism clearly transformed the Christian world, changing the course of several major Christian communions and radically altering how others presented the faith. Similarly, investigations into the origins of Judaism and the historical material contained within the Hebrew scriptures have affected the Jewish tradition. In Judaism as in Christianity, traditions developed that rejected literalism and reevaluated numerous elements of traditional orthodoxy. Reform Judaism, like the liberal Protestant denominations, generally rejected traditional understandings and the literalism that underlay them.

Yet Judaism and Christianity still live, and in many areas they thrive. They have survived the challenge. Can Islam survive the same historical-critical challenge?

No one knows, for it has never received this treatment on nearly the same scale.

Why should Islam and its leading figure be exempt from the scrutiny that has been applied to other religions?

## The Power of Legend

As a personality, Muhammad fairly leaps from the pages of the earliest available Islamic texts. What mortal hand or eye could frame this fearsome man? Who would dare to create such an outsize character, so immense in his claims, his loves, his hates?

In addition, there is little doubt that the political unification of Arabia took place around the time Muhammad is assumed to have lived. Scholars generally agree that the Arabian warriors swept out of Arabia beginning in the second quarter of the seventh century and within a hundred years had subdued much of the Middle East, North Africa, and Persia and had entered India and Spain.

Finally, of course, Muhammad has undeniably made a lasting impact as teacher and example to the Islamic world.

Given these three points—the richly detailed portrait of Muhammad found in the Islamic literature, the way he seemingly inspired his successors to found a vast empire, and his enduring legacy as founder of a religion that today claims more than a billion adherents—few have thought to question Muhammad's existence. Muslims and non-Muslims alike take it for granted that he did live and that he originated the faith we know as Islam. I understand the influence the traditional account has, for I spent more than two decades studying Islamic theology, law, and history in depth before seriously considering the historical reliability of what the early Islamic sources say the prophet of Islam said and did.

But the more I examined the evidence gathered by scholars who had bothered to apply the historical-critical method to Islam's origins, the more I recognized how little there was to confirm the canonical story. In my 2006 book, *The Truth about Muhammad*, a biography based on the earliest available Muslim sources, I pointed out "the paucity of early, reliable sources" and observed that "from a strictly historical standpoint, it is impossible to state with certainty even that a man named Muhammad actually existed, or if he did, that he did much or any of what is ascribed to him." Even, then, however, I said for a variety of reasons that "in all likelihood he did exist."[4]

That may have been an overly optimistic assessment. Even the pillars used to support the traditional account begin to crumble upon close scrutiny. True enough, beginning in the seventh century, Arabian conquerors went out and created an immense empire. But as this book will show, historical and archaeological records cast serious doubt on the claim that they did so under the sway of what was already a fully formed religion with a revealed book as its centerpiece and a revered prophet as its model for conduct.

Likewise, Muhammad's tremendous impact on history does not in itself provide irrefutable evidence of the accuracy of the portrait that the earliest available Islamic sources paint of him. Many legendary or semilegendary figures have inspired magnificent achievements by real people. One need only consider, for example, the Crusader literature, such as *The Song of Roland* and *The Poem of El Cid*, which romanticized historical figures and presented them as larger-than-life heroes, and which in turn inspired other warriors to new feats of bravery and heroism. Muhammad's great influence in providing the impetus for a remarkably resilient culture need not depend on his having been a historical figure; a historical legend, believed fervently, could account for the same effect.

The vividness of the picture of Muhammad that emerges from the Islamic sources is no guarantee of his reality, either. Literature is full of compelling, believable portraits of men who never existed but whose personalities are fully formed on the page, such that if the fictional narratives were mistaken for historical accounts, no one would take it amiss. Macbeth, the king of Scotland, is in Shakespeare's play easily as coherent and compelling a character as Islam's prophet. Macbeth was a real king, but the available historical records depict a figure far different from Shakespeare's troubled antihero. Sir Walter

Scott's historical novel *Ivanhoe* depicts many historical events accurately, but the primary story it tells is fictional. Robin Hood may have been an actual person, but his real exploits are shrouded in the mists of folklore. Take away Robin's robbing of the rich and giving to the poor, and consider his merry men, Friar Tuck, Sherwood Forest, and the rest as legendary accretions, and what is left? Perhaps some kernel of what gave rise to these legends, or perhaps nothing much at all. We will probably never know.

A careful look at the available historical evidence suggests, or at least opens up the possibility, that the case of Muhammad may be similar. Some early accounts do assert that a man named Muhammad existed, but what they say about him bears little resemblance to the Muslim prophet, the guiding light and inspiration of the army of Arabian nomads that stormed out of Arabia in the 630s and embarked on a stunningly successful string of conquests. The oldest records that tell us anything about this man, if they're definitely talking about him in the first place, differ sharply from the story told by the earliest Islamic texts, which date from many decades after Muhammad's reported death.

What's more, the available historical records contain a surprising number of puzzles and anomalies that strongly suggest that the standard Muslim story about Muhammad is more legend than fact. Muhammad, it appears, was much different from the perfect man of Islamic hagiography—if he existed at all.

## Standing on the Shoulders of Giants

In writing this book, I do not intend to break new ground. Instead, I aim to bring to wider public attention the work of a small band of scholars who have dared, often at great personal and professional risk, to examine what the available historical data reveals about the canonical account of Islam's origins.

This book is the fruit of my researches into the writings of scholars of earlier generations, including, among others, Ignaz Goldziher, Arthur Jeffery, Henri Lammens, David S. Margoliouth, Alphonse Mingana, Theodor Nöldeke, Aloys Sprenger, Joseph Schacht, and Julius Wellhausen, as well as modern-day scholars such as Suliman Bashear, Patricia Crone, Michael Cook, Ibn Warraq, Judith Koren, Christoph Luxenberg, Günter Lüling, Yehuda Nevo, Volker Popp, Ibn Rawandi, David S. Powers, and John Wansbrough.

Some of the bold scholars who have investigated the history of early Islam have even received death threats. As a result, some publish under pseudonyms, including scholars of the first rank, such as those who go by the names Christoph Luxenberg and Ibn Warraq. Such intimidation is an impediment to scholarly research that even the most radical New Testament scholar never had to deal with.

The investigation of Islam's origins, despite the obscurity in which the endeavor has been shrouded, is actually almost as old as the comparable investigations of Judaism and Christianity. The German scholar Gustav Weil (1808–1889) first attempted a historical-critical evaluation of the earliest Islamic sources in *Mohammed der prophet, sein Leben und sein Lehre* (*Muhammad the Prophet, His Life and His Teaching*) (1843), but he had only limited access to those sources. Weil noted in another work on Islam that "reliance upon oral traditions, at a time when they were transmitted by memory alone, and every day produced new divisions among the professors of Islam, opened up a wide field for fabrication and distortion."[5]

Ernest Renan, for all his enthusiasm about the historicity of Muhammad, actually approached the Islamic sources with something of a critical eye. Writing of the Qur'an, he pointed out that "the integrity of a work committed to memory for a long time is unlikely to be well preserved; could not interpolations and alterations have slipped in during the successive revisions?" But Renan himself did not investigate that possibility. He retreated into the unsupported assertion that "the veritable monument of the early history of Islam, the Koran, remains absolutely impregnable, and suffices in itself, independently of any historical accounts, to reveal to us Muhammad."[6]

The Scottish historian William Muir (1819–1905) published his massive work *A Life of Mahomet and History of Islam to the Era of the Hegira* in four volumes between 1858 and 1862. Muir expressed skepticism about some of the material about Muhammad in Islamic tradition, asserting that "even respectably derived traditions often contained much that was exaggerated and fabulous."[7] Nonetheless, in his huge biography of Muhammad he took the early Islamic sources essentially at face value, discarding little or nothing as "exaggerated and fabulous."

More skeptical was Wellhausen (1844–1918), whose studies of the five books of Moses led him to posit that those books were the product not of a single hand but of four separate sources that had been combined by later editors. He applied the same analysis to the sources of Islamic hadith. The Hadith, literally "reports," are the collections of Muhammad's words and deeds that form the foundation of Islamic law and practice. Wellhausen attempted to distinguish reliable transmitters of hadiths from those who were less reliable.[8]

The Austrian scholar Aloys Sprenger (1813–1893) contributed mightily to the study of Islam's origins by unearthing Islamic texts long thought to have been lost, including Ibn Hisham's ninth-century biography of Muhammad. Sprenger likewise doubted the historical accuracy of some of the hadiths.

The pioneering Hungarian scholar Ignaz Goldziher (1850–1921) took such investigations even further. He determined that the lateness of the Hadith collections relative to the time Muhammad was supposed to have lived, together with the widespread Muslim tendency to forge stories about Muhammad that supported a political position or religious practice, made it virtually impossible to regard the Hadith, which fill many volumes, as historically reliable.

It is noteworthy that Goldziher, although he never converted to Islam, had a deep and abiding love for the Islamic faith. As a young man he sojourned to Damascus and Cairo, and he came to admire Islam so fervently that he wrote in his diary: "I became inwardly convinced that I myself was a Muslim." In Cairo he entered a mosque and prayed as a Muslim: "In the midst of the thousands of the pious, I rubbed my forehead against the floor of the mosque. Never in my life was I more devout, more truly devout, than on that exalted Friday."[9]

It may seem strange, then, that Goldziher would cast scholarly doubt on the historicity of the entire corpus of the Hadith. But he did not intend his conclusions to be corrosive of Islamic faith. Instead, he hoped that they would lead to a critical evaluation of the Hadith as what they actually were: not sources of historical information, which they had been always assumed to be, but indications of how Islamic law and ritual practice developed. He hoped, in other words, that his scholarly findings would lead to a fuller understanding of Islam's origins and thereby positively affect its present character.

Likewise dubious about the historical legitimacy of the early Islamic texts was the Italian scholar of the Middle East Prince Leone Caetani, Duke of Sermoneta (1869–1935). Caetani concluded that "we can find almost nothing true on Muhammad in the Traditions [i.e., hadiths], we can discount as apocryphal all the traditional material that we possess."[10] His contemporary Henri Lammens (1862–1937), a Flemish Jesuit, made a critical study of the Islamic traditions about Muhammad, casting doubt on, among other things, the traditional dates of Muhammad's birth and death. Lammens noted "the artificial character and absence of critical sense" in the compilation of the earliest biographies of the prophet of Islam, although he warned that "there can be no question of rejecting the whole en bloc."[11]

Joseph Schacht (1902–1969), the foremost scholar of Islamic law in the Western world, wrote a study of the origins of Islamic law in which he observed that "even the classical corpus" of Hadith "contains a great many traditions which cannot possibly be authentic. All efforts to extract from this often self-contradictory mass an authentic core by 'historic intuition,' as it has been called, have failed." He backed up Goldziher's finding that "the great majority of traditions from the Prophet are documents not of the time to which they claim to belong, but of the successive stages of development of doctrines during the first centuries of Islam." But Schacht went beyond even

Goldziher's arguments, concluding, for instance, that "a great many traditions in the classical and other collections were put into circulation only after Shafii's time [the Islamic jurist ash-Shafii died in 820]; the first considerable body of legal traditions from the Prophet originated towards the middle of the second century"; and "the evidence of legal traditions carries us back to about the year 100 A.H. only"— that is, to the first decade of the eighth century, not any closer to the time Muhammad is supposed to have lived.[12]

John Wansbrough (1928–2002), an American historian who taught at the University of London, amplified the work of earlier scholars who doubted the historical value of the early Islamic texts. In his groundbreaking and complex work, Wansbrough postulated that the Qur'an was developed primarily to establish Islam's origins in Arabia and that the Hadith were fabricated in order to give the Arabian Empire a distinctive religion so as to foster its stability and unity.

Influenced by this, the historians Patricia Crone, a protégée of Wansbrough, and Michael Cook, a protégé of the eminent historian of the Middle East Bernard Lewis, published the wildly controversial book *Hagarism: The Making of the Islamic World* (1977). Like their predecessors, Crone and Cook noted the lateness and unreliability of the bulk of the early Islamic sources about Muhammad and the origins of Islam. Their objective was to reconstruct the birth and early development of the religion by examining the available historical, archaeological, and philological records about early Islam, including coins minted in the region during the seventh and eighth centuries and official inscriptions dating from that period. "We have set out with a certain recklessness," they wrote, "to create a coherent architectonic of ideas in a field over much of which scholarship has yet to dig the foundations."[13]

Crone and Cook posited that Islam arose as a movement within Judaism but centered on Abraham and his son Ishmael through his concubine Hagar—as many of the earliest non-Muslim sources refer to the Arabians not as "Muslims" but as "Hagarians" (or "Hagarenes"). This movement, for a variety of reasons, split from Judaism in the last decade of the seventh century and began developing into what would ultimately become Islam.

In 1987 Crone published *Meccan Trade and the Rise of Islam*, in which she demonstrated that one of the principal foundations of the canonical Islamic biography of Muhammad—its Arabian setting, with Mecca as a center for trade—was not supported by any contemporary records. The records indicate, she showed, that Mecca was not such a center at all. Crone, like Wansbrough, saw Islam's Arabian setting as read back into the religion's literature at a later date for political purposes.

Later, however, Crone asserted, "The evidence that a prophet was active among the Arabs in the early decades of the 7th century, on the eve of the Arab conquest of the middle east, must be said to be exceptionally good." She added that "we can be reasonably sure that the Qur'an is a collection of utterances that [Muhammad] made in the belief that they had been revealed to him by God." Although these statements represented a departure from her earlier position on Islam's origins, she offered no new findings or evidence to explain the change; instead, she left her earlier reasoning and the evidence presented standing untouched. Crone still acknowledged that "everything else about Mohammed is more uncertain," pointing out that the earliest Islamic sources about his life date from "some four to five generations after his death," and that in any case few scholars consider these sources "to be straightforward historical accounts."[14] This uncertainty, along with the provocative evidence Crone herself presented in her earlier books, inspired a number of other scholars to continue investigations into the historicity of Muhammad.

Meanwhile, other modern-day scholars have undertaken a close critical examination of the Qur'anic text itself. The German theologian Günter Lüling maintains that the original Qur'an was not an Islamic text at all but a pre-Islamic Christian document. Close examination of textual oddities and anomalies in the Qur'an finds many signs of that Christian foundation. Lüling believes that the Qur'an reflects the theology of a non-Trinitarian Christian sect that left traces on Islamic theology, notably in its picture of Christ and its uncompromising unitarianism.

The pseudonymous scholar Christoph Luxenberg, although he differs in many ways with Lüling's methods and conclusions, agrees that the Qur'an shows signs of containing a Christian substratum. Luxenberg argues that many of the Qur'an's puzzling words and phrases become clear only by reference to Syriac, a dialect of Aramaic that was the literary language of the region at the time the Qur'an was assembled. Through this method, he has come to numerous startling conclusions. Some of his findings have won international notoriety. Most notably, the famous Qur'anic passages promising virgins in Paradise to Islamic martyrs do not, in his reading, actually refer to virgins; the word usually translated as "virgins" is more accurately rendered as "raisins" or "grapes," he argues.

For this book, I have relied primarily on the recent authors, particularly Crone's earlier work, Luxenberg, Lüling, Popp, and Powers, with frequent recourse to the work of older scholars as well, especially Goldziher.

Reaction from Muslims to the revisionist reconstruction of early Islamic history has varied. Some have attempted to refute the various findings of the revisionist historians.[15] For example, Professor Ahmad Ali al-Imam has published a book-length examination of the variants in the text of the Qur'an. He explains those variants by pointing to Islamic traditions that detail the Qur'an's seven styles of recitation; he concludes that "the Qur'an's completeness and trustworthiness has been shown."[16] Meanwhile, Professor Muhammad Sven Kalisch, a German convert to Islam and the first professor of Islamic theology in Germany, examined the work of the historical critics of Islam and determined that Muhammad never existed in the form in which the Islamic texts depict him.[17] He subsequently left Islam.[18] In contrast, Khaled Abou El Fadl, a professor of law at the University of California, Los Angeles, has reacted to historical criticism of Islam with fury, calling it "bigotry." Abou El Fadl terms Ibn Warraq a "pitiful figure," as well as "an inanity, and an utter intellectual bore." He accuses

scholar Daniel Pipes, in recounting the work of the critics approv-
ingly, of "discharging the White Man's Burden." He even claims that
"revisionism, like all forms of incipient or established bigotry, rests on
several peculiar assumptions. Assumption number one is that Muslims invariably lie . . . and can hardly distinguish fiction from fact."[19]

That is not actually the case at all. The scholarly inquiries into
Islam's origins do not rest on the assumption that Muslims were
unable to distinguish fiction from fact. The issue is whether legend
supplemented a historical record to the extent that it was no longer
possible to determine what was legend and what was history. That
accretion of legendary detail is not a phenomenon peculiar to Muslims; it has taken place regarding the lives of numerous historical
figures whose actual deeds are forgotten but who have become the
heroes of legends that are told and retold to this day.

The scholars who are investigating the origins of Islam are moti-
vated not by hatred, bigotry, or racism but by a desire to discover the
truth. These are the scholars who laid the foundations for the explo-
rations in this book.

# 1

---

# The Man Who Wasn't There

## The Sources

One may assume that the first and foremost source for information about Muhammad's life is the Qur'an, the holy book of Islam. Yet that book actually reveals little about the life of Islam's central figure. In it, Allah frequently addresses his prophet and tells him what to say to the believers and unbelievers. Commentators and readers generally assume that Muhammad is the one addressed in these cases, but that—like so much else in this field—is not certain.

The name *Muhammad* actually appears in the Qur'an only four times, and in three of those instances it could be used as a title—the "praised one" or "chosen one"—rather than as a proper name. By contrast, Moses is mentioned by name 136 times, and Abraham, 79 times. Even Pharaoh is mentioned 74 times. Meanwhile, "messenger of Allah" (*rasul Allah*) appears in various forms 300 times, and "prophet" (*nabi*), 43 times.[1] Are those all references to Muhammad, the seventh-century prophet of Arabia? Perhaps. Certainly they have been taken as such by readers of the Qur'an through the ages. But even if they are, they tell us little to nothing about the events and circumstances of his life.

Indeed, throughout the Qur'an there is essentially nothing about this messenger beyond insistent assertions of his status as an emissary of Allah and calls for the believers to obey him. Three of the four times that the name *Muhammad* is mentioned, nothing at all is disclosed about his life.

The first of the four mentions of Muhammad by name appears in the third chapter, or sura, of the Qur'an: "Muhammad is nothing but a messenger; messengers have passed away before him" (3:144). The Qur'an later says that "the Messiah, the son of Mary, is nothing but a messenger; messengers have passed away before him" (5:75).[2] The identical language may indicate that in 3:144, Jesus is the figure being referred to as the "praised one"—that is, the *muhammad*.

In sura 33 we read that "Muhammad is not the father of any one of your men, but the Messenger of God, and the Seal of the Prophets; God has knowledge of everything" (33:40).[3] This is almost certainly a specific reference to the prophet of Islam and not simply to a prophetic figure being accorded the epithet the "praised one." It is also an extremely important verse for Islamic theology: Muslim scholars have interpreted Muhammad's status as "Seal of the Prophets" to mean that Muhammad is the last of the prophets of Allah and that anyone who pretends to the status of prophet after Muhammad is of necessity a false prophet. This doctrine accounts for the deep antipathy, often expressed in violence, that traditional Islam harbors toward later prophetic movements that arose within an Islamic milieu, such as the Baha'is and Qadiani Ahmadis.

Less specific is Qur'an 47:2: "But those who believe and do righteous deeds and believe in what is sent down to Muhammad—and it is the truth from their Lord—He will acquit them of their evil deeds, and dispose their minds aright." In this verse, "Muhammad" is someone to whom Allah has given revelations, but this could apply to any of the Qur'an's designated prophets as well as to Muhammad in particular.

Qur'an 48:29, meanwhile, probably refers only to the prophet of Islam: "Muhammad is the Messenger of God, and those who are with him are hard against the unbelievers, merciful one to another." Although the "praised one" here could conceivably refer to some other prophet, the language "Muhammad is the messenger of Allah"

(*Muhammadun rasulu Allahi*) within the Islamic confession of faith makes it more likely that 48:29 refers specifically to the prophet of Islam.

That is all as far as Qur'anic mentions of Muhammad by name go. In the many other references to the messenger of Allah, this messenger is not named, and little is said about his specific actions. As a result, we can glean nothing from these passages about Muhammad's biography. Nor is it even certain, on the basis of the Qur'anic text alone, that these passages refer to Muhammad, or did so originally.

Abundant detail about Muhammad's words and deeds is contained in the Hadith, the dizzyingly voluminous collections of Islamic traditions that form the foundation for Islamic law. The Hadith detail the occasions for the revelation of every passage in the Qur'an. But (as we will see in the next chapter) there is considerable reason to believe that the bulk of the hadiths about Muhammad's words and deeds date from a period considerably after Muhammad's reported death in 632.

Then there is the Sira, the biography of the prophet of Islam. The earliest biography of Muhammad was written by Ibn Ishaq (d. 773), who wrote in the latter part of the eighth century, at least 125 years after the death of his protagonist, in a setting in which legendary material about Muhammad was proliferating. And Ibn Ishaq's biography doesn't even exist as such; it comes down to us only in the quite lengthy fragments reproduced by an even later chronicler, Ibn Hisham, who wrote in the first quarter of the ninth century, and by other historians who reproduced and thereby preserved additional sections. Other biographical material about Muhammad dates from even later.

This is chiefly the material that makes up the glare of the "full light of history" in which Ernest Renan said that Muhammad lived and worked. In fact, arguably none of the biographical details about Muhammad date to the century in which his prophetic career was said to unfold.

## The Earliest Records of an Arabian Prophet

Yet surely there are abundant mentions of this man who lived and worked in the "full light of history" in contemporary records written by both friends and foes alike.

That is, at least, what one might expect. After all, he unified the hitherto ever-warring tribes of Arabia. He forged them into a fighting machine that, only a few years after his death, stunned and bloodied the two great powers of the day, the eastern Roman (Byzantine) Empire and the Persian Empire, rapidly expanding into the territory of both. It would be entirely reasonable to expect that seventh-century chroniclers among the Byzantines and Persians, as well as the Muslims, would note the remarkable influence and achievements of this man.

But the earliest records offer more questions than answers. One of the earliest apparent mentions of Muhammad comes from a document known as the *Doctrina Jacobi*, which was probably written by a Christian in Palestine between 634 and 640—that is, at the time of the earliest Arabian conquests and just after Muhammad's reported death in 632. It is written in Greek from the perspective of a Jew who is coming to believe that the Messiah of the Christians is the true one and who hears about another prophet arisen in Arabia:

> When the *candidatus* [that is, a member of the Byzantine imperial guard] was killed by the Saracens [*Sarakenoi*], I was at Caesarea and I set off by boat to Sykamina. People were saying "the candidatus has been killed," and we Jews were overjoyed. And they were saying that the prophet had appeared, coming with the Saracens, and that he was proclaiming the advent of the anointed one, the Christ who was to come. I, having arrived at Sykamina, stopped by a certain old man well-versed in scriptures, and I said to him: "What can you tell me about the prophet who has appeared with the Saracens?" He replied, groaning deeply: "He is false, for the prophets do not come armed with a

sword. Truly they are works of anarchy being committed today and I fear that the first Christ to come, whom the Christians worship, was the one sent by God and we instead are preparing to receive the Antichrist. Indeed, Isaiah said that the Jews would retain a perverted and hardened heart until all the earth should be devastated. But you go, master Abraham, and find out about the prophet who has appeared." So I, Abraham, inquired and heard from those who had met him that there was no truth to be found in the so-called prophet, only the shedding of men's blood. He says also that he has the keys of paradise, which is incredible.[4]

In this case, "incredible" means "not credible." One thing that can be established from this is that the Arabian invaders who conquered Palestine in 635 (the "Saracens") came bearing news of a new prophet, one who was "armed with a sword." But in the *Doctrina Jacobi* this unnamed prophet is still alive, traveling with his armies, whereas Muhammad is supposed to have died in 632. What's more, this Saracen prophet, rather than proclaiming that he was Allah's last prophet (cf. Qur'an 33:40), was "proclaiming the advent of the anointed one, the Christ who was to come." This was a reference to an expected Jewish Messiah, not to the Jesus Christ of Christianity (*Christ* means "anointed one" or "Messiah" in Greek).

It is noteworthy that the Qur'an depicts Jesus as proclaiming the advent of a figure whom Islamic tradition identifies as Muhammad: "Children of Israel, I am the indeed the Messenger of God to you, confirming the Torah that is before me, and giving good tidings of a Messenger who shall come after me, whose name shall be Ahmad" (61:6). *Ahmad* is the "praised one," whom Islamic scholars identify with Muhammad: The name *Ahmad* is a variant of *Muhammad* (as they share the trilateral root *h-m-d*). It may be that the *Doctrina Jacobi* and Qur'an 61:6 both preserve in different ways the memory of a prophetic figure who proclaimed the coming of the "praised one" or the "chosen one"—*ahmad* or *muhammad*.

The prophet described in the *Doctrina Jacobi* "says also that he has the keys of paradise," which, we're told, "is incredible." But it is not only incredible; it is also completely absent from the Islamic tradition, which never depicts Muhammad as claiming to hold the keys of paradise. Jesus, however, awards them to Peter in the Gospel according to Matthew (16:19), which may indicate (along with Jesus' being the one who proclaims the coming of *ahmad* in Qur'an 61:6) that the figure proclaiming this eschatological event had some connection to the Christian tradition, as well as to Judaism's messianic expectation. Inasmuch as the "keys of paradise" are more akin to Peter's "keys to the kingdom of heaven" than to anything in Muhammad's message, the prophet in the *Doctrina Jacobi* seems closer to a Christian or Christian-influenced Messianic millennialist than to the prophet of Islam as he is depicted in Islam's canonical literature.

## Was That Muhammad?

In light of all this, can it be said that the *Doctrina Jacobi* refers to Muhammad at all? It is difficult to imagine that it could refer to anyone else, as prophets who wielded the sword of conquest in the Holy Land—and armies acting on the inspiration of such prophets—were not thick on the ground in the 630s. The document's departures from Islamic tradition regarding the date of Muhammad's death and the content of his teaching could be understood simply as the misunderstandings of a Byzantine writer observing these proceedings from a comfortable distance, and not as evidence that Muhammad and Islam were different then from what they are now.

At the same time, there is not a single account of any kind dating from around the time the *Doctrina Jacobi* was written that affirms the canonical Islamic story of Muhammad and Islam's origins. One other possibility is that the unnamed prophet of the *Doctrina Jacobi* was one of several such figures, some of whose historical attributes were later subsumed into the figure of the prophet of Islam under the name of one of them, Muhammad. For indeed, there is nothing dating from the time of Muhammad's activities or for a considerable period thereafter that actually tells us anything about what he was like or what he did.

One apparent mention of his name can be found in a diverse collection of writings in Syriac (a dialect of Aramaic common in the region at the time) that are generally attributed to a Christian priest named Thomas and dated to the early 640s. But some evidence indicates that these writings were revised in the middle of the eighth century, and so this may not be an early reference to Muhammad at all.[5] Nonetheless, Thomas refers to "a battle between the Romans and the *tayyaye d-Mhmt*" east of Gaza in 634.[6] The *tayyaye*, or *Taiyaye*, were nomads; other early chroniclers use this word to refer to the conquerors. Thus one historian, Robert G. Hoyland, has translated *tayyaye d-Mhmt* as "the Arabs of Muhammad"; this translation and similar ones are relatively common. Syriac, however, distinguishes between *t* and *d*, so it is not certain (although it is possible) that by *Mhmt*, Thomas meant *Mhmd*—Muhammad. Even if "Arabs of Muhammad" is a perfectly reasonable translation of *tayyaye d-Mhmt*, we are still a long way from the prophet of Islam, the polygamous warrior prophet, recipient of the Qur'an, wielder of the sword against the infidels. Nothing in the writings or other records of either the Arabians or the people they conquered dating from the mid-seventh century mentions any element of his biography: At the height of the Arabian conquests, the non-Muslim sources are as silent as the Muslim ones are about the prophet and holy book that were supposed to have inspired those conquests.

Thomas may also have meant to use the word *Mhmt* not as a proper name but as a title, the "praised one" or the "chosen one," with no certain referent. In any case, the Muhammad to which Thomas refers does not with any certainty share anything with the prophet of Islam except the name itself.

## Sophronius and Umar

No one who interacted with those who conquered the Middle East in the middle of the seventh century ever seems to have gotten the impression that a prophet named Muhammad, whose followers burst from Arabia bearing a new holy book and a new creed, was behind the conquests.[7]

Consider, for example, a seventh-century Christian account of the conquest of Jerusalem, apparently written within a few years of that conquest (originally in Greek but surviving in a translation into Georgian). According to this account, "the godless Saracens entered the holy city of Christ our Lord, Jerusalem, with the permission of God and in punishment for our negligence."[8] A Coptic homily from the same period characterizes the "Saracens" as "oppressors, who give themselves up to prostitution, massacre and lead into captivity the sons of men, saying: 'We both fast and pray.'"[9]

Sophronius, the patriarch of Jerusalem who turned the city over to the caliph Umar after the Arabian conquest in 637, lamented the advent of "the Saracens who, on account of our sins, have now risen up against us unexpectedly and ravage all with cruel and feral design, with impious and godless audacity."[10] In a Christmas sermon in 634, Sophronius declares that "we, however, because of our innumerable sins and serious misdemeanours, are unable to see these things, and are prevented from entering Bethlehem by way of the road. Unwillingly, indeed, contrary to our wishes, we are required to stay at home, not bound closely by bodily bonds, but bound by fear of the Saracens." He laments that "as once that of the Philistines, so now the army of the godless Saracens has captured the divine Bethlehem and bars our passage there, threatening slaughter and destruction if we leave this holy city and dare to approach our beloved and sacred Bethlehem."[11]

It is not surprising that a seventh-century Christian like Sophronius would refer to the invaders as "godless." After all, even if those invaders had come brandishing the holy book of the deity they proclaimed as the sole true creator of all things, Sophronius denied that god's existence. Still, he makes no mention, even in the heat of the fiercest polemic, of the conquerors' god, their prophet, or their holy book.

In all his discussion of the "Saracens," Sophronius shows some familiarity with their disdain for the cross and the orthodox Christian doctrines of Christ, but he never calls the invaders "Muslims" and never refers to Muhammad, the Qur'an, or Islam. In a sermon from December 636 or 637, Sophronius speaks at length about the conquerors' brutality, and in doing so he makes some references to their beliefs:

> But the present circumstances are forcing me to think differently about our way of life, for why are [so many] wars being fought among us? Why do barbarian raids abound? Why are the troops of the Saracens attacking us? Why has there been so much destruction and plunder? Why are there incessant outpourings of human blood? Why are the birds of the sky devouring human bodies?

The invaders are not randomly vicious but apparently have a particular contempt and hatred for Christianity:

> Why have churches been pulled down? Why is the cross mocked? Why is Christ, who is the dispenser of all good things and the provider of this joyousness of ours, blasphemed by pagan mouths (*ethnikois tois stomasi*) so that he justly cries out to us: "Because of you my name is blasphemed among the pagans," and this is the worst of all the terrible things that are happening to us.

Sophronius's sermon coincides with the Islamic rejection of the cross—a rejection that also made its way into the Qur'an, which asserts that the Jews "did not slay him [Jesus], neither crucified him" (4:157). And in speaking of pagans' blaspheming of Christ, Sophronius could be referring to the denial of Christ's divinity and salvific sacrifice—denials that are part of Islamic doctrine.

Sophronius sees the Saracens as the instrument of God's wrath against Christians who have grown lax, although he describes the Saracens themselves are "God-hating" and "God-fighters," and their unnamed leader as the "devil." It is unclear whether Sophronius refers to the devil himself or to the caliph Umar, who conquered Jerusalem, or to Muhammad or to someone else. Sophronius declares:

> That is why the vengeful and God-hating Saracens, the abomination of desolation clearly foretold to us by the prophets, overrun the places which are not allowed to them, plunder cities, devastate fields, burn down villages, set on fire the holy churches, overturn the sacred monasteries, oppose the Byzantine armies arrayed against them, and in fighting raise up the trophies [of war] and add victory to victory. Moreover, they are raised up more and more against us and increase their blasphemy of Christ and the church, and utter wicked blasphemies against God. Those God-fighters boast of prevailing over all, assiduously and unrestrainably imitating their leader, who is the devil, and emulating his vanity because of which he has been expelled from heaven and been assigned to the gloomy shades. Yet these vile ones would not have accomplished this nor seized such a degree of power as to do and utter lawlessly all these things, unless we had first insulted the gift [of baptism] and first defiled the purification, and in this way grieved Christ, the giver of gifts, and prompted him to be angry with us, good though he is and though he takes no pleasure in evil, being the fount of kindness and not wishing to behold the ruin and destruction of men. We are ourselves, in truth, responsible for all these things and no word will be found for our defence. What word or place will be given us for our defence when we have taken all these gifts from him, befouled them and defiled everything with our vile actions?[12]

Such descriptions of violence and brutality are hard to reconcile with the better-known accounts of the Arabian conquest of Jerusalem. Those accounts depict Umar meeting Sophronius and treating him respectfully, even magnanimously declining to pray in the Church of the Holy Sepulchre so that his followers will not be able to seize the church and convert it into a mosque.[13] Umar and Sophronius conclude a pact that forbids Christians from building new churches, carrying arms, or riding on horses, and that requires them to pay a poll tax, *jizya*, to the Muslims; but Christians are generally allowed to practice their religion and live in relative peace.[14] This is the foundation of the Islamic legal superstructure of dhimmitude, which denies equality of rights to non-Muslims in the Islamic state and is oppressive in numerous ways by modern standards, but which in the seventh century was comparatively tolerant.

This "Pact of Umar," however, is of doubtful historical authenticity.[15] The earliest reference to it comes in the work of the Muslim historian Tabari, who died nearly three centuries later, in 923. According to Tabari, Umar wrote to the neighboring provinces about how he was treating the newly conquered people in Jerusalem:

> In the name of God, the Merciful, the Compassionate. This is the assurance of safety (*aman*) which the servant of God, Umar, the Commander of the Faithful, has granted to the people of Jerusalem. He has given them an assurance of safety for themselves, for their property, their churches, their crosses, the sick and the healthy of the city, and for all the rituals that belong to their religion. Their churches will not be inhabited [by Muslims] and will not be destroyed. Neither they, nor the land on which they stand, nor their cross, nor their property will be damaged. They will not be forcibly converted. No Jew will live with them in Jerusalem. The people of Jerusalem must pay the poll tax (*jizya*) like the people of the [other] cities, and they must expel the Byzantines and the robbers. As for those who leave the city, their lives and property will be safe until they reach their place of safety;

and as for those who remain, they will be safe. They will have to pay the poll tax like the people of Jerusalem. Those of the people of Jerusalem who want to leave with the Byzantines, take their property, and abandon their churches and their crosses will be safe until they reach their place of safety. . . . If they pay the poll tax according to their obligations, then the contents of this letter are under the covenant of God, are the responsibility of His Prophet, of the caliphs, and of the faithful.[16]

The atmosphere of this purported letter from Umar and the writings of Sophronius couldn't be more different. Umar promises to preserve the churches and to allow the Christians to travel freely and even take their property and leave his domains, although he is not wholly tolerant, saying he will restrict the Jews from Jerusalem. Sophronius, on the other hand, laments the destruction of the churches and the restrictions on the Christians' ability to travel. The most striking difference is that the caliph's letter is unmistakably written within the Islamic milieu; it begins with the familiar Islamic invocation of Allah the compassionate and merciful, and refers matter-of-factly to "His Prophet." By contrast, Sophronius, writing at the time that Umar actually conquered Jerusalem, shows no awareness that the Arabians had a prophet at all or were even Muslims.

### Pagan Arabians?

Arabia before Muhammad was pagan; the Arabians were polytheists. Islam, of course, is supposed to have ended all that. Muhammad, according to the standard account, united and Islamized Arabia. Shortly after his death, some of the Arabians rebelled, leading to the Wars of Apostasy in 632 and 633, but the Muslims won these. Arabian polytheism and paganism quickly became relics of history.

Here again, however, contemporary accounts paint a significantly different picture. In 676, a Nestorian synod declared in Syriac of the

Christians in the "islands of the south"—that is, Arabia—that "women who once believed in Christ and wish to live a Christian life must keep themselves with all their might from a union with the pagans [*hanpê*]. . . . Christian women must absolutely avoid living with pagans."[17]

Many later Christian writers referred to Muslims as pagans, and some historians have taken this as an early example of such usage. There are telling indications, however, that when seventh-century Christian writers referred to "pagans," they meant exactly that and not Muslims. The Nestorian synod stipulated that "those who are listed among the ranks of the faithful must distance themselves from the pagan custom of taking two wives." Islam, of course, allows a man to take as many as four wives, as well as slave girls as concubines (Qur'an 4:3). This synodal instruction may therefore be an imprecise reference to Islamic polygamy—or a precise reference to a pagan custom. In addition, the synod directs that "the Christian dead must be buried in a Christian manner, not after the manner of the pagans. Now, it is a pagan custom to wrap the dead in rich and precious clothing, and to make . . . loud lamentations regarding them. . . . Christians are not permitted to bury their dead in silk cloth or in precious clothing."[18] None of this has anything to do with Islam as we know it, which does not allow for burial in rich clothing, eschews silk, and frowns on loud lamentations for the dead.

It appears, therefore, that the Nestorian synod was talking about real pagans, forty years after they were supposedly cleared from Arabia.

Another telling indication comes from Athanasius II, the Monophysite patriarch of Antioch (683–686), the Syrian city that was at that time the fourth most important see in Christendom. Athanasius laments that Christians "take part unrestrainedly with the pagans in their festivals," and "some unfortunate women unite themselves with the pagans." He describes practices that sound more genuinely pagan than Islamic: "In short they all eat, making no distinction, any of the pagans' [sacrificial] victims, forgetting thus . . . the orders and exhortations of the Apostles . . . to shun fornication, the [flesh of] strangled [animals], blood, and food from pagan sacrifices."[19]

This is a reference to the apostles' instructions to Gentile converts from paganism to "abstain from the pollutions of idols and from unchastity and from what is strangled and from blood" (Acts 15:20), but Athanasius doesn't seem to be simply repeating this as a formulaic prohibition. The pagans he is concerned about seem to be engaging in at least some of these practices, as Athanasius continues: "Exhort them, reprimand them, warn them, and especially the women united with such men, to keep themselves from food [derived] from their sacrifices, from strangled [meat], and from their forbidden congregations."[20]

Muslims do sacrifice animals once a year, on the feast of Eid ul-Adha, marking the end of the time of the hajj, the great pilgrimage to Mecca; they do not, however, strangle the animals thus sacrificed. It is thus extremely unlikely that Athanasius had Islam or Eid ul-Adha in mind, and much more probable that there were actual pagans in the precise areas from which Islam is supposed to have eradicated paganism fifty years earlier.

It may be that the conquerors themselves were more pagan than Muslim—not because they had recently converted to Islam and retained some of their old practices, but because Islam itself, as we know it today, did not exist.[21] In any case, whether it existed or not, neither the Arabians nor the people they conquered mentioned the fact.

## No Muslims

In 639 the Monophysite Christian patriarch John I of Antioch held a colloquy with the Arabian commander Amr ibn al-As; it survives in a manuscript dating from 874.[22] In it the author refers to the Arabians not as Muslims but as "Hagarians" (*mhaggraye*)—that is, the people of Hagar, Abraham's concubine and the mother of Ishmael. The Arabic interlocutor denies the divinity of Christ, in accord with Islamic teaching, but neither side makes any mention of the Qur'an, Islam, or Muhammad.[23]

Similarly, in 647 Ishoyahb III, the patriarch of Seleucia, wrote in a letter about the "Tayyaye" and "Arab Hagarians" who "do not help those who attribute sufferings and death to God, the Lord of everything."[24] In other words, the Hagarians reject the divinity of Christ. Here again, there is no mention of Muslims, Islam, the Qur'an, or Muhammad the Islamic prophet. Ishoyahb's account agrees with the disputation from eight years earlier in saying that the Arabian conquerors denied Christ's divinity, but it says nothing about any new doctrines they might have been bringing to their newly conquered lands.

When the early non-Muslim sources do mention Muhammad, their accounts, like the *Doctrina Jacobi*, diverge in important ways from the standard Islamic story. A chronicle attributed to the Armenian bishop Sebeos and written in the 660s or 670s portrays a "Mahmet" as a merchant and preacher from among the Ishmaelites who taught his followers to worship the only true God, the God of Abraham. So far, so good: That sounds exactly like the prophet of Islam. But other elements of Sebeos's account have no trace in Islamic tradition. The bishop's chronicle begins with the story of a meeting between Jewish refugees and the Ishmaelites in Arabia, after the Byzantine reconquest of Edessa in 628:

> They set out into the desert and came to Arabia, among the children of Ishmael; they sought their help, and explained to them that they were kinsmen according to the Bible. Although they [the Ishmaelites] were ready to accept this close kinship, they [the Jews] nevertheless could not convince the mass of the people, because their cults were different.
>
> At this time there was an Ishmaelite called Mahmet, a merchant; he presented himself to them as though at God's command, as a preacher, as the way of truth, and taught them to know the God of Abraham, for he was very well-informed, and very well-acquainted with the story of Moses. As the command came from on high, they all united under the authority of a single man, under a single law, and, abandoning vain cults,

returned to the living God who had revealed Himself to their
father Abraham. Mahmet forbade them to eat the flesh of any
dead animal, to drink wine, to lie or to fornicate. He added:
"God has promised this land to Abraham and his posterity after
him forever; he acted according to His promise while he loved
Israel. Now you, you are the sons of Abraham and God fulfills in
you the promise made to Abraham and his posterity. Only love
the God of Abraham, go and take possession of your country
which God gave to your father Abraham, and none will be able
to resist you in the struggle, for God is with you."

Then they all gathered together from Havilah unto Shur
and before Egypt [Genesis 25:18]; they came out of the desert
of Pharan divided into twelve tribes according to the lineages
of their patriarchs. They divided among their tribes the twelve
thousand Israelites, a thousand per tribe, to guide them into
the land of Israel. They set out, camp by camp, in the order of
their patriarchs: Nebajoth, Kedar, Abdeel, Mibsam, Mishma,
Dumah, Massa, Hadar, Tema, Jetur, Naphish and Kedemah
[Genesis 25:13–15]. These are the tribes of Ishmael. . . . All that
remained of the peoples of the children of Israel came to join
them, and they constituted a mighty army. Then they sent an
embassy to the emperor of the Greeks, saying: "God has given
this land as a heritage to our father Abraham and his posterity after him; we are the children of Abraham; you have held
our country long enough; give it up peacefully, and we will not
invade your territory; otherwise we will retake with interest
what you have taken."[25]

It is extraordinary that one of the earliest accounts of Muhammad
as a prophet that contains any detail at all depicts him as insisting
on the Jews' right to the Holy Land—even if in the context of claiming that land for the Ishmaelites, acting in conjunction with the Jews.
Many elements in Islamic tradition do show Muhammad proclaiming
himself as a prophet in the line of the Jewish prophets and enjoining

various observances adapted from Jewish law upon his new community. He even originally had the Muslims praying toward the Temple Mount in Jerusalem, before the revelation came from Allah that they should face Mecca instead. It is odd, however, that this account gives no hint of any of the antagonism toward the Jews that came to characterize Muhammad and the Muslims' posture toward them; the Qur'an characterizes Jews as the worst enemies of the Muslims (5:82).

Of course, Sebeos's account here is wildly unhistorical. There is no record of twelve thousand Jews partnering with Arabians to invade Byzantine holdings. Nonetheless, the mention of Muhammad is one of the earliest on record, and it corresponds with Islamic tradition both in depicting Muhammad as a merchant and in recording that, at least at one point in his career, he fostered an alliance with the Jews. Yet from Sebeos's account, one gets the impression that as late as the 660s, the Muslims and the Jews were spiritual kin and political allies. This doesn't correspond to anything in Islamic tradition or the conventional account.

If this does reflect, even in a radically distorted way, an actual historical incident, it is certain that the Jews who entered into this alliance did not think of it as what modern-day ecumenists term "Muslim-Jewish engagement." There is still no mention of Muslims or Islam. As we have seen, the contemporary chroniclers from the lands they invaded called them "Hagarians," "Saracens," or "Taiyaye." The invaders referred to themselves as *Muhajirun,* "emigrants"—a term that would eventually take on a particular significance within Islam but that at this time preceded any clear mention of Islam as such. Greek-speaking writers would sometimes term the invaders "Magaritai," which appears to be derived from *Muhajirun.* But conspicuously absent from the stock of terms that invaded and conquered people used to name the conquering Arabians was "Muslims."[26]

Sebeos also records that Muawiya, governor of Syria and later caliph, sent a letter to the Byzantine emperor Constantine "the Bearded" in 651. The letter calls on Constantine to renounce Christianity—in favor not of Islam but of a much vaguer Abrahamic monotheism:

If you wish to live in peace . . . renounce your vain religion, in which you have been brought up since infancy. Renounce this Jesus and convert to the great God whom I serve, the God of our father Abraham. . . . If not, how will this Jesus whom you call Christ, who was not even able to save himself from the Jews, be able to save you from my hands?[27]

Islam's contempt for the idea of Christ crucified is evident, but once again, no Muhammad, no Qur'an, no Islam as such. Muawiya's call to Constantine to convert to the religion of "the God of our father Abraham" recalls the Qur'an's quasi-creedal formulation: "We believe in God, and in that which has been sent down on Abraham, Ishmael, Isaac, and Jacob, and the Tribes, and that which was given to Moses and Jesus and the Prophets, of their Lord; we make no division between any of them, and to Him we surrender" (2:136). But this Qur'an passage is itself noteworthy for not mentioning the new revelations purportedly delivered to the prophet who was reciting that very book, and who was supposed to confirm the message that the earlier prophets brought.

It is also odd that Sebeos makes no mention of the Ishmaelite merchant Mahmet in connection with Muawiya's letter; maybe this mysterious Arabian leader was not as central to this Abrahamic religion as he would later become.

And so the earliest accounts depict an Arabic monotheism, occasionally featuring a prophet named Muhammad who situated himself in some way within the religion of Abraham, but there is little else to go by. An anonymous non-Muslim chronicler writing around the year 680 identifies Muhammad as the leader of the "sons of Ishmael," whom God sent against the Persians "like the sand of the sea-shores." He specifies the Ka'ba—the cubed-shaped shrine in Mecca—as the center of the Arabians' worship, identifying it with Abraham, "the father of the head of their race." But he offers no details about Muhammad's particular teachings, and like all other early chroniclers, he never mentions the Qur'an or uses the words *Muslim* or *Islam*.[28]

Writing ten years later, in 690, the Nestorian Christian chronicler John bar Penkaye writes of the authority of Muhammad and of the Arabians' brutality in enforcing that authority, but he still knows of no new holy book among the conquerors. He also paints a picture of a new religious practice that is far closer to Judaism and Christianity than Islam eventually became:

> The Arabs . . . had a certain order from the one who was their leader, in favour of the Christian people and the monks; they held also, under his leadership, the worship of one God, according to the customs of the Old Covenant; at the outset they were so attached to the traditions of Muhammad who was their teacher, that they inflicted the pain of death upon any one who seemed to contradict his tradition. . . . Among them there were many Christians, some from the Heretics, and some from us.[29]

## The First Use of the Term *Muslim*?

Also in the 690s, a Coptic Christian bishop, John of Nikiou, makes the first mention of Muslims:

> And now many of the Egyptians who had been false Christians denied the holy orthodox faith and lifegiving baptism, and embraced the religion of the Muslims, the enemies of God, and accepted the detestable doctrine of the beast, that is, Mohammed, and they erred together with those idolaters, and took arms in their hands and fought against the Christians. And one of them . . . embraced the faith of Islam . . . and persecuted the Christians.[30]

There is, however, reason to believe that this text as it stands is not as John of Nikiou wrote it. It survives only in an Ethiopic translation from the Arabic, dating from 1602. The Arabic was itself a translation from the original Greek or some other language. There is no other record of the terms *Muslim* and *Islam* being used either by the Arabians or by the conquered people in the 690s, outside of the inscription on the Dome of the Rock, which itself has numerous questionable features, as we shall see. Thus it seems likely that John of Nikiou used other terms—*Hagarian? Saracen? Ishmaelite?*—which a translator ultimately rendered as *Muslim.*[31]

If the term *Muslim* was used in the 690s, it wasn't in as widespread usage as *Hagarian, Saracen, Muhajirun,* and *Ishmaelite.* In 708 the Christian writer Jacob of Edessa is still referring to *Mahgrayé*—a Syriac rendering of *Muhajirun,* or "emigrants":

> That the Messiah is of Davidic descent, everyone professes, the Jews, the *Mahgrayé* and the Christians. . . . The *Mahgrayé* too, though they do not wish to say that this true Messiah, who came and is acknowledged by the Christians, is God and the Son of God, nevertheless confess firmly that he is the true Messiah who was to come. . . . On this they have no dispute with us, but rather with the Jews. . . . [But] they do not assent to call the Messiah God or the Son of God.[32]

Jacob's statement demonstrates that by the first decade of the eighth century, the Muhajirun were known to confess belief in Jesus but denied his divinity—echoing the depiction of Jesus in the Qur'an as a prophet of Islam but not as divine.

### John of Damascus on the Hagarians, Ishmaelites, or Saracens

Around 730, the renowned Christian theologian John of Damascus published *On the Heresies,* a smorgasbord of nonmainstream Christianity from the perspective of Byzantine orthodoxy. He included a chapter on the strange new religion of the people he identified by three names: Hagarians, Ishmaelites, and Saracens. John writes of a "false prophet" named Muhammad (*Mamed*) who, "having happened upon the Old and the New Testament and apparently having conversed, in like manner, with an Arian monk, put together his own heresy. And after ingratiating himself with the people by a pretence of piety, he spread rumours of a scripture (*graphe*) brought down to him from heaven. So, having drafted some ludicrous doctrines in his book, he handed over to them this form of worship."[33]

John repeats some details of the Saracens' beliefs that correspond to Islamic doctrine—specifically, its critique of Christianity. "They call us," he says, "associators (*hetairiastas*) because, they say, we introduce to God an associate by saying Christ is the Son of God and God. . . . They misrepresent us as idolaters because we prostrate ourselves before the cross, which they loathe." In responding to this he also demonstrates some familiarity with Islamic practice: "And we say to them: 'How then do you rub yourselves on a stone at your Kaʿba (*Chabatha*) and hail the stone with fond kisses?'"[34]

Likewise John shows some familiarity with at least some of the contents of the Qur'an, although he never names it as such, referring instead to particular suras by their names. "Women" is the title of the fourth sura of the Qur'an, and John writes: "This Muhammad, as it has been mentioned, composed many frivolous tales, to each of which he assigned a name, like the text (*graphe*) of the Woman, in which he clearly prescribes the taking of four wives and one thousand concubines, if it is possible." This sura does indeed allow a man four wives as well as the use of slave girls, "what your right hands own" (4:3), although it doesn't specify a thousand, or any number of these. That may simply be John indulging in a bit of polemical hyperbole or using a thousand to indicate a virtually unlimited number of concubines.

John also refers to "the text of the Camel of God, about which he [that is, Muhammad] says that there was a camel from God"—a story that appears twice in the Qur'an, albeit told elliptically both times (7:77, 91:11–14). Moreover, John notes that "Muhammad mentions the text of the Table," a vestigial account of the Christian Eucharist found in Qur'an 5:112–115, and "the text of the Cow," which is the title of the Qur'an's second sura, "and several other foolish and ludicrous things which, because of their number, I think I should pass over."[35]

John demonstrates a detailed knowledge of the Qur'an's teaching about Jesus Christ, ascribing them to Muhammad. Note that the material in brackets below has been added by the translator, generally referring to Qur'an verses; it does not appear in John's original. John writes:

> He [that is, Muhammad] says that Christ is the Word of God and His Spirit [cf. Qur'an 9:171], created [3:59] and a servant [4:172, 9:30, 43:59], and that he was born from Mary [3:45 and cf. Isa ibn Maryam], the sister of Moses and Aaron [19:28], without seed [3:47, 19:20, 21:91, 66:12]. For, he says, the Word of God and His Spirit entered Mary [19:17, 21:91, 66:12], and she gave birth to Jesus, a prophet [9:30, 33:7] and a servant of God. And [he says] that the Jews, acting unlawfully, wanted to crucify him, but, on seizing [him], they crucified [only] his shadow; Christ himself was not crucified, he says, nor did he die [4:157]. For God took him up to heaven to Himself. . . . And God questioned him saying: "Jesus, did you say that 'I am son of God and God'?" And, he says, Jesus answered, "Mercy me, Lord, you know that I did not say so" [5:116].[36]

This is an impressive summary of the Qur'an's teaching on Jesus, but note again that the verse citations have been added by the translator into English; John does not cite sura and verse, and his summary contains small but significant departures from the actual Qur'anic text. In Qur'an 5:116, for example, Allah does not ask Jesus whether he called himself the Son of God and God, but rather: "Didst thou say unto men, 'Take me and my mother as gods, apart from God?'" And Jesus does not respond, "Mercy me, Lord, you know that I did not say so," but instead: "To Thee be glory! It is not mine to say what I have no right to. If I indeed said it, Thou knowest it, knowing what is within my soul, and I know not what is within Thy soul; Thou knowest the things unseen."

These discrepancies, as well as the fact that John leaves out of his summary significant things the Qur'an says about Jesus that would have been of interest to him as a Christian theologian (particularly Jesus' apparent prophecy of the coming of Muhammad in 61:6), give rise to the possibility that John was working not from an actual copy of the Qur'an but from oral tradition or some text that was later adapted as part of the Qur'an.

Another reason to suggest that John was not summarizing from a Qur'an that he had open in front of him is the fact that he never refers to the book by name. Instead he gives the impression that the "text of the Woman" and the "text of the Camel of God" and the "text of the Cow" are all separate documents rather than parts of a single collection. "Women" (not the singular "Woman," as John has it) and "The Cow" are titles of two Qur'anic suras (4 and 2, respectively); "Camel of God" is not. It seems more likely that John is working from what the Hagarians or those who had contact with them may have told him, and not from a written text, or at least not a written text exactly like the Qur'an as we know it.

It is also possible that this manner of citation is simply an idiosyncrasy of John's, with no larger significance. In any case, John betrays considerably more knowledge, and more accurate knowledge, of actual Islamic teaching than did earlier non-Muslim writers who took up the subject of the beliefs of their Arabian conquerors. But note that he is writing a century after the purported revelation of the Qur'an and establishment of Islam.

And even at this point, nearly a hundred years after the reported death of Muhammad, the image of the prophet of Islam remained fuzzy. Indeed, a full-blown picture of Muhammad, recipient through the angel Gabriel of Allah's revelations of the Qur'an, living and working in the "full light of history," would not appear for several more decades.

# 2

## Jesus, the Muhammad

### Muhammad: A Late Arrival on the Scene

Non-Muslim chroniclers who were writing at the time of the early Arabian conquests made no mention of the Qur'an, no mention of Islam, no mention of Muslims, and scant mention of Muhammad.

The situation is no different when one turns to the contemporary Muslim artifacts of the time. The Arabian invaders who swept into North Africa in the 650s and 660s and besieged Constantinople in the 670s were energized, in the traditional view, by the Qur'an and Muhammad's teaching and example. But they made no mention of what was supposed to be their primary inspiration. References to Qur'anic passages and Islam do not appear until near the end of the seventh century, and when the Arabian invaders mentioned Muhammad, they did so in ways that departed significantly from the canonical Islamic account.

For example, in 677 or 678, during the reign of the first Umayyad caliph, Muawiya (661–680), a dam was dedicated near Ta'if in Arabia. (The Umayyads were the dynasty that ruled the Near East from the middle of the seventh century to the middle of the eighth.) The official inscription reads:

This is the dam [belonging] to the Servant of God Muawiya Commander of the Faithful. Abdullah bn Saxr[1] built it

with God's permission in the year 58.
Allah! Forgive the Servant of God Muawiya,
Commander of the Faithful, confirm him in his position and
　　help him and
let the faithful
rejoice in him. Amr bn Habbab/Jnab wrote it.[2]


Muawiya is the "Commander of the Faithful," but the nature of
the faith, besides being faith in Allah, is left undefined. There is no
hint of the Islamic religious culture that would soon and ever after
be all-pervasive in inscriptions like this one and other official proclamations.[3] Exactly what Muawiya did believe in is unclear, but if he
believed that Muhammad was the prophet of Allah and the Qur'an
was Allah's book delivered to mankind by means of that prophet, he
gave no indication of it.

Likewise the official inscription on a canal bridge in Fustat in
Egypt, dating from the year 688, reads: "This is the arch which Abd
al-Aziz bn Marwan, the Emir, ordered to be built. Allah! Bless him in
all his deeds, confirm his authority as You please, and make him very
satisfied in himself and his household, Amen! Sa'd Abu Uthman built
it and Abd ar-Rahman wrote it in the month Safar of the year 69."[4]
Here again, no Muhammad, no Qur'an, no Islam.

One of the best records of the worldview of the conquerors is
found in the coins they struck. Coins carry official sanction and bear
inscriptions that generally reflect the foundational principles of the
polity that struck them. In the Islamic world today it is difficult to go
very long through any given day without encountering some mention of Islam, Muhammad, or the Qur'an. The *shahada*, the Islamic
confession of faith, is featured on the Saudi flag. Coins all over the
Islamic world carry inscriptions containing some Islamic element.
The most obvious and proudly held aspect of the Islamic world is that
it is *Islamic*. But in the earliest days of Islam, that is the one element
most conspicuously lacking.

The earliest known coins that the conquerors produced bore the inscription *bism Allah*, "in the name of Allah." *Allah* is simply the Arabic word for God, used by Arabic-speaking Jews and Christians as well as by Muslims. Yet coins minted in the 650s and possibly as late as the 670s bore this inscription alone, without making any reference to Muhammad as Allah's prophet or to any other distinctive element of Islam. This is the period of the first flush of Arabian conquest, when one would most expect the Arabians to stress the particular features of their religion, which they considered to have been made victorious over other, competing religions in the region.

Other coins dating from the same period feature inscriptions such as *bism Allah rabbi* ("In the name of Allah my Lord"), *rabbi Allah* ("my Lord is Allah"), and *bism Allah ul-malik* ("in the name of Allah the King").[5] Conspicuously absent is coinage bearing any reference to *Muhammad rasul Allah* ("Muhammad is the messenger of Allah").

One coin that the Arabian conquerors apparently struck in Palestine between 647 and 658 does bear the inscription *muhammad*. And yet there is no way it can be taken as a product of pious, informed, believing Muslims: It depicts a figure, apparently of a ruler—in violation of Islam's prohibition of images. Even odder is the fact that the figure is carrying a cross, a symbol that is anathema to Islam.[6]

Numismatist Clive Foss explains this coin's obverse (shown at left) as depicting a "crude standing figure with detached crown, flanked by long cross r., محمد, *muh[ammad]*."[7]

Muhammad, the prophet of Islam, is supposed to have been the principal agent of a new civilizational order based on a holy book that admonished Christians that Jesus was neither killed nor crucified: "They did not slay him, neither crucified him" (Qur'an 4:157). Would the caliph, the leader of a religious group that claimed it a blasphemy for a rival religion to regard Jesus as the Son of God, really place the crowning symbol of that rival religion on his public inscriptions? Would the leader of a religious group whose founding prophet claimed that Jesus would return at the end of the world and "break all crosses"—as an insult to himself and a testament to the transcendent majesty of Allah—really allow a cross to be featured on any inscription carved anywhere in his domains?[8]

Would the followers of this new prophet, whose new religious and political order was defiantly at odds with that of the "cross worshippers," have placed any figure bearing a cross on any of their coinage? Perhaps this can be interpreted as a gesture of Islam's tolerance, given that Christians overwhelmingly populated the domains of the new Arabian Empire. Yet Islamic law as codified in the ninth and tenth centuries forbade Christians to display the cross openly—even on the outside of churches—and there is no indication that the imposition of this law was a reversal of an earlier practice.[9] So it is exceedingly curious that Muslim conquerors of Christians would strike a coin bearing the central image of the very religion and political order they despised, defeated, and were determined to supplant.[10]

Other coins from this period also bear the cross and the word *Muhammad*.[11] A Syrian coin that dates from 686 or 687, at the earliest, features what numismatist Volker Popp describes as "the *muhammad* motto" on the reverse side (right).[12] The obverse depicts a ruler crowned with a cross and holding another cross.[13]

The most obvious explanation is that the "muhammad" to whom the coin refers is not the prophet of Islam. Alternatively, the figure on the coin could have evolved into the Muhammad of Islam but was not much like him at the time the coin was issued. Or it may be that the word *muhammad* is not a name at all but a title, meaning the "praised one" or the "chosen one." Popp, noting that some of these seventh-century cross-bearing coins also bear the legend *bismillah*—"in the name of God"—as well as *muhammad*, suggests that the coins are saying of the depicted ruler, "He is chosen in the name of God," or "Let him be praised in the name of God."[14]

This could be a derivative of the common Christian liturgical phrase referring to the coming of Christ: "Blessed is he who comes in the name of the Lord." In that case, the *muhammad*, the praised or blessed one, would be Jesus himself.

Supporting this possibility is the fact that the few times the Qur'an mentions Muhammad by name, the references are not clearly to the prophet of Islam but work equally well as general exhortations to obey that which was revealed to the "praised one," who could be someone else. Jesus is the most likely candidate, because, as we have seen, the Qur'an tells believers that "Muhammad is nothing but a messenger; messengers have passed away before him" (3:144), using language identical to that it later uses of Jesus: "the Messiah, the son of Mary, is nothing but a messenger; messengers have passed away before him" (5:75).[15] This opens the possibility that here, as elsewhere, Jesus is the one being referred to as the "praised one," the *muhammad*.

The first biographer of Muhammad, Ibn Ishaq, lends additional support to this possibility. Recall that in Qur'an 61:6, Jesus is depicted as prophesying the coming of a new "Messenger of God," "whose name shall be Ahmad." Because *Ahmad*—the "praised one"—is a variant of *Muhammad*, Islamic scholars take this passage to be a reference to the prophet of Islam. Ibn Ishaq amplifies this view in his biography of Muhammad, quoting "the Gospel," the New Testament, where Jesus says that "when the Comforter [*Munahhemana*] has come whom God will send to you from the Lord's presence, and the spirit of truth which will have gone forth from the Lord's presence, he (shall bear) witness of me and ye also, because ye have been with me from the beginning. I have spoken unto you about this that ye should not be in doubt." Ibn Ishaq then explains: "the *Munahhemana* (God bless and preserve him!) in Syriac is Muhammad; in Greek he is the paraclete."[16]

Ibn Ishaq's English translator Alfred Guillaume notes that the word *Munahhemana* "in the Eastern patristic literature . . . is applied to our Lord Himself"—that is, not to Muhammad but to Jesus. The original bearer of the title "praised one" was Jesus, and this title and the accompanying prophecy were "skillfully manipulated to provide the reading we have" in Ibn Ishaq's biography of Muhammad—and, for that matter, in the Qur'an itself.[17]

Whichever of these possibilities is correct, the weakest hypothesis is that these *muhammad* coins refer to the prophet of the new religion as he is depicted in the Qur'an and the Hadith.[18] For there are no contemporary references to Muhammad, the Islamic prophet who received the Qur'an and preached its message to unify Arabia (often by force) and whose followers then carried his jihad far beyond Arabia; the first clear records of the Muhammad of Islam far postdate these coins.

## The Cross and the Crescent Together

Equally curious is a coin that was to all appearances minted officially in northern Palestine or Jordan during the reign of Muawiya. The sovereign depicted on it (it is unclear whether it is Muawiya himself or someone else) is shown not with the cross topping a globe, which

was a feature of Byzantine coinage of the period, but with a cross that features a crescent at the top of its vertical bar.[19]

The crescent appears at the top of the cross on the obverse, at the right of the image of the sovereign. Could this unusual design be a remnant of a long-forgotten synthesis? Or was it struck at a time when the distinction between Christianity and Arabic/Islamic monotheism was not as sharp as it eventually became? Whatever the case may be, it is hard to imagine that such a coin would have been minted at all had the dogmatic Islamic abhorrence of the cross been in place at the time, as one would expect if Islam had really burst from Arabia fully formed.[20]

## The Caliph and the Cross

There is another arresting item among the surviving artifacts from the reign of Muawiya: an inscription, dating from the year 662, on a bathhouse in Gadara in Palestine. (Gadara is one possible setting of the Gospel story in which Jesus casts demons out of a young man and into a herd of pigs.) The Greek inscription identifies Muawiya as "the servant of God, the leader of the protectors," and dates the dedication of the bathhouse to "the year 42 following the Arabs." At the beginning of the inscription is a cross.[21]

This was a public installation, bearing the official sanction of the governing authorities. Muawiya himself most likely visited there, so he probably saw this inscription and apparently did not consider it to be anything amiss.[22] Although the Umayyads were notorious (or at least so Islamic tradition tells us) for the laxity of their Islamic observance, it is one thing to be relaxed in one's Islam and another thing to allow for the promotion of the symbols of another religion altogether—much less one that is rebuked numerous times in the Qur'an.

Unless, of course, there was no Qur'an, and no Islam, at least in the form in which we know it today, when the public baths in Gadara were dedicated, as also when the cross-bearing Muhammad coin was minted in Palestine.

Still more striking is the identification on the bathhouse inscription of the year as "following the Arabs"—that is, the "era of the Arabs," rather than the more expected "era of Islam" or "era after the Hijra." The Arabian conquests are a historical fact; that the Arabian conquerors actually came out of Arabia inspired by the Qur'an and Muhammad is less certain. This inscription becomes perfectly understandable if the centrality of the Hijra—Muhammad's move from Mecca to Medina in 622, marked as the beginning of the Islamic calendar—and Islam to the Arabian conquerors was projected back into history, but was not actually a contemporary phenomenon when the bathhouse was dedicated.

What, then, was the beginning of the "era of the Arabians"? The Arabians used a lunar calendar, and a year in the lunar calendar was ten days shorter than the solar year. So forty-two lunar years equal forty solar years, and thus the year 622 was forty-two lunar years before the dedication of the bathhouse in 662. The year 622 saw the Byzantine Empire win a surprising and decisive victory over the Persians, which led to the collapse of Persian power. Not long thereafter the Arabians filled the power vacuum and took control of the Persian Empire. Soon they threatened Byzantine holdings as well. What became the date of the Hijra may have originally marked the beginning of the Arabians as a political force to be reckoned with on the global scene.

Similarly dating some momentous event to the year 622, and yet containing no specifically Islamic characteristics, is an inscription that dates itself from the year 64—that is, the Gregorian year 683, which is sixty-four lunar years from the year 622. This graffito found near Karbala in Iraq states:

> In the name of Allah the Merciful, the Compassionate
> Allah [is] great in greatness and great is His Will
> and prayer / praise to Allah morning, evening and a long night.
> Allah! Lord of Gabriel and Michael and Asrafil,
> forgive Tabit bin Yazid al-Asari [i.e., from Ashar]

his earlier transgression and his later one
and him who says aloud, Amen, Lord of Creation
and this document (*kitab*) was inscribed in
Sawal of the year 64.[23]

Sawal is the tenth month of the Islamic calendar, as well as of
the pre-Islamic lunar calendar that the pagan Arabs used. Gabriel,
Michael, and Asrafil are angels in the biblical tradition; it is extremely
odd, if Tabit bin Yazid al-Asari was a Muslim who revered Muhammad as the last and greatest prophet, that he invoked Allah as the
Lord of these angels rather than in some more conventionally Islamic
manner. Likewise it is unlikely that Tabit bin Yazid al-Asari could
have been a Christian or a Jew, for the same reason: Invoking God
as Lord of the angels was not a common practice for either. After
all, other inscriptions from roughly the same period invoke Allah as
the "Lord of Musa and Isa," that is, Moses and Jesus—but not, once
again, Muhammad.[24]

This kind of inscription may, however, have been more common
among those who considered themselves to be monotheists with a
kinship to Jews and Christians but nonetheless distinct from them.
This would fit in with what we have seen of Muawiya's Abrahamic
but apparently creedally vague monotheism. Muawiya objected to the
divinity of Christ but was apparently not hostile enough to Christianity to forbid the cross altogether, as Islam ultimately did. No
surviving inscription indicates that he was aware of Muhammad or
Islam, but he does mention Abraham and thus seems to have some
knowledge of the founding figures of the Hebrew scriptures. Tabit
bin Yazid al-Asari, who apparently lived in Muawiya's domains during his reign, could have been one who subscribed to precisely this
religious perspective—indeed, it may have been an imperative for
subjects of the new Arab domains.

If the explanation for the cross on the Gadara inscription is lost in
the mists of history, it is reasonable to surmise that Islamic strictures
against the cross and Christianity were ignored because those stric-

tures did not yet exist, at least in their present form. Coins that appear to depict Muawiya's successor, Yazid I (680–683), also feature a cross.[25]

It is even possible, given these coins and the official nature of the Gadara inscription, that Muawiya and Yazid thought of themselves in some way as Christian rulers. They would have been exponents not of any form of Christianity that survives today but rather of a faith that encompassed Christianity and was not incompatible with some form of it. A clue as to the nature of the Christianity to which Muawiya, Yazid, and many of their subjects may have adhered can be found in the inscriptions inside the Dome of the Rock, the imposing mosque that was constructed late in the seventh century on Jerusalem's Temple Mount, the holiest site in Judaism and holy for Christians as well.[26]

### The Dome of the Rock:
### The First Exposition of Islamic Theology?

Traditionally the Dome of the Rock has been understood as a manifestation of the triumph and superiority of Islam. Completed in 691, eleven years after the death of Muawiya, on the order of the caliph Abd al-Malik (685–705), the mosque contains inscriptions that appear to be taken directly from the Qur'an, although not in any orderly fashion.

Here is the text of the inscription on the southeast portion of the octagonal arcade within the Dome of the Rock. The translator, Estelle Whelan, has added in brackets material indicating where various portions of the inscription appear (and do not appear) in the Qur'an:

> "In the name of God, the Merciful the Compassionate. There is no god but God. He is One. He has no associate" [this is the beginning of the *shahada*]. "Unto Him belongeth sovereignty and unto Him belongeth praise. He quickeneth and He giveth death; and He is Able to do all things" [a conflation of 64:1 and

57:2]. "Muhammad is the servant of God and His messenger" [variant completion of the *shahada*]. "Lo! God and His angels shower blessings on the Prophet. O ye who believe! Ask blessings on him and salute him with a worthy salutation" [33:56 complete]. "The blessing of God be on him and peace be on him, and may God have mercy" [blessing, not in the Qur'anic text]. "O, People of the Book! Do not exaggerate in your religion (*dinikum*) nor utter aught concerning God save the truth. The Messiah, Jesus son of Mary, was only a messenger of God, and His Word which He conveyed unto Mary, and a spirit from Him. So believe in God and His messengers, and say not 'Three'—Cease! (it is) better for you!—God is only One God. Far be it removed from His transcendent majesty that He should have a son. His is all that is in the heavens and all that is in the earth. And God is sufficient as Defender. The Messiah will never scorn to be a servant unto God, nor will the favoured angels. Whoso scorneth His service and is proud, all such will He assemble unto Him" [4:171–72 complete]. "Oh God, bless Your messenger and Your servant Jesus son of Mary" (interjection introducing the following passage). "Peace be on him the day he was born, and the day he dies, and the day he shall be raised alive!" [19:33 complete, with change from first to third person]. "Such was Jesus, son of Mary, (this is) a statement of the truth concerning which they doubt. It befitteth not (the Majesty of) God that He should take unto Himself a son. Glory be to Him! When He decreeth a thing, He saith unto it only: Be! and it is" [19:34–35 complete]. Lo! God is my Lord and your Lord. So serve Him. That is the right path" [19:36 complete, except for initial "and"]. "God (Himself) is witness that there is no God save Him. And the angels and the men of learning (too are witness). Maintaining His creation in justice, there is no God save Him, the Almighty, the Wise. Lo! religion with God (is) The Surrender (to His will and guidance). Those who (formerly) received the Book differed only after knowledge came unto them, through transgression among themselves. Whoso disbelieveth the revelations of God (will find that) lo! God is swift at reckoning" [3:18–19 complete].

Another Dome of the Rock inscription, on the outer portion of the arcade, reads this way:

"In the name of God, the Merciful the Compassionate. There is no god but God. He is One. He has no associate" [beginning of the *shahada*]. "Say: He is God, the One! God, the eternally Besought of all! He begetteth not nor was begotten. And there is none comparable unto Him" [112 complete except for the introductory *basmala*]. "Muhammad is the Messenger of God" [completion of the *shahada*], "the blessing of God be on him" [blessing]. "In the name of God, the Merciful the Compassionate. There is no god but God. He is One. He has no associate. Muhammad is the Messenger of God" [*shahada*, complete]. "Lo! God and His angels shower blessings on the Prophet. O ye who believe! Ask blessings on him and salute him with a worthy salutation" [33:56 complete].

"In the name of God, the Merciful the Compassionate. There is no god but God. He is One" [beginning of the *shahada*]. "Praise be to God, Who hath not taken unto Himself a son, and Who hath no partner in the Sovereignty, nor hath He any protecting friend through dependence. And magnify Him with all magnificence" [17:111 complete except for the initial "And say"]. "Muhammad is the Messenger of God" [completion of the *shahada*], "the blessing of God be on him and the angels and His prophets, and peace be on him, and may God have mercy" [blessing].

"In the name of God, the Merciful the Compassionate. There is no god but God. He is One. He has no associate" [beginning of the *shahada*]. "Unto Him belongeth sovereignty and unto Him belongeth praise. He quickeneth and He giveth death; and He is Able to do all things" [conflation of 64:1 and 57:2]. "Muhammad is the Messenger of God" [completion of the *shahada*], "the blessing of God be on him. May He accept his intercession on the Day of Judgment on behalf of his people" [blessing and prayer].

"In the name of God, the Merciful the Compassionate. There is no god but God. He is One. He has no associate. Muhammad is the Messenger of God" [the *shahada* complete], "the blessing of God be on him" [blessing].

"The servant of God Abd [Allah the *Imam al-Ma'mun*, Commander] of the Faithful, built this dome in the year two and seventy. May God accept from him and be content with him. Amen, Lord of the worlds, praise be to God" [foundation notice].[27]

This Qur'anic material is the earliest direct attestation to the existence of the book—sixty years after the Arab armies that had presumably been inspired by it began conquering neighboring lands. And yet the mixture of Qur'anic and non-Qur'anic material is odd. Would pious Muslims really have composed an inscription that combined Qur'anic material—which they would have understood as the perfect and unalterable, eternal word of Allah—with merely human words, however eloquent? Would Muslims who believed that the Qur'an was the perfect and unalterable word of Allah have dared to change the Qur'an's words "Peace be upon me, the day I was born, and the day I die, and the day I am raised alive!" (19:33) to the Dome of the Rock's "Peace be on him the day he was born, and the day he dies, and the day he shall be raised alive!"? The change is not substantial, but it would still involve taking liberties with the perfect word of Allah, which presumably would give the pious pause.

Likewise, the presentation of material from all over the book, although it is thematically related, is curious. If the authors of the inscription intended to include all the Qur'an's statements that rebuke Trinitarian Christianity, there are some notable omissions—especially the claim that "they did not slay him, neither crucified him" (4:157). Or if the main thrust of the inscription is to deny the divinity of Christ and assert the prophethood of Muhammad, the omission of the Qur'anic passage in which Jesus prophesies the coming of Muhammad is odd: "Children of Israel, I am indeed the Messenger of God to you, confirming the Torah that is before me, and giving good tidings of a Messenger who shall come after me, whose name shall be Ahmad" (61:6).

Given the seamlessly mixed Qur'anic / non-Qur'anic nature of the inscription and the way the Qur'an passages are pulled together from all over the book, some scholars, including Christoph Luxenberg, have posited that whoever wrote this inscription was not quoting from a Qur'an that already existed. Rather, they suggest, most of this material was added to the Qur'an only later, as the book was compiled.

Not everyone agrees, of course. Estelle Whelan, writing in the *Journal of the American Oriental Society* in 1998, argues that if the Dome of the Rock inscriptions now found in the Qur'an actually predated the Qur'an, they would have gone into the Qur'an the way they appear on the famous mosque: "It seems particularly unlikely that the combination of phrases from 64:1 and 57:2, repeated twice, could originally have been a unitary statement that was then 'deconstructed' and incorporated into different parts of the Qur'an." She thus argues that the Qur'an must have predated the inscription and served as its source.[28]

Although the two verses do go together very well in the Dome of the Rock inscriptions, they are not notably out of place in their contexts in the Qur'an as it stands—unlike other verses that appear to be fairly obvious interpolations (as we will see in chapter 8). It may be that both the Dome of the Rock and the Qur'an incorporated material from earlier sources that contained similar material in different forms. After all, if anything is a characteristic of early Islamic literature, it is repetition: Even the Qur'an itself, as brief as it is (shorter than the New Testament), tells numerous stories more than once and frequently repeats phrases. Yet all its repetitions of the same story, whether that of Moses and Pharaoh, or of Satan's refusal to bow down to Adam, contain minor variations. This is what one might expect if this material was held in the minds of poets, prophets, and orators rather than committed to writing.

It is thus possible that the Dome of the Rock inscriptions predated the Qur'an but did not serve as its source, or at least its sole source. Qur'an 64:1 and 57:2 may simply have come from different sources, not from someone deciding to divide what appears in the Dome of the Rock inscriptions as a unified passage.

What is most unusual about the Dome of the Rock inscriptions, however, is that they may not refer to Islamic theology at all. This may seem to be an outrageous statement at first glance: After all, when the inscription warns the "People of the Book"—primarily Jews and Christians, and in this context, Christians only—not to "exaggerate in your religion" by claiming that Jesus is the Son of God, it is articulating a staple of Islamic theology and an oft-repeated assertion of the Qur'an.

But there is a grammatical difficulty with the traditional explanation of the first inscription above. *Muhammad*, remember, means "praised one" in Arabic—and, accordingly, could be a title as well as a proper name. *Al-muhammad* would be precisely the "praised one," but the word *muhammad* here without the definite article *al-* could be a gerundive meaning "praising" or "being praised," and hence also "the one who is being praised." Christoph Luxenberg, a philologist, explains that in the context of the Dome of the Rock inscription, the phrase commonly translated as "Muhammad is the servant of God and His messenger" is more correctly understood as reading "praised be the servant of God and His messenger." Luxenberg elaborates with reference to Arabic grammar: "Therefore, by using this gerundive, the text here is not speaking of a person named *Muhammad*, which was made only later metaphorically into a personal name attributed analogically to the prophet of Islam."[29]

A compelling case can be made that this inscription refers not to the prophet of Arabia at all but to Jesus himself, whom the inscription clearly calls "a messenger of God," "a servant unto God," and finally "Your messenger and Your servant."[30]

In fact, the entire inscription makes much more sense as a literary and theological statement if one understands *muhammad* as referring to Jesus. Then the whole passage is about Jesus being but a messenger of God rather than his son. By the standard Islamic interpretation, the inscription mentions Muhammad essentially in passing, identifying him as a messenger from God and his servant; then, without explanation, it turns away from Muhammad to Jesus, calling him also a messenger from and a servant of God, and spends the bulk of its time correcting Christian Christology.

If the inscription does not speak of Muhammad or reflect Islamic theology, why would it challenge the divinity of Christ? It may well offer a version of *Christian* theology differing from that of the Eastern Roman (Byzantine) Empire and the great church in Constantinople.

At the time the Dome of the Rock was constructed, the Church of Constantinople was still in the throes of a centuries-long battle to determine the exact nature of Jesus Christ. Five ecumenical councils had been held to discuss aspects of this; those who believed that Jesus was a created being, albeit a demigod, were anathematized at the first of these, held across the Bosphorus from Constantinople in Nicaea in 325. Because of the institutionalized discrimination that these heretical groups then faced, many of them left the Byzantine Empire and headed for points east. It is therefore possible that the Dome of the Rock inscription is a surviving expression of the theology of a heretical Christian group that viewed Jesus solely as a divine messenger, not as the Son of God or Savior of the world.[31]

The specific theology of such a group has not come down to us in the many denunciations of heresies that orthodox theologians produced in these centuries. But that may be due to other factors: It could have been a politically driven attempt at theological compromise, much like Monothelitism in Christianity; such a compromise would not have corresponded exactly to the theology of any particular group. Or the silence could be due simply to the remoteness of this group from the imperial centers by the time such works were being produced, or to the group's gradual coalescing with non-Christian monotheistic communities to the extent that most of what was distinctively Christian about the group was effaced.

The Dome of the Rock inscription, then, could be an expression of a theologically uncomplicated Arab monotheism that is deeply concerned with Christ and Christianity—to the point of polemicizing against claims of Christ's divinity. This preoccupation with Christ leaves us far short of Islam in any clearly recognizable form as the religion of Muhammad and the Qur'an. By that point in history, the specifics of that religion still had been nowhere elaborated.

## Abd al-Malik and Hajjaj ibn Yusuf Introduce Islam

Seen in this light, an official inscription from 693 (or possibly 702), found on a road near Tiberias, does not necessarily refer to a fully formed Islam, with its prophet Muhammad:

> In the name of Allah, the Merciful, the Compassionate[.]
> There is no God but Allah alone, He has no *sharik* [partner in
>     receiving worship]
> Muhammad is the messenger of Allah.
> The Servant of God Abd al-Malik, Commander of the Faithful,
>     ordered
> the straightening of this mountain road.
> It was made by Yahya bn al- . . .
> In Muharram of the year three [and 70 *or* and 80].[32]

Here it may seem that we finally breathe in the full atmosphere of Islam, with the denunciation of *shirk*—that is, placing partners alongside Allah—and the proclamation of Muhammad as Allah's prophet. But this inscription actually gets no more specific than those on the Dome of the Rock, which is to say that it is just as compatible with Muawiya's vague Abrahamic monotheism as with traditional Islam.

It was not until 696, five years after the Dome of the Rock was dedicated, that the caliph Abd al-Malik began to have coins minted without images of a sovereign (in line with Islam's prohibition of images) and bearing the *shahada*, the Islamic confession of faith.[33]

Thus it was Abd al-Malik who proclaimed Islam as the state religion of the empire of the Umayyads—an oddly late proclamation for an empire that was supposed to have been inspired by and founded upon Islam six decades earlier.[34] The historian Robert G. Hoyland concludes that "it was pressure from rebel factions" that induced Abd al-Malik and his successors "to proclaim Islam publicly as the ideological basis of the Arab state."[35]

Indeed, Abd al-Malik's rival Abdullah ibn Az-Zubair, who had revolted against the Umayyad caliphate and now controlled Arabia, Iraq, and Iran, had started minting coins that proclaimed Muhammad as the prophet of Allah as early as 685—the first such official proclamation.[36] The coins carried the inscription "In the name of God, Muhammad is the messenger of God (*bismillah Muhammad rasul Allah*)."[37] Hoyland remarks that this "would mean that the earliest attested Islamic profession comes from an opposition party. This is not implausible. That the revolt of Abdullah ibn Az-Zubair had religious implications is confirmed by a contemporary Christian source, which says of him that 'he had come out of zeal for the house of God and he was full of threats against the Westerners, claiming that they were transgressors of the law.'"[38]

Abd al-Malik emulated Ibn Az-Zubair in minting coins bearing the inscription *Muhammad rasul Allah*—"Muhammad is the messenger of God." In 696 Abd al-Malik's associate Hajjaj ibn Yusuf (d. 714), who served as governor of Iraq after the defeat of Ibn Az-Zubair, had coins minted that contained the full text of the Islamic confession of faith: *bism Allah la ilah ila Allah wahdahu Muhammad rasul Allah* ("In the name of God, there is no deity but God on His own; Muhammad is the messenger of God").[39] (This text is different from the common phrasing of the *shahada* in some ways—for example, in placing the *bismallah* at the start.)

Even as these proclamations appeared on coins, the situation remained in considerable flux: Some coins minted in this era bore the confession of faith but still pictured rulers; one depicted rulers with crosses on their crowns.[10]

Regardless, the reign of Abd al-Malik marked an all-important turning point. His reign also witnessed the first references by non-Muslims to "Muslims," as opposed to "Hagarians," "Ishmaelites," "Muhajirun," and "Saracens," and to the Qur'an itself. Nothing of this sort was recorded for sixty or seventy years after the Arab conquests began.

Did Abd al-Malik essentially invent Islam, or begin investing it with details about Muhammad and his teaching, to unify and strengthen his empire? The Muhammad coin that Ibn Az-Zubair minted make it unlikely that Abd al-Malik originated the idea of the Islamic prophet, but it is possible that he expropriated and greatly expanded on the nascent Muhammad myth for his own political purposes.

There are hints of this. Much of what we know of Islam may be traced to Abd al-Malik's reign. According to a hadith reported by the respected Islamic scholar as-Suyuti (d. 1505) and others, the caliph himself claimed, "I have collected the Qur'an (*jama'tul-Qur'ana*)."[41] This report emerged very late, and it contradicted well-established traditions holding that the caliph Uthman, who reigned from 644 to 656, collected and standardized the text of the Qur'an. But it is hard to explain why this hadith would have been invented at such a late date unless it contained some kernel of authenticity. Other hadiths back the claim that the Qur'an came together during the reign of Abd al-Malik. Some traditions record that Hajjaj ibn Yusuf collected and edited the Qur'an. And several hadiths affirm that Hajjaj added the bulk of the diacritical marks to the core text of the Qur'an, making it possible for the first time to read it without confusion—and, not incidentally, fixing the Islamic character of the text.[42] According to one hadith, the jurist Malik ibn Anas (d. 795) recalled that "reading from the *mushaf*"—that is, a codex of the Qur'an—"at the Mosque was not done by people in the past. It was Hajjaj b. Yusuf who first instituted it."[43]

Intriguingly, the fifteenth-century Hadith scholar Ibn Hajar (1372–1448) notes that Hajjaj "had a pure Arabic language, he was eloquent and well-versed in the law," and he said that "obedience to the Caliph in his every demand was compulsory for the population."[44] It is striking that, six centuries after Hajjaj's life, his "pure Arabic language" would persist in the memory of the Islamic community. A pure Arabic language would be useful for writing or editing Arabic scripture out of concern for obedience to the caliph and the political unity of his empire. And, for reasons we will explore later in this book, it may well have been the case that the Qur'an *needed* to be Arabicized.

The Umayyad court of Abd al-Malik and those of his successors began to expand on the hadiths about Muhammad and edit and augment the Qur'anic text to buttress their own practices and political position—a practice that the enemies of the Umayyads, the Abbasids, skillfully employed when they supplanted the Umayyads in 750.

If Abd al-Malik built up the Islamic religion for political purposes, then the earlier silence from all quarters about Muhammad, Islam, and the Qur'an can be explained very simply: There was no reference to these things because Muhammad, Islam, and the Qur'an did not exist yet, or did so only in an inchoate state.

Further evidence that Islam was newly developing during the reign of Abd al-Malik can be seen in the fact that the ideas did not take root immediately. Even after Abd al-Malik and Hajjaj ibn Yusuf did their work, the official statements that the Umayyads left behind are not unanimously or unambiguously Islamic. Qasr Kharana, a desert castle that Abd al-Malik's successor, Walid I (705–715), built in eastern Jordan, bears this inscription:

> Allahumma have mercy on Abd al-Malik ibn Umar [not Abd
>     al-Malik the caliph, who was the son of Marwan, but
>     rather the son of Umar] and forgive him his transgressions,
>     the earlier and the later ones, the hidden and the disclosed;
> No one of himself draws nigh unto Thee but that Thou for-
>     givest him and hast mercy upon him

if he believes. I believe in my Lord. Therefore bestow on me
    Thy benefits,
for Thou art the Benefactor, and have mercy
upon me, for Thou art the Merciful. Oh God, I beg of Thee to
accept from him his prayer and his donation. Amen Lord of
    Creation,
Lord of
Moses and Aaron. May God have mercy on him who reads it
    and says
Amen, Amen, Lord of Creation,
the Mighty, the Wise! Abd al-Malik bn [*sic*] Umar wrote [it] on
Monday, three [nights] remaining from Muharram of the year
    two and ninety [A.D. 710].
[Witnessed by] Lam bn [*sic*] Harun.
And lead us so we meet with my prophet and his prophet
in this world and the next.[45]

The Lord is the Lord of Moses and Aaron. No mention is made of
Muhammad. It is an odd omission, unless this newly created prophet
Muhammad was not yet established enough in the popular mind to
figure in such an invocation alongside the likes of Moses and Aaron.

But fame would soon come to the warrior prophet of Arabia. In
the year 735 another inscription betrayed a very different popular
religious sensibility:

In the name of Allah, the Compassionate, the Merciful
Allah! forgive! Hasan bn [*sic*] Maysarah
and his two parents and their offspring
Amen Lord of Muhammad and Ibrahim
Allah! consider my deeds great exertion (*jihad*)
and accept my compassion as martyrdom in Your cause
and Hasan wrote (it) on Tuesday
the 22th [*sic*] of the month of Rabiy' al-Awwal, in which
passed away

Banu Ha[t]im may God have mercy on all of them
And this in the year 117 [735][46]

By this time, accounts of the heroic life and exemplary deeds of Muhammad, the prophet of Islam, had begun to circulate widely. He had become a figure with whom the faithful could identify—someone they felt they knew.

This familiarity was the product of a remarkable court industry, first among the Umayyads and then among the Abbasids, of unabashedly manufacturing material about what Muhammad said and did.

# Inventing Muhammad

## If Muhammad Did Not Exist, It Was Necessary to Invent Him

From the foregoing it is clear that when it comes to the history of early Islam, the records, both of the Arab conquerors and of the conquered people, are sketchy in the extreme. Instead of what we might expect—depictions of Muslim warriors shouting "Allahu akbar," invoking Muhammad, and quoting the Qur'an—we see hardly any presence of the Qur'an, Muhammad, or Islam at all. The early Arab rulers, while styling themselves as "servant of God" or "agent of God" (*khalifat allah*) and "commander of the faithful," are vague at best about the content of their creed and make no mention whatsoever of the putative founder of their religion or his holy book for decades after beginning to conquer and transform huge expanses of territory across the Middle East and North Africa.

Compounding this curiosity are the shaky historical foundations of the Hadith, the voluminous accounts of Muhammad's words and deeds. The importance of the Hadith in Islam cannot be overstated. They are, when Islamic scholars deem the accounts authentic, second in authority only to the Qur'an itself. Along with the Qur'an that they elucidate, the Hadith form the basis for Islamic law and practice regarding both individual religious observance and the governance of the Islamic state. And in fact, so much of the Qur'an is obscure and opaque, and explained only in the Hadith, that functionally, if not officially, the Hadith are the primary authority in Islam.

Much of the Muslim holy book—not only its Arabic neologisms and turns of phrase—would be incomprehensible without the Hadith. The Qur'an is prohibitively uninviting to those unschooled in its particularities; reading much of it is like walking into a conversation between two people one doesn't know who are talking about incidents in which one was not involved—and they aren't bothering to explain matters.

Thus the Hadith become a necessity. They are the prism through which the vast majority of Muslims understand the Qur'an. According to Islamic tradition, these accounts clarify the import of cryptic Qur'an verses by providing the *asbab an-nuzul*, or occasions of revelation. These are stories about when, where, and why Muhammad was given a certain verse—usually in order to settle a question in dispute among Muslims, or to answer a query that one of the believers posed to the Islamic prophet.

Some of the hadiths are fairly straightforward. In one, Ibn Abbas, forefather of the Abbasids and a companion of Muhammad, recalls that the Qur'anic command to "obey Allah, and obey the Messenger, and those charged with authority among you" (4:59) was revealed to Muhammad "in connection with Abdullah bin Hudhafa bin Qais bin Adi when the Prophet appointed him as the commander of a *Sariya* (army unit)."[1] That is as plausible an explanation for the verse as any, but the context and setting are entirely imposed from without: Nothing in the Qur'anic verse itself refers to this particular appointment by Muhammad; it could just as easily refer to any number of similar incidents.

The same can be said of an explanation of a Qur'an verse excoriating hypocrites: "Will you bid others to piety, and forget yourselves while you recite the Book? Do you not understand?" (2:44). According to one hadith, Ibn Abbas explains, "This was revealed about the Jews of Medina," who would "enjoin people to follow Islam while abstaining themselves from doing so."[2] This verse certainly *could* refer to the Jews of Medina who pretended allegiance to Muhammad while plotting against him, but there is no internal indication of that.

A more elaborate explanation can be found for Qur'an 5:67: "O Messenger, deliver that which has been sent down to thee from thy Lord, for if thou dost not, thou wilt not have delivered His Message. God will protect thee from men. God guides not the people of the unbelievers."

The eleventh-century Qur'anic scholar al-Wahidi (d. 1075), who collected the occasions of revelation and published them together in a book, *Asbab an-Nuzul*, quotes a hadith asserting that this verse was revealed because of apprehensions that Muhammad felt. The hadith tells us that al-Hasan, one of Muhammad's companions, reported: "The Prophet, Allah bless him and give him peace, said: 'When Allah, exalted is He, sent me His message, I felt oppressed by it, for I knew that some people will give me the lie.' The Messenger of Allah, Allah bless him and give him peace, was apprehensive of the Quraysh, Jews and Christians, and so Allah, exalted is He, revealed this verse."

Al-Wahidi also reports, however, that another Muslim, Abu Said al-Khudri, recounted a different story, saying that the verse "was revealed on the day of 'Ghadir Khumm' about Ali ibn Abi Talib, may Allah be well pleased with him." The Shiites contend that in the last year of his life, Muhammad, while on his way to Medina, stopped at "Ghadir Khumm," the pond of Khumm, near the town of al-Juhfah in Arabia, and delivered a sermon in which he appointed his son-in-law Ali ibn Abi Talib his successor—or indicated, by taking his hand, that he wanted Ali to succeed him.

According to hadiths, Muhammad's favorite wife, Aisha, and Ali had been at odds ever since Ali treated her dismissively when she was accused of adultery; decades later, their forces actually clashed during the Battle of the Camel. And so after relating the Shiite explanation of the verse, al-Wahidi quotes Aisha offering an explanation of this verse that has nothing to do with Ali: "The Messenger of Allah, Allah bless him and give him peace, stayed up one night and so I said: 'What's the matter, O Messenger of Allah?' He said: 'Is there not any righteous man who would stand to watch over us tonight?' Then we heard commotion caused by arms and the Messenger of Allah asked: 'Who's there?' 'It is Sa'd and Hudhayfa, we have come to keep watch over you,' came the response. The Messenger of Allah, Allah bless him and give him peace, went to sleep, and he slept so deeply that I heard his snoring; this verse was then revealed. The Messenger of Allah, Allah bless him and give him peace, then popped his head out of the collar of his garment and said: 'O people, you can leave, for Allah has protected me.'"

Finally, al-Wahidi quotes Ibn Abbas, who gives a similar explanation: "The Messenger of Allah, Allah bless him and give him peace, used to be guarded. Abu Talib used to send every day men from the Banu Hashim to guard him until this verse was revealed (O Messenger! Make known that which hath been revealed unto thee from thy Lord) up to His words (Allah will protect thee from mankind). And so when his uncle wanted to send with him people to protect him, he said: 'O uncle! Indeed Allah has protected me from the jinn and humans.'"[3]

The multiplicity of explanations suggests the authenticity of none of them. If one of these four explanations of the verse was the true one, and was therefore as old as the verse itself, it is hard to see how the others would have arisen or, if they were formulated for political reasons, how they would have gained widespread credence. It is evident that no one really knew the circumstances of the verse, and so stories were constructed to explain it.

The accounts of the circumstances of the Qur'anic revelations generally emerged late, with the Hadith dating from the ninth century. There is no evidence contemporary with the Qur'an explaining its origins. In light of that, it could be that these accounts were invented in order to explain Qur'an verses, rather than actually presenting the historical circumstances of revelations to Muhammad.

## The Centrality of the Hadith

However questionable many hadiths may be, they form the basis for the standard Islamic understanding of Qur'anic verses that are less than clear on their surface (and the number of those is considerable).

The Hadith are also pivotal because of the tremendous importance that Islamic theology and tradition attaches to Muhammad, whom the Qur'an terms a "good example . . . for whosoever hopes for God and the Last Day" (33:21).

It may seem curious that Muhammad is made so important when the Qur'an itself says so little specific about him, but that is precisely why the biographical material elaborated in the Hadith was so urgently needed. The Qur'an tells believers that Muhammad is "upon a mighty morality" (68:4), and "whosoever obeys God, and the Messenger— they are with those whom God has blessed" (4:80). Exhortations to obey Allah's messenger, who is assumed to be Muhammad, occur frequently in the Qur'an (3:32, 3:132, 4:13, 4:59, 4:69, 5:92, 8:1, 8:20, 8:46, 9:71, 24:47, 24:51, 24:52, 24:54, 24:56, 33:33, 47:33, 49:14, 58:13, 64:12). What does it mean to obey Muhammad? To answer that, one must know what he said and did.

Muhammad himself, according to one hadith, asserted the centrality of his words and deeds: "I have given orders, exhortations and interdictions which count as much as the Koran if not more."[4] They became in Islamic tradition the guideposts for even the most minute aspects of individual behavior. The modern-day Islamic apologist Muqtedar Khan of the Center for the Study of Islam and Democracy explains that "the words, deeds and silences (that which he saw and did not forbid) of Muhammad became an independent source of Islamic law. Muslims, as a part of religious observance, not only obey, but also seek to emulate and imitate their Prophet in every aspect of life. Thus Muhammad is the medium as well as a source of the divine law."[5] In Islam the centrality of Muhammad allows no room whatsoever for innovation (*bida*): What the prophet approved is approved, and what he rejected is rejected, for all time. Thus the fifteenth-century Islamic scholar al-Qastallani rejected "anything that is practiced without a relevant example from olden times and, more especially in religion, anything that was not practiced in the time of the Prophet."[6]

The prophet of Islam himself sums up these Islamic beliefs when he says in a hadith: "Verily, the most truthful communication is the Book of Allah, the best guidance is that of Muhammad, and the worst of all things is innovation; every innovation is heresy, every heresy is error, and every error leads to hell."[7] In another hadith, however, Muhammad seems to retreat from this hard-line stance. He promises a reward to "anyone who establishes in Islam a good sunna"—that is, an "accepted practice"—and warns against "anyone who establishes in Islam an evil sunna."[8] This presupposes that Islamic leaders will establish new practices and that some of these practices may be good and some evil—a clear departure from the idea that "every innovation is heresy."

Did Muhammad equivocate? Did he forbid innovation and then change his mind, or vice versa? Possibly; however, these two traditions can be harmonized by coming down against innovation while interpreting the second hadith as meaning that as new issues arise, they must be judged in light of Muhammad's words and deeds. In any case, in this as in all matters pertaining to Islamic law, Muhammad's example (along with the word of the Qur'an) is paramount, and hadiths recording that example are decisive.

## The Contentless Sunna

One of the most curious aspects of Muhammad's paramount importance in Muslim law and practice is that there is absolutely no evidence that the Muslims who actually knew the prophet of Islam kept records of what he said and did. If the canonical account of the origins of Islam is true, then the material in the Hadith about Muhammad's words and deeds existed, and presumably circulated in Muslim communities, for nearly two centuries before it was finally sifted, judged for authenticity, collected, and published. Yet there is no indication of this material's presence.

The early caliphs do not appear ever to have invoked Muhammad's example. The word *caliph* means "successor" or "representative," and in the traditional understanding the caliphs were successors to the prophet. But the first four caliphs who ruled after Muhammad's death—known as the "rightly guided caliphs"—issued coins that proclaimed them to be the "caliphs of Allah," rather than the expected "caliphs of the prophet of Allah." Apparently the early caliphs saw themselves as vice-regents or vicars of Allah on earth, not as the successors of Allah's prophet.

One scholar of Islam, Nabia Abbott, contends that there is no record of the early caliphs invoking the hadiths of Muhammad because the caliph Umar (634–644) ordered hadiths destroyed. He did so, she says, because he feared that a collection of the Hadith would rival and compete with the Qur'an.[9] But if Umar really did order the records of Muhammad's words and deeds destroyed, despite the Qur'an's numerous exhortations to obey and imitate him, how could later Muslims have preserved them in such quantity? Did Muslims really preserve wheelbarrows full of hadiths against the express orders of the Leader of the Believers, or hold it all in their memories with absolute fidelity?

We begin to hear about Muhammad's example from the same caliph who built the Dome of the Rock, claimed to have collected the Qur'an (after the caliph Uthman was supposed to have done it decades earlier), and created the first coins and inscriptions mentioning Muhammad as the prophet of Allah: the Umayyad caliph Abd al-Malik. Reigning from 685 to 705, Abd al-Malik called rebels to obey Allah and the sunna of his prophet.[10] (By contrast, an earlier caliph, Muawiya, had referred to the "sunna of Umar," his predecessor.[11]) The Umayyad governor of Iraq, Hajjaj ibn Yusuf, whom some hadiths report as having edited the Qur'an and destroyed variant texts, scolded a Kharijite rebel: "You have opposed the book of God and deviated from the sunna of his prophet."[12]

One would think, given such references, that the sunna of the prophet was by that period a recognized corpus of laws. But just as Umayyad rulers charged their opponents with departing from the prophet's example, those same opponents invoked the sunna of the prophet to justify their own, competing perspectives and rulings.[13] The historians Patricia Crone and Martin Hinds conclude that in the early decades of the Arab Empire, the sunna of the prophet did not

refer to a specific set of rulings at all: "To say that someone had followed the sunna of the Prophet was to say that he was a good man,
not to specify what he had done in concrete terms. . . . In concrete
terms, the 'sunna of the Prophet' meant nothing."[14]

But Abd al-Malik and his successors emphasized Muhammad's
example: They presented the words and deeds of the prophet as nor-
mative for Islamic faith and practice. The necessity for every Muslim
to obey Muhammad became a central and oft-repeated doctrine of
the Qur'an. Consequently, the hunger for them became so intense
that some Muslims traversed the entire Islamic world searching for
the prophet's solution to a disputed question. An eighth-century
Egyptian Muslim named Makhul, a freed slave, recounted how he
searched for what Muhammad might have decreed about the particulars of distributing the spoils of war:

> I did not leave Egypt until I had acquired all the knowledge that
> seemed to me to exist there. I then came to al-Hijaz and I did
> not leave it until I had acquired all the knowledge that seemed to
> be available. Then I came to al-Iraq, and I did not leave it until
> I had acquired all the knowledge that seemed to be available. I
> then came to Syria, and besieged it. I asked everyone about giv-
> ing rewards from the booty. I did not find anyone who could tell
> me anything about it.

Finally, he found what he was looking for: "I then met an old man
called Ziyad ibn Jariyah at-Tamimi. I asked him: Have you heard anything about giving rewards from the booty? He replied: Yes. I heard
Maslama al-Fihri say: I was present with the Prophet (peace be upon
him). He gave a quarter of the spoils on the outward journey and a
third on the return journey."[15]

That settled that—for Makhul, anyway. Not every Muslim could
travel the world in search of answers. In the face of commands to
obey Allah's messenger, there was an immense need for a collection of
the prophetic word on various disputed issues. Islamic tradition gen-

erally identifies the second Abbasid caliph, al-Mansur, who reigned from 754 to 775, as the first to commission a legal manual: the *Muwatta*. Because Islamic law is based to such a tremendous degree on the words and example of Muhammad, this manual of Islamic law records a great many hadiths of the prophet of Islam. The imam who wrote the *Muwatta*, Malik ibn Anas (715–795), died a mere sixteen decades after Muhammad, making him the nearest in time of all the collectors of hadiths to the life of the man whose every action and every utterance is the focus of the Hadith.

Various editions of Malik's *Muwatta* differ from one another so widely as to raise the question of whether they are the same book at all. Different versions (*riwayat*) of Malik's teachings were written down and transmitted by different students of his. On one occasion a man approached the imam and showed him a manuscript. "This is your Muwatta, O Abu Abd Allah," the man said to Malik, "which I have copied and collated; please grant me your permission to hand it down." Without looking at the manuscript, Malik responded, "This permission is granted, and when handing down the text you may use the formula: Malik has told me, Malik has reported to me."[16] Some of the variant manuscripts were probably compiled after Malik died. In any case, the variations hardly inspire confidence regarding the authenticity of the *Muwatta*'s material about Muhammad.

But with Muhammad held up as an exemplar, the Hadith became political weapons in the hands of warring factions within the Islamic world. And as is always the case with weapons in wartime, they began to be manufactured wholesale. The early Islamic scholar Muhammad ibn Shihab az-Zuhri, who died in 741, sixty years before the death of Malik ibn Anas, complained even in his day that the "emirs forced people to write hadiths."[17] Even the caliph al-Mahdi (775–785) was known as someone who fabricated hadiths.[18]

Some of these were useful in justifying the rapid expansion of the Arab Empire, by placing its manifest destiny in the mouth of Muhammad. One such hadith describes an incident during the siege of Medina by the pagan Quraysh of Mecca. After ordering his followers to dig a trench around the city, Muhammad jumps in with a pickax to help out with a particularly large rock. Three times when he strikes the rock, lightning shoots out from it.[19] Muhammad then explains: "The first means that God has opened up to me the Yaman [Yemen]; the second Syria and the west; and the third the east."[20] In another version of the tale, he says the lightning indicates that the Muslims will conquer "the palaces of al-Hirah" in southern Iraq "and al-Madaiin of Kisra," the winter capital of the Sassanian Empire, as well as "the palaces of the pale men in the lands of the Byzantines" and "the palaces of San'a."[21] In another, Muhammad predicts that "the Greeks will stand before the brown men (the Arabs) in troops in white garments and with shorn heads, being forced to do all that they are ordered, whereas that country is now inhabited by people in whose eyes you rank lower than a monkey on the haunches of a camel."[22]

Muslims also fabricated hadiths in the heat of political and religious controversies that they hoped to settle with a decisive, albeit hitherto unknown, word from the prophet. Abd al-Malik at one point wanted to restrict Muslims from making pilgrimages to Mecca, because he was afraid one of his rivals would take advantage of the pilgrimage to recruit followers. Accordingly, he prevailed upon the hapless az-Zuhri to fabricate a hadith to the effect that a pilgrimage to the mosque in Jerusalem (*Bayt al-Maqdis*) was just as praiseworthy in the sight of Allah as one to Mecca. Az-Zuhri went even further, having Muhammad say that "a prayer in the Bayt al-Maqdis of Jerusalem is better than a thousand prayers in other holy places"—in other words, even better than going to Mecca. This hadith duly appears in one of the six canonical Hadith collections that Muslim scholars consider most reliable: the *Sunan* of Muhammad ibn Maja (824–887).[23]

## Factionalism and the Hadith

Sometimes hadiths were manufactured in order to support one party or another among early Muslim factions. The caliph Muawiya had supplanted the last "rightly guided caliph," Muhammad's son-in-law Ali ibn Abi Talib, and Ali's son and chosen successor Husayn, and he continued to struggle against the nascent party of Ali (*shiat Ali*), which ultimately became the Shiites. Muawiya is presented in a hadith as having told his lieutenant al-Mughira: "Do not tire of abusing and insulting Ali and calling for God's mercifulness for Uthman [Ali's predecessor and Muawiya's cousin], defaming the companions of Ali, removing them and omitting to listen to them; praising, in contrast, the clan of Uthman, drawing them near to you and listening to them."[24] Accordingly, a hadith appeared in which Muhammad declared that Ali's father and Muhammad's guardian, Abu Talib, was burning in hell: "Perhaps my intercession will be of use to him at the day of resurrection, so that he may be transferred into a pool of fire which reaches only up to the ankles but which is still hot enough to burn his brain."[25]

For its part, the party of Ali had Muhammad designate Ali as the guarantor of the proper understanding of the Muslim holy book: "I go to war for the recognition of the Koran and Ali will fight for the interpretation of the Koran."[26] In another hadith that came to be beloved of the Shiites, Muhammad declares, "So know then that whose master I am, their master is Ali's also." Then he takes Ali's hand and prays, "O God, protect him who recognizes Ali and be an enemy to all who oppose Ali." Hearing this, Umar (who later became caliph, after the death of Abu Bakr in 634), says to Ali: "I wish you luck, son of Abu Talib, from this hour you are appointed the master of all Muslim men and women."[27] In another pro-Ali hadith, Muhammad exclaims to one of his companions: "O Anas! Is there anyone amongst the Ansar who is better than or preferable to Ali?"[28] The Ansar, or "helpers," were the people of Medina who had converted to Islam after Muhammad moved there from Mecca in the Hijra, twelve years into his career as a prophet.

The Umayyads fought back with new hadiths of their own. In one, Muhammad's favorite wife, Aisha, who hated Ali for his ungallant advice to Muhammad to discard her and get a new wife when she was accused of adultery, is told after the death of the prophet of Islam that Muhammad appointed Ali as his successor in his will. Aisha responds fiercely: "When did he appoint him by will? Verily, when he died he was resting against my chest (or said: in my lap) and he asked for a washbasin and then collapsed while in that state, and I could not even perceive that he had died, so when did he appoint him by will?"[29]

In another, Muhammad showers praise on the three men who immediately succeeded him: Abu Bakr, Umar, and Uthman, each of whom was chosen as caliph instead of Ali. After Muhammad climbs the mountain of Uhud with the three successors, the mountain starts shaking, and he speaks to it: "Be firm, O Uhud! For on you there are no more than a Prophet, a *Siddiq* and two martyrs."[30] *Siddiq*, or "truthful," is an honorary title bestowed on one who is entirely trustworthy.

The Umayyads even put words in the mouth of Ali, having him praise his two foremost rivals as Muhammad's closest companions. In a hadith, Ibn Abbas recalls:

> While I was standing amongst the people who were invoking Allah for Umar bin Al-Khattab who was lying (dead) on his bed, a man behind me rested his elbows on my shoulder and said, "(O Umar!) May Allah bestow His Mercy on you. I always hoped that Allah will keep you with your two companions, for I often heard Allah's Apostle saying, 'I, Abu Bakr and Umar were (somewhere). I, Abu Bakr and Umar did (something). I, Abu Bakr and Umar set out.' So I hoped that Allah will keep you with both of them." I turned back to see that the speaker was Ali bin Abi Talib.[31]

The partisans of Ali made fun of Uthman for having run away during some of the early battles of the Muslims. One follower of Ali mocked Uthman in verse: "You can accuse me of no other sin than that I have mentioned him who ran away from Khaybar. I mention the man who fled from Marhab, like a donkey runs from the lion."[32]

Uthman exonerated himself by referring to the words of Muhammad. One hadith tells the story of an Egyptian who has come to Mecca for the hajj and asks an elderly Muslim, Abdullah ibn Umar, son of the second caliph: "Do you know that Uthman fled away on the day (of the battle) of Uhud?"

When Ibn Umar says that yes, he did know that, the Egyptian has more: "Do you know that Uthman was absent on the day (of the battle) of Badr and did not join it?"

When Ibn Umar again says yes, the Egyptian comes back with a third question: "Do you know that he failed to attend the Ar-Ridwan pledge and did not witness it?" This pledge was a declaration of loyalty to Muhammad that his closest companions made after the Islamic prophet concluded a treaty with the pagan Quraysh; the treaty of Hudaibiya, as it is known in Islamic tradition, was disadvantageous to the Muslims in numerous particulars.

For the third time, Ibn Umar says, "Yes." The Egyptian responds, "Allahu akbar!"—in this case, an expression of indignation and dismay. Then Ibn Umar explains, saying that Allah "excused" Uthman and forgave him for being absent from Uhud, although he does not explain the absence. As for Badr, Ibn Umar says that Uthman was not there because he was obeying Muhammad: "The daughter of Allah's Apostle was his wife and she was sick then. Allah's Apostle said to him, 'You will receive the same reward and share (of the booty) as any one of those who participated in the battle of Badr (if you stay with her).'" Finally, Ibn Umar explains Uthman's nonappearance at the Ar-Ridwan pledge of allegiance by saying that Muhammad sent Uthman elsewhere, and "had there been any person in Mecca more respectable than Uthman (to be sent as a representative), Allah's Apostle would have sent him instead of him." In fact, while Uthman was absent, Muhammad "held out his right hand saying, 'This is Uthman's hand.' He stroked his (other) hand with it saying, 'This (pledge of allegiance) is on the behalf of Uthman.'" Ibn Umar tells the Egyptian: "Bear (these) excuses in mind with you."[33]

Not only did this tale exonerate Uthman by invoking Muhammad himself; it also exalted him beyond all rivals as being "more respectable," and even showed Muhammad acting as his proxy. How, then, could anyone favor Ali's claim to the caliphate over Uthman's? That is, at least until the party of Ali invented another hadith in favor of its champion. This hadith describes the siege of the oasis of Khaybar, home of the last Jewish settlement in Arabia after Muhammad (according to still other hadiths) exiled two of the three Jewish tribes of Medina and massacred the third. Muhammad sends Abu Bakr, Umar, and Uthman—here again, the first three caliphs and Ali's rivals—in turn against one of the Khaybar forts, but they cannot capture it. When he sends out Uthman, Muhammad refers to his reputation for cowardice and sticks up for him: "Tomorrow I will give the flag to a man who loves Allah and his apostle. Allah will conquer it by his means; he is no runaway." But even Uthman fails, so Muhammad summons Ali, heals him miraculously from an eye ailment, and sends him against the fort. Ali, of course, succeeds.[34]

The various Muslim factions produced a steady stream of hadiths defending their leaders or attacking those of their opponents. The Umayyad side invented a hadith defending the Umayyad governor of Iraq, Khalid al-Qasri (d. 743), whom pious Muslims hated for his brutality in governing. Khalid is redeemed in a hadith in which Muhammad is made to say, "O God, let thy victory and the victory of thy religion take place through the offspring of Asad b. Kurz," Khalid's ancestor.[35] But opponents of the Umayyads had Muhammad disparage the caliph al-Walid (705–715). In the hadith, Muhammad confronts a man who has just named his newborn son al-Walid: "You name your children by the names of our Pharaohs. Verily, a man with the name al-Walid will come who will inflict greater injury upon my community than ever did Pharaoh upon his people."[36] A later transmitter of this hadith notes that while it was initially believed to refer to al-Walid I, once al-Walid II (743–744) began committing his own atrocities, it became clear that Muhammad had actually been referring to *him*.[37]

## Riddled with Contradictions

The consequence of all this was inevitable: utter confusion. Since warring parties were all fabricating hadiths that supported their positions, the Hadith are riddled with contradictions. Many of these, but by no means all of them, revolve around differences in Islamic ritual practice, probably reflecting regional variations. For example, among the hadiths compiled by the renowned ninth-century imam Muhammad Ibn Ismail al-Bukhari is one recording that, according to Ibn Abbas, "the Prophet performed ablution by washing the body parts only once."[98] But Bukhari reports that another companion of Muhammad, Abdullah bin Zaid, said that "the Prophet performed ablution by washing the body parts twice."[39] And yet another hadith collected by Bukhari has Muhammad praising Uthman for performing the ablutions not once or twice but thrice, saying that if he does it that way while avoiding distractions, "his past sins will be forgiven."[40] Bukhari puts these three hadiths together without comment or attempt at harmonization.

In a hadith recorded by another ninth-century imam, Muslim ibn al-Hajjaj al-Qushayri, we are told that Muhammad "disapproved the drinking of water while standing."[41] Yet Muslim also reports that when Ibn Abbas gave Muhammad some sacred water from the well of Zamzam in Mecca, Muhammad—whose conduct is always exemplary for Muslims—"drank it while standing."[42]

Contemporary Islamic apologists point to a hadith in which Muhammad "forbade the killing of women and children" as evidence of the humaneness, unusual for its time, of Islam's rules of warfare.[43] Immediately following that prohibition, however, Muslim includes another hadith in which Muhammad, "when asked about the women and children of the polytheists being killed during the night raid, said: They are from them."[44] In other words, the children of the polytheists are from the polytheists and deserve to share their fate.

Other contradictions involve details of Muhammad's own life, the Islamic eschatological scheme, and more. Consequently, the ninth-century scholar Asim an-Nabil (d. 827) threw up his hands in despair: "I have come to the conclusion that a pious man is never so ready to lie as in matters of the hadith."[45]

## Collecting and Codifying the Hadith

Islamic authorities realized that some effort had to be made to bring order out of all this chaos. In the latter part of the eighth century, the Abbasids initiated the collection and codification of the Hadith. By doing so, they exponentially expanded specific knowledge about what the prophet of Islam had commanded and condemned, approved and disapproved. The poet Marwan ibn Abi Hafsa accordingly exulted about the Abbasid caliph Muhammad ibn Mansur al-Mahdi (775–785): "The *amir al-mu'minin* [commander of the believers] Muhammad has revived the sunna of the Prophet with regard to what is permitted, what forbidden."[46]

This great effort came to full fruition in the next century, with the appearance of the six most important Hadith collections, none of which date from earlier than two centuries after Muhammad's death. Together these are known as *as-Sahih as-Sittah*: the authentic and trustworthy ones (*sahih* means "sound" or "reliable"). These include, in order of their importance and general reputation for reliability, *Sahih Bukhari*, the most respected and authoritative Hadith collection, compiled by Bukhari (810–870); *Sahih Muslim*, by Muslim ibn al-Hajjaj (821–875); the *Sunan* of Abu Dawud as-Sijistani (818–889); *As-Sunan as-Sughra*, by Ahmad ibn Shuayb an-Nasai (829–915); the *Jami* of Abu Isa Muhammad At-Tirmidhi (824–892); and the *Sunan* of Muhammad ibn Maja (824–887). Although Muslims consider Bukhari's and Muslim's collections to be the most trustworthy, the others are held in high regard as well. Abu Dawud as-Sijistani, for example, reportedly traveled to Arabia, Iraq, Khurasan, Egypt, Syria, Iran, and elsewhere collecting hadiths. One respected imam, Zakariya bin Yahya as-Saji, declared: "The Qur'an is the foundation of Islam and *Sunan Abu Dawud* is its pillar." Another, Ibn al-Arabi, added: "There is no need of acquaintance of anything after acquiring the knowledge of the Qur'an and of *Sunan Abu Dawud*."[47]

The most respected Hadith collection, Bukhari's, began in a dream, according to Dr. Muhammad Muhsin Khan, a Saudi Islamic scholar and Qur'an translator. Dr. Khan writes that Bukhari dreamed that he was "standing in front of Prophet Muhammad having a fan in his hand and driving away the flies from the Prophet." The imam interpreted this dream as a divine sign that he would "drive away the falsehood asserted against the Prophet." Accordingly, he spent his life attempting to distinguish authentic hadiths from forgeries. According to Islamic tradition, Bukhari traversed the Islamic world collecting stories about Muhammad's words and deeds—fully 300,000 of them.[48] Ultimately he rejected nearly 293,000 of them as fabricated, or at least impossible to evaluate as to their reliability. He chose and published 7,563 hadiths, though these included repetitions; in all, he included 2,602 separate hadiths that he deemed authentic. Even these run to nine volumes in a modern-day English-Arabic edition published in Saudi Arabia.

The imam Muslim ibn al-Hajjaj was Bukhari's disciple. Born in Nishapur in what is now Iran, he is said to have traveled to Arabia, Egypt, Syria, and Iraq to collect hadiths. According to Islamic tradition, he also collected 300,000 hadiths, of which he preserved 4,000 as authentic in his *Sahih*. Most Muslim scholars consider his collection, as well as that of Bukhari, to be almost entirely reliable; Muslims raise virtually no question about the authenticity of traditions that appear in both *Sahih Bukhari* and *Sahih Muslim*—of which there are many. One Internet-based introduction to Islamic faith and practice, which assures readers that "nothing on this site violates the fixed principles of Islamic law," sums up the prevailing opinion among Muslims: "Sahih Bukhari is distinguished with it's [sic] strong reliability." It adds that the imam Muslim chose the hadiths that he included in *Sahih Muslim* "based on stringent acceptance criteria."[49]

## The Proliferation of Forgeries

Yet if the imams Bukhari and Muslim had to go to such extraordinary lengths to find a relatively small number of authentic hadiths, this means that hundreds of thousands of stories about Muhammad were either completely unreliable or of doubtful authenticity. The problem was beyond their, or anyone's, ability to control. Ignaz Goldziher, the pioneering critical historian of the Hadith, notes that "the simplest means by which honest men sought to combat the rapid increase of faked hadiths is at the same time a most remarkable phenomenon in the history of literature. With pious intention, fabrications were combated with new fabrications, with new hadiths which were smuggled in and in which the invention of illegitimate hadiths were condemned by strong words uttered by the Prophet."[50] Muhammad was accordingly made to acknowledge: "After my departure, the number of sayings ascribed to me will increase in the same way as sayings have been ascribed to previous prophets."[51] In another hadith he prophesies, "In the later days of my community, there will be people who will hand you communications which neither you nor your forefathers have ever heard. Beware of them." And even more strongly: "At the end of time there will be forgers, liars who will bring you hadiths which neither you nor your forefathers have heard. Beware of them so that they may not lead you astray and into temptation."[52]

But how was a pious Muslim to know the true hadiths from the false? A hadith cites Muhammad proposing a solution: "What therefore is told you as a saying of mine you will have to compare with the Book of God (the Qur'an), and what is in accordance with it is by men, whether I have in fact said it myself or not."[53] Ibn Abbas adds another criterion, community acceptance: "If you hear from me a communication in the name of the Prophet and you find that it does not agree with the Book of God or is not liked by the people, know that I have reported a lie about the Prophet."[54]

Note that in these hadiths, neither Muhammad nor Ibn Abbas is made to say that Muslims should make a careful effort to winnow out the Islamic prophet's authentic sayings from those that are inauthentic. Rather, they are simply to measure his purported sayings against the Qur'an, and follow those that aren't contradicted by the Muslim holy book. To this day, one of the criteria by which Muslims evaluate hadiths is by how well they accord with the Qur'an. Those that contradict the words of Allah are rejected. That is a reasonable criterion, but it doesn't get us any closer to what Muhammad actually said and did.

Nonetheless, Bukhari and the other hadith collectors made a valiant attempt. They claimed to be able to distinguish genuine material about Muhammad from forged hadiths largely by examining the chain of transmitters (*isnad*), the list of those who had passed on the story from the time of Muhammad to the present. Islamic scholars grade individual traditions according to their chains of transmitters, as "sound," "good," "weak," "forged," and so on.

A hadith is considered sound if its chain of transmitters includes reliable people and goes back to a recognized authority. A typical strong chain is recorded by the Shiite scholar Sheikh al-Mufid (Ibn Muallim, 948–1022) as going all the way back to Ali himself. Al-Mufid said: "Abul Hasan Ali b. Muhammad b. Khalid al-Maythami reported to me from Abu Bakr Muhammad b. al-Husain b. al-Mustanir, who reported from al-Husain b. Muhammad b. al-Husain b. Masab, who reported from Abbad b. Yaqoob, who reported from Abu Abdil Rahman al-Masoodi, from Katheer al-Nawa, from Abu Maryam al-Khawlani, from Malik b. Dhamrah, that *Amir ul-Mu'mineen* [leader of the believers] Ali b. Abi Talib (A.S.) said . . ."[55]

If the chain of transmission includes unreliable people or a broken link, Muslim scholars consider the authenticity of the hadith doubtful. Ibn Maja notes that one hadith is considered weak "because of Khalid b. Ubaid," one of its transmitters. He quotes Bukhari saying of Khalid: "His hadith is debatable" and points out that two other Islamic authorities, Ibn Hibban and Hakim, "have stated that he narrates *maudu* (spurious) *ahadith* (traditions) on Anas's authority."[56]

The apparent reliability of the *isnad* chain was what determined authenticity. It didn't matter if a hadith was self-contradictory or absurd on its face; so long as its *isnad* chain was clear of anomalies, and it did not contradict the Qur'an, the tradition had no obstacles to being accepted as reliable.[57] Bukhari and Muslim, as well as their counterparts, also tended to favor traditions that they received from multiple sources, but this indicates only that a hadith had circulated widely, not that it was authentic.

If a hadith could be forged, however, so could its chain of transmission. There are numerous indications that *isnads* were forged with the same alacrity with which *matns*—that is, the content of the hadiths—were invented. The scholar of Islamic law Joseph Schacht notes one anomalous hadith that indicates the liberties taken with the *isnads*. He points out that ash-Shafii, a renowned Islamic jurist of the early ninth century, described a particular hadith as *mursal*, meaning "hurried," and "generally not acted upon." Shafii's description implies that the hadith "is not confirmed by any version with a complete *isnad*," Schacht explains. But, he continues, the same hadith "appears with a different, full *isnad* in Ibn Hanbal . . . and Ibn Maja."[58]

Schacht notes many instances of hadiths with obviously forged or altered *isnads*. He recounts one passed on by Malik in his *Muwatta*. Malik heard from Muhammad ibn Abdalrahman ibn Sad ibn Zurara, who heard from one of Muhammad's wives, Hafsa, that once Hafsa killed one of her slaves who practiced witchcraft and had cast a spell on her. In another place we learn that Malik heard from Abul-Rijal Muhammad ibn Abdalrahman ibn Jariya, who heard from his mother, Amra, that another one of Muhammad's wives, Aisha, sold one of her slaves who practiced witchcraft and had cast a spell on her. "One of these versions is modeled on the other," Schacht observes, "and neither can be regarded as historical."[59]

## But Are They *All* Unreliable?

That hadiths were forged is admitted by Muslim and non-Muslim scholars alike. For the Muslim scholar Muhammad Mustafa Azami, the existence of obviously faulty *isnads* is in itself enough to establish the reliability of the hadiths that have been deemed authentic.[60] After all, he argues, if the *isnads* were forged, why would the forger buttress his work with an unsatisfactory chain of transmission? If the whole thing is fictional in the first place and fabricated for political reasons, why not attribute the tradition to none but respected members of the Islamic community, passing on Muhammad's words in an unbroken and clearly reliable chain? But Amazi's argument falters on the fact that hadiths were manufactured by competing factions, and the old adage that the victors write the history books applies: If a well-known hadith did not promote a perspective favorable to the ruling faction, altering the *isnad* was an easy way to cast doubts on its authenticity. Moreover, a transmitter whom one faction saw as a reliable and pious could be considered a villainous fabricator by another faction.

The contemporary scholar Harald Motzki has also challenged on several fronts the idea that the Hadith as a whole is unreliable. He points to the hadiths collected by scholar Abd ar-Razzaq (744–826) as evidence that hadiths were circulating by at least the early eighth century. But in truth, Abd ar-Razzaq did the bulk of his work toward the end of the eighth century.[61] Like Azami, Motzki cites the very existence of suspect *isnads* to argue that the other hadiths must be authentic. He notes that Abd ar-Razzaq sometimes attributes hadiths to sources that he considers of doubtful reliability, and even presents hadiths with no known source. If hadiths were being manufactured wholesale and fitted out with impressive *isnads*, why would hadiths with weak attribution, or no attribution at all, even exist?[62]

Despite such claims, there is strong reason to question the reliance on *isnads* as a guide to the authenticity of hadiths. The *isnads* themselves didn't start appearing until after hadiths had begun circulating. Islamic tradition attributes a telling statement about the *isnads* to Muhammad ibn Sirin, an eighth-century Qur'anic scholar who was also renowned as an interpreter of dreams in Iraq. The collectors of hadiths, he said, "were not used to inquiring after the *isnad*, but when the *fitna* (= civil war) occurred they said: Name us your informants."[63] The *fitna* is usually understood as a reference to the unrest that followed the assassination of the caliph Uthman in 656—more than thirty years after the death of Muhammad, the subject of the hadiths. Thus even according to Islamic tradition, hadiths circulated for a considerable period without *isnads*. It strains credulity to imagine that thirty years after Muhammad's death, Muslims could remember exactly who among the Islamic prophet's companions was responsible for transmitting each of thousands of stories about him.

Significantly, the use of *isnads* apparently became mandatory in the early 700s—around the time of Abd al-Malik and Hajjaj ibn Yusuf, or shortly thereafter.[64]

Even the idea that the *isnad* is an indication of authenticity rests on shaky foundations. Anyone who has played the child's game of telephone, involving a story passed on by whispers through multiple transmitters and then compared with the original at the end of the chain, knows how unreliable oral tradition can be.[65] If Muhammad could be made to warn the Muslims that they "must keep on reciting the Qur'an because it escapes from the hearts of men faster than camels do when they are released from their tying ropes," would not the same tendency to evanesce apply even more to the Hadith?[66] To be sure, Arabia had an established practice of memorizing poetry, and the memorization of Islamic texts would accord with that practice. It is equally true that in ancient Greece, trained bards recited the *Iliad* and *Odyssey* from memory. But the original transmitters of the Hadith were not poets or trained bards; they were simply companions of Muhammad who saw him do or say something at a given moment. What's more, the Hadith are far more voluminous than the ancient epics that the ancient bards committed to memory. And yet the canonical account of Islam's origins assumes that Muhammad's companions had essentially total recall of the prophet's words and deeds, and that they passed on with scrupulous care what they saw and heard in literally thousands of incidents. It further assumes that subsequent transmitters applied equal care over the course of many decades, passing on these traditions without embellishment, clarification, or alteration of any kind until the hadiths were finally collected and written down in the ninth century.

Seldom, if ever, has such a feat of memory been documented.

## What Did Muhammad Really Say and Do?

Ultimately, it is impossible to tell whether or not Muhammad himself actually said or did any of what the traditional Islamic sources depict him as saying or doing, or even if there was a Muhammad at all. We have already seen that the Abbasids to a great degree sponsored the proliferation, and ultimately the collection, of the prophetic hadiths. This was in keeping with their opposition to the Umayyads on religious grounds. Ignaz Goldziher observes that the Abbasids overthrew the Umayyads because of the latter's "godlessness and opposition to religion." The Abbasids, led by the general Abu Muslim—who, Goldziher writes, was "the man with the 'cudgel for the unbelievers'"—rose up against the Umayyads primarily to establish "the pillar of *din* [religion]."[67]

On the other hand, it may be that the charges of impiety leveled at the Umayyads were simply Abbasid polemic, intended to discredit their great rivals. After all, it is exceedingly strange that the Umayyads, who took over the caliphate in 661, following the murder of Ali, would have been so notorious for their irreligion. They ostensibly took power less than three decades after the death of the prophet of Islam, and among them were supposedly many who knew Muhammad personally and loved him above all creatures. Muawiya, the first Umayyad caliph, was a cousin of the caliph Uthman, who is credited with standardizing the text of the Qur'an. Is it really plausible that the Umayyads would have essentially discarded Muhammad's religion so soon after he gave it to them? Why did the Islamic community so quickly fall into the hands of rulers who cared little for its central organizing principle and reason for being?

This could have been simply due to the vicissitudes of a violent age, and of a religion that sanctioned that violence. Muawiya, after all, was the son of Abu Sufyan, the Quraysh chieftain who (according to Islamic tradition) fought several battles against Muhammad and converted to Islam only reluctantly once defeated. In a meeting with the vanquished general, Muhammad asked, "Woe to you, Abu Sufyan, isn't it time that you recognize that I am God's apostle?" Abu Sufyan answered, "As to that I still have some doubt." Muhammad's companion Ibn Abbas, forefather of the Abbasids, would have none of that. He said to Abu Sufyan: "Submit and testify that there is no God but Allah and that Muhammad is the apostle of God before you lose your head." Abu Sufyan duly obeyed.[68]

In light of all this, it is not outrageous to wonder about Muawiya's commitment to Islam. Then again, there are hadiths saying that he actually became very devout and even served as a scribe to Muhammad. The hadith about Abu Sufyan could be the product of Abbasid polemic.

Even if Muawiya was not devout, it is difficult to imagine that he would have passed on his irreligion to his successors, ruling as they did for a hundred years over Muslims who, according to the standard account, were inspired by the words of the Qur'an and the example of Muhammad. Perhaps what Islamic tradition characterizes as Umayyad irreligion could simply reflect a time (the early Umayyad period) when the words and deeds of Muhammad, and the text of the Qur'an, had not yet been fixed.

The unreliability of the Hadith makes it impossible to know for certain anything about Muhammad. Further doubts arise because, as we shall soon see, there is scant evidence establishing Mecca as the center for trade and pilgrimage that it was reputed to be in Muhammad's time. But in the eighth century, the first biography of the prophet of Islam appeared. And that book, combined with the beginning of the collection of the scattered and chaotic hadiths, heralded a momentous event: The mysterious and shadowy figure of the prophet of Islam began to move ever more confidently into "the full light of history."

# 4

## Switching On the Full Light of History

### Muhammad's First Muslim Biographer

T he "full light of history" supposedly shining on Muhammad's life results largely from the work of a pious Muslim named Muhammad Ibn Ishaq Ibn Yasar, generally known as Ibn Ishaq, who wrote the first biography of Muhammad. But Ibn Ishaq was not remotely a contemporary of his prophet, who died in 632. Ibn Ishaq died in 773, and so his work dates from well over a hundred years after the death of his subject.

What's more, Ibn Ishaq's *Sirat Rasul Allah*—*Biography of the Messenger of Allah*—has not survived in its original form. It comes down to us today only in a later, abbreviated (although still quite lengthy) version compiled by another Islamic scholar, Ibn Hisham, who died in 834, sixty years after Ibn Ishaq, as well as in fragments quoted by other early Muslim writers, including the historian Muhammad ibn Jarir at-Tabari (839–923).

The lateness of this material doesn't in itself mean that it is unreliable. Historians generally tend to favor earlier sources over later ones, but an early source is not always more trustworthy than a later one. A hurriedly written biography of a politician rushed into print within weeks of his death, for example, would not be likely to have greater value than a more considered account published several years later, after exhaustive research. But in light of the rampant forging of material concerning Muhammad's words and deeds, and the way various factions in the eighth and ninth centuries used Muhammad's supposed statements and actions to support their positions, Muhammad's first biographers would have faced an extraordinary challenge in winnowing out authentic material from forgeries and fabrications.

Ibn Hisham, moreover, warns that his version is sanitized: He left out, he says, "things which it is disgraceful to discuss; matters which would distress certain people; and such reports as al-Bakkai [Ibn Ishaq's student, who edited his work] told me he could not accept as trustworthy."[1] Abdallah ibn Numayr, a collector of hadiths who died in 814, complained that although Ibn Ishaq's work contained much that was authentic, the authentic material was mixed with "worthless sayings" that Ishaq had obtained from "unknown people."[2] The renowned hadith specialist Ahmad ibn Hanbal (d. 855) did not regard Ibn Ishaq as a trustworthy source for Islamic law.[3] Since much of that corpus of law is derived from the example of what Muhammad said and did, embraced and avoided, that is extremely significant: Ibn Hanbal's delicacy in this matter implies that he considered the great bulk of what Ibn Ishaq reported about Muhammad to be unreliable. On another occasion, however, Ibn Hanbal clarified his view, explaining that while he did not believe Ibn Ishaq was trustworthy on matters of law, he saw Ibn Ishaq's work as reliable regarding material about Muhammad that was more purely biographical, such as accounts of battles. A less favorable view comes from another early Islamic jurist, Malik ibn Anas (d. 795), who called Ibn Ishaq "one of the antichrists."[4] Others simply called him a liar.[5]

## Defending Ibn Ishaq

Ibn Ishaq had his defenders as well. The early Muslim writer who collected all these unfavorable statements about Ibn Ishaq, and many more as well, ultimately dismissed the criticisms and affirmed the trustworthiness of the biographer's work. And indeed, many of those who objected to Ibn Ishaq's work did so because he had Shiite tendencies or affirmed the free will of mankind, which many Muslims considered to be a heresy. Some believed that he wrote too favorably of the Jewish tribes of Arabia.

None of this actually bears upon the veracity of what he reports, and many early Muslims affirmed that veracity. One eighth-century Muslim, Shuba, dubbed Ibn Ishaq the "amir of traditionalists" (that is, hadith specialists) because of his prodigious memory. A late-ninth-century writer, Abu Zura, said that Ibn Ishaq's work had been scrutinized for accuracy and had passed the test. The early ninth-century jurist ash-Shafii said that Ibn Ishaq was an indispensable source for the battles of the prophet, and even exclaimed that "knowledge will remain among men as long as Ibn Ishaq lives."[6]

These widely divergent views may be attributable to the fact that the picture of Muhammad that emerges from Ibn Ishaq's biography is not what one might expect from the founder of one of the world's great religions. The Muhammad of Ibn Ishaq is not a peaceful teacher of the love of God and the brotherhood of man but rather a warlord who fought numerous battles and ordered the assassination of his enemies. "The character attributed to Muhammad in the biography of Ibn Ishaq," observes the twentieth-century historian David Margoliouth, "is exceedingly unfavorable. In order to gain his ends he recoils from no expedient, and he approves of similar unscrupulousness on the part of his adherents, when exercised in his interest."[7]

It isn't so much Muhammad's wars that embarrass modern-day Muslims in the West—those they can attribute to their prophet's particular time and place, glossing over his status as a "good example" (Qur'an 33:21) for Muslims in all times and places. Harder to explain away are incidents such as the notorious "satanic verses" episode: Muhammad received a revelation naming three goddesses of the pagan Quraysh as daughters of Allah, worthy of veneration. But when the prophet of Islam realized that he had compromised his message of monotheism, he claimed that Satan had inspired those verses, and indeed that Satan interfered with the messages of all the prophets (cf. Qur'an 22:52). Muhammad quickly canceled the offending passages. Ibn Ishaq tells the story of this incident, which most other early chroniclers of Muhammad's life omit from their accounts. Ibn Ishaq also recounts the horrific story of Kinana bin ar-Rabi, a Jewish leader at the oasis of Khaybar, which Muhammad raided and conquered. Thinking that Kinana knew where the Jews of Khaybar had hidden their treasure, the prophet gave this order to his men: "Torture him until you extract what he has." The Muslims then built a fire on Kinana's chest, and when Kinana still wouldn't tell them where the treasure was, they beheaded him.[8]

A modern-day Islamic apologist named Ehteshaam Gulam, a youthful writer at the website Answering Christian Claims, offers a typical Islamic objection to this story when he rejects it for its lack of a proper chain of transmitters (*isnad*): Ibn Ishaq doesn't name his source. Gulam also says that the story simply can't be true, because Muhammad would not have acted this way: "That a man should be tortured with burns on his chest by the sparks of a flint is too heinous a deed for a Prophet (Peace and blessings of Allah be upon him) who had earned for himself the title of *Rahma'lil Alamin* (Mercy for all the worlds)."[9] He suggests that Jews may have concocted the story and passed it along to a credulous Ibn Ishaq.


## Ibn Ishaq's Reliability

So are these all "worthless sayings" that Ibn Ishaq received from "unknown people"? Possibly. Yet left unexplained in these criticisms is Ibn Ishaq's motive. If there were indeed Jews who were enemies of Islam (as they are for all generations, as designated by Qur'an 5:82) and were feeding Ibn Ishaq false information about Muhammad in order to discredit Islam, their motive is relatively clear, but Ibn Ishaq's isn't. Ibn Ishaq, says Margoliouth, paints "a disagreeable picture for the founder of a religion," but it "cannot be pleaded that it is a picture drawn by an enemy."[10] Even if the Muhammad of Ibn Ishaq's portrait is more of a cutthroat than a holy man, his biographer's reverence for his protagonist is obvious and unstinting. Clearly Ibn Ishaq has no interest in portraying his prophet in an unfavorable light; Muhammad, after all, is Ibn Ishaq's moral compass, just as he is for so many Muslims today. Ibn Ishaq seems not to be troubled by the moral implications of the stories he tells or to believe that the incidents place Muhammad in a negative light. Such stories cannot be rejected as unhistorical simply because modern-day Muslims wish they weren't there.

Islamic sources mention earlier historians, but their works have not survived, and what has come down to us about them is uncertain. For example, the man generally acknowledged as the founding father of Islamic history, Urwa ibn Az-Zubair ibn al-Awwam, according to Islamic tradition was a cousin of Muhammad and nephew of Aisha who died in 712. Ibn Ishaq, Tabari, and another early Muslim historian, Ibn Sa'd, attribute many traditions to him, but if he wrote anything at all, it has not come down to us.[11]

There is no way to evaluate the veracity of Ibn Ishaq's various accounts of Muhammad. Material that circulated orally for as many as 125 years, amid an environment in which forgery of such material was rampant, is extremely unlikely to have maintained any significant degree of historical reliability. What's more, as the Dutch scholar of Islam Johannes J. G. Jansen observes:

> Nothing from the contents of Ibn Ishaq is confirmed by inscriptions or other archeological material. Testimonies from non-Muslim contemporaries do not exist. Greek, Armenian, Syriac and other sources about the beginnings of Islam are very difficult to date, but none of them is convincingly contemporary with the Prophet of Islam. Under such circumstances, no biography can be a scholarly work in the modern sense of that word, not even with the help of an omniscient Ibn Ishaq.[12]

## Historical Embroidery

Later biographers were even more knowing, often embroidering on Ibn Ishaq's accounts. Historian Patricia Crone adduces one particularly egregious example. According to Ibn Ishaq's account, the raid of Kharrar appears to have been a nonevent in Muhammad's life: "Meanwhile the Messenger of God had sent Sa'd b. Abi Waqqas on campaign with eight men from among the Muhajirun. He went as far as Kharrar in the Hijaz, then he returned without having had a clash with the enemy." [13]

Two generations later, al-Waqidi (d. 822), in his *Book of History and Campaigns*, a chronicle of the battles of Muhammad, embellishes this spare account:

> Then the Messenger of God (may God bless him and give him peace) appointed Sa'd b. Abi Waqqas to the command against Kharrar—Kharrar being part of Juhfa near Khumm—in Dhu'l-Qa'da, eighteen months after the *hijra* of the Messenger (may God bless him and give him peace). Abu Bakr b. Ismail b. Muhammad said on the authority of his father on the authority of Amir b. Sa'd on the authority of his father [*sc.* Sa'd b. Abi Waqqas]: the Messenger of God (may God bless him and give him peace) said, "O Sa'd, go to Kharrar, for a caravan belonging to Quraysh will pass through it." So I went out with twenty or twenty-one men, on foot. We would hide during the day and travel at night until we arrived there on the morning of the fifth day. We found that the caravan had passed through the day before. The Messenger had enjoined upon us not to go beyond Kharrar. Had we not done so, I would have tried to catch up with it. [14]

Al-Waqidi knows so much more about this expedition than did Ibn Ishaq—and, as Crone notes, "he knows all this on the impeccable authority of the leader of the expedition himself"! But how is it that these details eluded Ibn Ishaq and yet made their way to al-Waqidi some fifty years later? Though it is possible that al-Waqidi had access to oral traditions that had been passed on from people close to Muhammad but had escaped Ibn Ishaq's notice, it is more likely that these details were legendary elaborations developed for the purposes of dramatic storytelling.[15]

## Legendary Elaboration

The scholar of Islam Gregor Schoeler contends that the traditional Islamic material about Muhammad's life and work is substantially reliable. He points out that although the work of Urwa ibn Az-Zubair, Muhammad's first biographer, is lost, Ibn Ishaq and other early Muslim writers quote it extensively. Because Urwa died in 712 and collected the bulk of his stories about Muhammad from the 660s to the 690s, he had ample occasion to gather reliable information. Urwa, says Schoeler, "still had the opportunity to consult eye witnesses and contemporaries of many of the events in question—irrespective of whether he mentions his informant in the *isnad* or not. For this reason, it is much more likely that he asked his aunt Aisha about many events she had witnessed. . . . In addition, he was able to collect first-hand reports on numerous incidents occurring (slightly) before, during and after the *hijra*, e.g. the *hijra* itself (including the 'first *hijra*' to Abyssinia and the circumstances and events leading to the *hijra* proper), the Battle of the Trench and al-Hudaibiya."[16]

These are all important events in Muhammad's life: The Hijra is the Muslims' move from Mecca to Medina in 622, when Muhammad became for the first time a military and political leader as well as a spiritual one. Before that, some Muslims had fled to Abyssinia to escape persecution from the Quraysh of Mecca. The Battle of the Trench, in 627, was the siege of Medina by the pagan Arabs of Mecca—a siege the Muslims eventually broke, with momentous consequences for all concerned. The Treaty of Hudaibiya was the truce Muhammad reached with the Quraysh around the year 628;

it permitted Muslims to make the pilgrimage to Mecca. This treaty set the standard in Islamic law for all treaties between Muslims and non-Muslims. If Urwa was really able to gather and transmit reliable information about all this from his aunt Aisha and others eyewitnesses of the events in question, then the biography of Muhammad in the standard Islamic accounts is essentially trustworthy.

Schoeler's claim, however, falters in light of the comparison above between Ibn Ishaq's and al-Waqidi's accounts of the nonevent at Kharrar. If that material could be subject to so much legendary elaboration within a few decades, what was to prevent those who passed on Urwa's material from altering it substantially, whether they did so in light of other material they had received from different sources, or in the service of some political calculation, or out of a pious interest in exaggerating Muhammad's virtues, or a combination of such motives? In fact, this process of legendary elaboration was already taking place when Ibn Ishaq compiled his account.

The clearest evidence of this comes from the Qur'an's repeated assumption that the messenger who received its revelations was not a miracle worker. The unbelievers demand a miracle: "And they that know not say: Why does God not speak to us? Why does a sign not come to us?" (2:118; cf. 6:37, 10:20, 13:7, 13:27). Allah tells his messenger that even if the prophet did come to the unbelievers with a miracle, they would reject him anyway: "Indeed, We have struck for the people in this Koran every manner of similitude; and if thou bringest them a sign, those who are unbelievers will certainly say, 'You do nothing but follow falsehood'" (30:58). Elsewhere in the Qur'an, Allah delivers a similar message: "Yet if thou shouldst bring to those that have been given the Book every sign, they will not follow thy direction [*qibla*, "direction for prayer"]; thou art not a follower of their direction; neither are they followers of one another's direction. If thou followest their caprices, after the knowledge that has come to thee, then thou wilt surely be among the evildoers" (2:145). The repetition of this theme suggests that one of the primary criticisms the unbelievers brought against the prophet was that he had no miracles to perform; the Qur'an was intended to be sufficient sign in itself: "What, is it not sufficient for them that We have sent down upon thee the Book that is recited to them? Surely in that is a mercy, and a reminder to a people who believe" (29:51).

Yet the Muhammad of Ibn Ishaq's biography is an accomplished miracle worker. Ibn Ishaq relates that during the digging of the trench that ultimately thwarted the Meccans' siege of the Muslims in Medina, one of Muhammad's companions prepared "a little ewe not fully fattened" and invited the prophet to dinner. Muhammad, however, surprised his host by inviting all of those who were working on the trench to dine at the man's home. The prophet of Islam solved the problem just as Jesus in the Gospels multiplied bread and fish: "When we had sat down we produced the food and he blessed it and invoked the name of God over it. Then he ate as did all the others. As soon as one lot had finished another lot came until the diggers turned from it."[17] On another occasion, Ibn Ishaq writes, one of the companions seriously injured his eye, so that it actually hung from its socket; Muhammad "restored it to its place with his hand and it became his best and keenest eye afterwards."[18] In other stories, Muhammad drew water from a dry waterhole and called down the rain with a prayer.[19]

There are many, many such stories in Ibn Ishaq. If any of them had been known at the time the Qur'an was written, it is inexplicable that Muhammad would have been portrayed in his own holy book as a prophet with a book alone and no supporting miracles. It is remarkable that a man who could heal the sick, multiply food, draw water from dry ground, and shoot out lightning from the strike of a pickax would nonetheless be portrayed as a prophet whose message was unsupported by miraculous signs.

Ibn Ishaq also includes stories of how Muhammad was repeatedly identified as a future prophet when he was a mere child. In one, Muhammad was taken as a child to Syria, where a Christian monk named Bahira studied him, "looking at his body and finding traces of his description (in the Christian books)." Ibn Ishaq affirms that

Bahira found the boy to be a stout monotheist, although his people were polytheists; young Muhammad told the monk that "by Allah nothing is more hateful to me" than al-Lat and al-Uzza, two goddesses of the Quraysh. Bahira also "looked at his back and saw the seal of prophethood between his shoulders in the very place described in his book." Accordingly, the monk gave Muhammad's uncle a warning that foreshadowed, or echoed, the later demonization of the Jews in Islamic tradition: "Take your nephew back to his country and guard him carefully against the Jews, for by Allah! If they see him and know about him what I know, they will do him evil; a great future lies before this nephew of yours, so take him home quickly."[20]

Johannes Jansen explains the motivation behind such stories:

The storytellers intended to convince their public that Muhammad has indeed been a prophet from God. In order to do so, they assured their public that already Christians, even monks, had recognized him as such. They had no real memory of such an event, but they wanted to convince their public that to recognize Muhammad as the prophet of God was a good thing. If a neutral, Christian authority had already recognized Muhammad, they must have argued, how much more should others do so!

In this case, the storytellers could only get their message across if they could create a setting in which Muhammad might have actually met a monk. Hence, they tell several stories of how Muhammad as a child went to Syria, together with one of his uncles. There he met his monk, and the monk recognized him. The many stories about Muhammad's travels to Syria are not the product of real historical memory, however vague, but a creation that was made necessary by the theological need to have Muhammad recognized as a prophet by Christians, preferably a monk.

The story about the meeting of Muhammad and the monk is improbable, it appears in many contradictory versions, but it served its purpose.[21]

Such stories are also strange in light of the opposition that Muhammad faced among his own people, the Quraysh, once he did proclaim himself as a prophet: If he really fulfilled the prophecies of a prophet who was to come, why were the Quraysh so slow and obstinate about recognizing that fact? In this the life of Muhammad resembles that of Jesus, whom the Gospel of Matthew in particular depicts as fulfilling the prophecies of the coming Messiah and yet being rejected by the religious leaders most familiar with those prophecies. This close resemblance indicates that the stories of Muhammad's being identified as a prophet while a youth have a typological, legendary cast.

The legendary character of these accounts is especially obvious in light of their absolute incompatibility with other Islamic traditions about how surprised and terrified Muhammad was by the first visitation of the angel Gabriel. Ibn Ishaq himself reports that this encounter left Muhammad in such extreme agitation that he said to his wife: "Woe is me poet [i.e., one who receives ecstatic visions and may be insane] or possessed."[22] If Muhammad had been repeatedly identified as a prophet when he was a child and a young man, one might be forgiven for thinking that he should have seen it coming.

On this basis alone, the historical reliability of Ibn Ishaq is severely compromised. The material he includes in his biography must have arisen long after the collection of the Qur'an. Even in that case, it is odd that he would have included so much material that clearly contradicts the testimony of the Qur'an, a book with which Ibn Ishaq was familiar at least in some form, as he frequently quoted passages that appear in it.

If Ibn Ishaq's biography of Muhammad is largely or even wholly pious fiction, all the information about Muhammad that is generally regarded as historical evaporates. Ibn Ishaq's overarching intention is to demonstrate to his readers that Muhammad is indeed a prophet. But in doing so, he recounts so many legends that fact cannot be separated from fiction. There is no reliable way to distinguish the miraculous material in Ibn Ishaq's account from that which appears to be more straightforwardly historical.

Jansen administers the coup de grâce to any claims that Ibn Ishaq's biography is historical. He points out that "for every event which took place in the life of Muhammad, Ibn Ishaq meticulously recorded in his *Sira* in which month it took place," and "this meticulous and systematic dating by month which is Ibn Ishāq's wont, is, of course, one of the main reasons why Western historians classified his book as historiography in the normal sense of that word." Yet this supposedly painstaking record keeping simply does not line up with the Arabic calendar. The pre-Islamic Arabic calendar, like the Islamic calendar, was lunar, consisting of 354 days rather than the 365 days of the solar calendar. To make up this difference, Arabians added leap months—one every three solar years. They discontinued that practice in the year 629; the Qur'an actually forbids adding leap months (9:36–37). But by that point, Muhammad had acted as a prophet for almost twenty years, according to the standard Islamic account. "How then," asks Jansen, "is it possible that not a single one of the numerous events Ibn Ishaq describes and attaches a date to, took place during a leap month? If his narrative of the life of Muhammad would be based on historical memories and on real events, however distorted, but remembered by real people, how can half a solar year (or more) remain unmentioned and have disappeared from the record?"

Ibn Ishaq's biography, Jansen observes, "can only date from a period in which people had forgotten that leap months had once existed."[23] That period would have to have been a considerably long time after Muhammad is supposed to have lived. "These stories by Ibn Ishaq," concludes Jansen, "do not attempt to describe memories of events that took place in the past, but they want to convince the reader that the protagonist of these stories, Muhammad, is the Messenger of God."

### Having It Both Ways with Ibn Ishaq

Nonetheless, the twentieth-century scholar of Islam W. Montgomery Watt (1909–2006) purported to separate the historical from the legendary in Ibn Ishaq in his two-volume biography of the prophet of Islam, *Muhammad at Mecca* and *Muhammad at Medina*. He did so simply by ignoring the miraculous elements of Ibn Ishaq's work and presenting the rest as historically accurate, a procedure that is, in the final analysis, completely arbitrary: There is no reason to give any more credence to the nonmiraculous elements of Ibn Ishaq's biography than to the miraculous ones. Neither the miraculous nor the nonmiraculous accounts are attested by any other contemporary source, or any source closer to the actual lifetime of Muhammad.

Patricia Crone explains some of what is wrong with Watt's methodology: "He accepts as historically correct the claim that Muhammad traded in Syria as Khadija's agent, even though the only story in which we are told as much is fictitious. It is similarly, to him, a historical fact that Abd al-Muttalib dug the well of Zamzam in Mecca, though the information is likewise derived from a miracle story."[24] Watt informs his readers with impressive precision that "the siege of Medina, known to Muslims as the expedition of the Khandaq or Trench, began on 31 March 627 (8/xi/5) and lasted about a fortnight."[25] He does not say anything about the lightning that shot from Muhammad's pickax during the digging of the trench, or note that his source for the precise start of the siege was al-Waqidi, whose ahistorical elaborations on Ibn Ishaq's already legendary narrative we have seen. Why Watt believes the precise dating for the start of the siege to be historically reliable, but not Muhammad's portentous pickax, he does not explain.

Neither Watt nor other historians who depend on Ibn Ishaq for their knowledge of Muhammad can have it both ways. And if Ibn Ishaq cannot be counted on as a reliable historical source, there is nothing else. Essentially every biography of Muhammad down to this day depends at least to some degree on Ibn Ishaq. Johannes Jansen observes: "Later books about Muhammad essentially limit themselves to retelling Ibn Ishaq's story. Sometimes they are a little more detailed than Ibn Ishaq, but the extra details they supply do not inspire much confidence in modern skeptics. The modern Western biographies of

Muhammad, too, all completely depend upon Ibn Ishaq. Equally, all encyclopedia articles about Mohammed, whether popular or academic, are nothing but summaries of Ibn Ishaq's narrative."[26]

So if Ibn Ishaq is not a historically trustworthy source, what is left of the life of Muhammad? If nothing certain can be known about him, Islam stands as a momentous effect in search of a cause. If there was no warrior prophet teaching jihad warfare against unbelievers and presenting this teaching as the perfect and eternal word of the only true God, then how and why did the great Arab conquests of the seventh century and thereafter really come about? What was the energizing force behind them, if they were not inspired by a fiery prophet's promise of reward in this world and the next for his warriors?

If Islam did not develop as Muslims believe it did and as the earliest Islamic sources explain, then how and why did it develop at all?

A clue to this comes from the anomalies surrounding Islam's Arabian setting.

## Muhammad: Arabian Prophet?

Muhammad was an Arab messenger, born in Mecca, speaking Arabic, and bringing the message of Allah to the Arabs (cf. Qur'an 41:44) and thence to the world at large.

Every element of that sentence is a commonplace that both Muslims and non-Muslims take for granted; yet every element, upon closer scrutiny, begins to dissolve. From the extant historical records, it is not at all clear that there was an Arab prophet named Muhammad anywhere near Mecca, who brought any kind of message to the world. Or at the very least, the records indicate that if there was a Muhammad, he was not in Mecca and didn't preach anything that closely resembles Islam—until long after his death, when his biography and holy book as we know them began to be constructed.

The centrality of Arabia and the Arabic language to the message of Islam cannot be overstated. Although Islam presents itself as a universal religion for all people on earth, it has a decidedly Arabic character. Converts to Islam, whatever their nationality, usually take Arabic names. Wherever they are in the world, and whatever their native language, Muslims must pray in Arabic and recite the Qur'an in Arabic.

Many converts in non-Muslim countries adopt traditional Arabic dress. Arabic culture has a pride of place in the Islamic world that has frequently given rise to tensions between Arab and non-Arab Muslims. Arabic supremacists have in our own time made war against non-Arab Muslims in the Darfur region of the Sudan; such conflicts are a recurring feature of Islamic history.[27]

Central to Islam, therefore, is the traditional account of how Muhammad, an Arabian merchant, received the Qur'an through the angel Gabriel from Allah, first in Mecca and then in Medina. According to the canonical Islamic account, armed with its message, Muhammad had united the entire Arabian Peninsula under the banner of Islam by the time of his death in 632.

It was not an easy task, according to the standard Islamic sources. The prophet and his new religion faced stiff resistance from his own tribe, the Quraysh, who were pagans and polytheists. The Quraysh, according to the Islamic story of the religion's origins, lived in Mecca, which was a center for both trade and pilgrimage, such that people went there from all over Arabia and from outside Arabia as well. The Quraysh, say the Muslim sources, profited from those who made pilgrimages to the Ka'ba (the cube-shaped shrine in Mecca) to worship its many idols. Mecca, according to Islamic tradition, was central to both the religion and the commerce of the area.

The canonical account of the origins of Islam holds that the Quraysh initially rejected Muhammad's prophetic claim for reasons that were economic more than spiritual. Watt notes that "by the end of the sixth century A.D.," the Quraysh "had gained control of most of the trade from the Yemen to Syria—an important route by which the West got Indian luxury goods as well as South Arabian frankincense."[28] Much of this trade depended on the Arabs who came to

Mecca as pilgrims. With pagan Arabs traveling from all over the Arabian Peninsula to worship their gods at the Ka'ba, a proclamation that all these gods did not exist or were demons—exactly what Muhammad preached with his uncompromising monotheism—would not only cost the Quraysh their pilgrimage business but also cut into their trade interests.

And so for the twelve years he remained in Mecca, Muhammad attracted few followers but aroused the antagonism of the Quraysh. That antagonism flared up regarding both the idols in the Ka'ba and the Quraysh trading caravans. Ibn Ishaq tells us that when Muhammad migrated to Medina twelve years into his prophetic career, he ordered the Muslims to raid the Quraysh caravans that were returning from Syria laden with goods. The prophet himself led many of these raids, which kept the Muslim movement solvent. Though driven by economic need, the raids became the occasion for certain elements of Islamic theology to take hold, according to Islamic tradition. In one notorious incident, a band of Muslims raided a Quraysh caravan during one of the four sacred months of the pre-Islamic Arabic calendar. These were the months during which fighting was forbidden, meaning that the Muslim raiders had violated a sacred principle. But the Qur'an says that Allah permitted the Muslims to violate the sacred month if they were persecuted—in other words, to set aside the moral principle for the good of Islam: "They will question thee concerning the holy month, and fighting in it. Say: 'Fighting in it is a heinous thing, but to bar from God's way, and disbelief in Him, and the Holy Mosque, and to expel its people from it—that is more heinous in God's sight; and persecution is more heinous than slaying'" (2:217). The "Holy Mosque" is, according to Islamic tradition, a reference to the Ka'ba.

This was a key incident for the development of Islamic ethics, establishing that good was what benefited Islam, and evil anything that harmed it. It also set the relations between the Muslims and the Quraysh on war mode. Their battles, according to the standard Islamic account of the origins of Islam, became the occasion for Allah to reveal to Muhammad many of the Qur'an's key passages regarding warfare against unbelievers.

Therefore, the Arabian setting of the Qur'an and the antagonism of the Quraysh to Muhammad's message are crucial for both Islamic history and theology. This was the context in which some of the most important Islamic doctrines unfolded. Islamic tradition establishes that at root, the Quraysh opposed Muhammad's prophetic message because it could end pilgrimages to Mecca and disrupt trade.

Just as Arab identity is central to Islam, the holiest city in Islam, Mecca, is central to Islam's Arab identity. Yet for all its centrality to Islam, Mecca is mentioned by name only once in the Qur'an: "It is He who restrained their hands from you, and your hands from them, in the hollow of Mecca, after that He made you victors over them. God sees the things you do" (48:24).

What incident this refers to is—as is so often the case in the Qur'an—completely unclear. The medieval Qur'an commentator Ibn Kathir explains the verse this way: "Imam Ahmad recorded that Anas bin Malik said, 'On the day of Hudaibiya, eighty armed men from Makkah went down the valley coming from Mount At-Tan'im to ambush the Messenger of Allah. The Messenger invoked Allah against them, and they were taken prisoners.' Affan added, 'The Messenger pardoned them, and this Ayah ["sign," or Qur'anic verse] was later on revealed.'"[29] But the Qur'an itself says nothing about Hudaibiya in the verse in question. What's more, as foundational as the Treaty of Hudaibiya became for the Islamic doctrine regarding treaties and truces with non-Muslim forces, no record outside of the Islamic sources verifies that the treaty was ever concluded at all.

As is true of so much about early Islamic history, the closer one looks at the relevant sources about Mecca's importance in the Arabia of Muhammad's time, the less there is to see. If Watt were correct that the Meccans controlled a pivotal trading empire that included the route from Europe to India, one would reasonably expect some indication of it in the contemporary literature. As Crone puts it, "It is obvious that if the Meccans had been middlemen in a long-distance trade of the kind described in the secondary literature"—that is, works by Watt and other historians who take for granted the canonical Islamic account—"there ought to have been some mention of them in the writings of their customers. Greek and Latin authors had, after all, written extensively about the south Arabians who supplied them with aromatics in the past, offering information about their cities, tribes, political organization, and caravan trade."[30]

But in all such sources, there is silence. No mention of Mecca. Nothing about its appearance, the nature of the business conducted there, the demeanor of the Quraysh—the usual kind of details one finds in chronicles of travelers and tradesmen from classical times into the Middle Ages. Instead, there is a yawning gap. Muslim writers make much of the mathematician and astrologer Ptolemy's mention of a place in Arabia called Macoraba, but even if this does refer to Mecca (which Crone disputes), Ptolemy died in A.D. 168.[31] Just as no one would take the account of a traveler in Constantinople in 1400 as evidence that the city was a thriving center of Christianity in the mid-nineteenth century, so would one be ill advised to take Ptolemy's writing about Mecca as proof that it was a thriving center for trade nearly five centuries after his death.

In contrast, Procopius of Caesarea (d. 565), the leading historian of the sixth century, does not mention Mecca—which is strange indeed if it were really the center of trade in Arabia and between the West and India during the time of Muhammad, who allegedly was born only five years after Procopius's death.[32] Centers of trade do not spring up instantaneously.

No non-Muslim historian mentions Mecca in any accounts of trade in the sixth and seventh centuries. (Nor, for that matter, do Muslim historians: There are no surviving Islamic records regarding this trade earlier than the eighth century.) Crone notes: "The political and ecclesiastical importance of Arabia in the sixth century was such that considerable attention was paid to Arabian affairs, too; but of Quraysh and their trading center there is no mention at all, be it in the Greek, Latin, Syriac, Aramaic, Coptic, or other literature composed outside Arabia before the conquests. This silence is striking and significant."[33] Specifically, she says, "Nowhere is it stated that Quraysh, or the 'Arab kings,' were the people who used to supply such-and-such regions with such-and-such goods: it was only Muhammad himself who was known to have been a trader."[34] And that is known only from sources written long after his death.

There is more, too. The location of Mecca is wrong if it was to have served as a center for trade. It is located in western Arabia, such that, in the words of historian Richard Bulliet, "only by the most tortured map reading can it be described as a natural crossroads between a north-south route and an east-west one."[35] Travelers along the route Watt envisions, between Yemen and Syria, might have reason to stop at Mecca, but his contention that Mecca was central to an "important route by which the West got Indian luxury goods as well as South Arabian frankincense" is both unsupported by the contemporary evidence and unlikely geographically.

The same thing goes for the idea of Mecca as a major pilgrimage site in the early seventh century. Contemporary evidence indicates that pilgrimages were conducted to at least three other sites in Arabia—Ukaz, Dhu'l-Majaz, and Majanna—but not to Mecca.[36] Crone also notes that Mecca differed from these other sites in being a populated city, whereas the established places for Arabian pilgrimage were uninhabited except during the times of the pilgrimage. She adds, "The pilgrimage was a ritual performed at times and places in which everybody downed arms and nobody was in control: a sanctuary owned by a specific tribe"—that is, the Quraysh—"does not belong in this complex."[37]

The significance of this is enormous. If Mecca was a center only for local, small-scale trade and pilgrimage in the early seventh century, then the entire canonical story of the origins of Islam is cast into doubt. If the Quraysh did not object to Muhammad's message on the grounds that it would harm their trade and pilgrimage business, on what grounds did they object to it? If Muhammad did not encounter stiff resistance from the Quraysh during the first twelve years of his prophetic career, as he preached his message of monotheism to an unreceptive Meccan audience, then what *did* happen?

Without Mecca as a trading and pilgrimage center, there is no foundation for the accounts of antagonism between Muhammad and the Quraysh in Mecca. Nor is there any foundation for accounts of Muhammad's subsequent migration to Medina and warfare against the Quraysh. Likewise unsupported are stories of how he defeated the Quraysh, returned to Mecca toward the end of his life, and converted the Ka'ba into a Muslim shrine, the centerpiece of what would forever after be a site of Islamic, rather than pagan, pilgrimage.

Today, Muslim pilgrims flock to Mecca for the hajj, as they have done for many centuries. But the entire account of the Meccan origins of Islam stands on shaky foundations. Although there is evidence that a shrine of some kind existed at Mecca, it does not appear to have been a major one.[38] Either Muhammad or later Muslims transformed the shrine into the center for Islamic pilgrimage that it is today. In doing so, they elevated Mecca to an importance it did not have, if we scrutinize the record, even at the time Muhammad is supposed to have lived.

Islam thus grows less Arabic and Arabian by the minute. The Arabic holy book, as we have seen, contains significant non-Arabic elements. Now it turns out that one of the key pieces anchoring Islam's origins in Arabia—Muhammad's increasingly antagonistic interaction with a Quraysh tribe jealous of its economic and religious prerogatives—turns out to be historically unsupported.

If that is the case, how did the stories of Muhammad arise at all, and for what reason? Why were they apparently cast back into an Arabia that was not home to his pagan tribe or a thriving trade and pilgrimage business, so meticulously recounted in the Islamic texts?

# The Embarrassment of Muhammad

## Muhammad: Resourceful and Opportunistic

One chief objection to the idea that Muhammad is either wholly or in large part a fictional character is the fact that the canonical Islamic texts contain a significant amount of material that portrays him in a negative light.

For if Muhammad was invented, or invested with a legendary biography, this would have been done in order to provide a nascent culture with a hero. Why would anyone invent a hero and then invest him with weaknesses? Why would anyone fashion a portrait of a founding father, the fashioner and unifier of the community, the exemplar in all things, and make him anything less than admirable in every way?

A singular figure appears to come alive on the pages of the Hadith: a resourceful, inventive, supremely intelligent man who seems to have known just what to do or say to inspire in his followers the maximum of awe and respect. How one evaluates the details of the portrait of Muhammad that emerges from the Islamic sources depends on what one thinks of the man and his claims. But could such a figure be wholly legendary?

Islamic tradition recounts that a rabbi of Medina, whose name comes down to us as Abdullah bin Salam, was impressed by what he was hearing about Muhammad and decided to give him a test to see whether he was really a prophet. Abdullah asked Muhammad three questions that, said Abdullah, "nobody knows unless he be a Prophet." They were these: "What is the first portent of the Hour? What is the first meal of the people of Paradise? And what makes a baby look like its father or mother?"

It was an odd scenario: How could Abdullah have known whether Muhammad's answers were correct unless Abdullah were himself a prophet? Muhammad took Abdullah's questions in stride, informing him coolly that "just now" the angel Gabriel had given him the answers to precisely those questions. He duly passed the responses on to Abdullah, who was so impressed that he immediately converted to Islam.[1]

The reader, confronted with such a story, has three options:

1.  Accept that Muhammad's answers were correct, and that this was a sign of his special prophetic knowledge.
2.  See Muhammad's willingness to supply answers to Abdullah that Abdullah had no way of verifying as evidence that he was a false prophet engaged in manipulating credulous people like Abdullah.
3.  Regard the entire account as a later embellishment designed to show that Muhammad was a prophet.

The problem with the third option is the logical difficulty embedded within the story: Anyone who reflects on this account for any time at all will realize that Abdullah had no way of knowing whether Muhammad's answers were correct. Nor does the reader, which makes the first option problematic. These considerations make the second option more likely: Muhammad knew Abdullah had presented him with a game that he could not lose, and he exploited the opportunity.

But if Muhammad was an invented character, why fabricate a story that enemies could use to portray him—and the nascent Islamic community—in a less than flattering light?

Of course, the most likely explanation here is that this story was constructed by people who took for granted that Muhammad was a prophet and did not consider that some readers might take the account as evidence he was a con artist. Supporting this explanation is the fact that establishing Muhammad's prophetic status is not the primary point of the story; the account of Abdullah bin Salam and Muhammad ultimately focuses on demonizing the Jews, whom Abdullah helps Muhammad catch in a lie after he converts to Islam.

But other aspects of the canonical Islamic account of Muhammad clearly did embarrass those who regarded him as a prophet. Some of the earliest Islamic material on Muhammad contains attempts to explain away certain actions of the prophet. One of the most notable examples is the episode in which Muhammad married his former daughter-in-law.

## The Comely Zaynab and the Historicity of Muhammad

On several occasions Allah seemed anxious to grant his prophet his heart's desires—as in the notorious story of one of Muhammad's wives, Zaynab bint Jahsh. Noted for her striking beauty, Zaynab was originally married to Muhammad's adopted son, Zayd bin Muhammad (formerly known as Zayd bin Haritha), who was so close to the prophet that he was known as the Beloved of the Messenger of Allah. Zayd has the distinction of being the only contemporary of Muhammad, or purported contemporary, to be mentioned by name in the Qur'an.

One day Muhammad chanced to visit Zayd's home while his adopted son was away, and Zaynab answered the door in a state of semi-undress. "He looked at her," says the *Tafsir al-Jalalayn*, a respected commentary on the Qur'an, "and felt love for her whereas Zayd disliked her."[2] Zayd offered to divorce her so that Muhammad could marry her; Muhammad's response is recorded in an elliptical passage in the Qur'an: "Keep thy wife to thyself, and fear God" (33:37).

One would think that being overcome with desire for one's daughter-in-law would bring a blush to the cheeks of the most ardent proponent of free love, but the part of the story that embarrassed

Muhammad, at least according to Islamic tradition, was not that at all. Rather, it was the fact that he told Zayd to keep his wife. Of this, one of his other wives, Aisha, later remarked: "If Allah's Apostle were to conceal anything (of the Qur'an) he would have concealed this verse."[3]

Why would Muhammad be embarrassed by this point? Because Allah wanted Muhammad to marry Zaynab, and therefore the prophet was rejecting Allah's will. Indeed, Allah rebuked Muhammad for not wanting to receive what the deity wanted to give him, saying that the prophet feared public opinion (as the people might justifiably be upset at Muhammad's new union with his comely former daughter-in-law) more than he feared Allah: "And thou wast concealing within thyself what God should reveal, fearing other men; and God has better right for thee to fear him" (33:37).

So Muhammad resolved to do Allah's will. He went into the trancelike state that often attended his reception of divine revelations, and when he came to, he asked happily: "Who will go to Zaynab to tell her the good news, saying that God has married her to me?"

Allah explained that he had staged the whole event in order to impress upon Muslims that adopted sons should not be treated as natural sons and that adoption itself was illegitimate: "God has not assigned to any man two hearts within his breast; nor has He made your wives, when you divorce, saying, 'Be as my mother's back,' truly your mothers, neither has He made your adopted sons your sons in fact. That is your own saying, the words of your mouths; but God speaks the truth, and guides on the way" (33:4). And specifically in Muhammad's case: "So when Zayd had accomplished what he would of her, then We gave her in marriage to thee: so that there should not be any fault in the believers, touching the wives of their adopted sons, when they have accomplished what they would of them" (33:37). Zayd bin Muhammad went back to being known as Zayd bin Haritha, and to this day adoption is not considered legitimate in Islamic law.

This new divine decree had the added benefit of absolving Muhammad of any guilt for violating the laws of consanguinity by marrying Zaynab. When, according to a hadith in Bukhari's collection, Muhammad announced that Allah had married him to Zaynab, Aisha remarked—with what degree of irony is up to the reader—"I feel that your Lord hastens in fulfilling your wishes and desires."[4]

Could this story possibly have been fabricated as a pious legend? It is hard to imagine why any pious Muslim would have invented it: The Zaynab incident depicts Muhammad as a rogue prophet, enslaved to his lust, and stooping to construct a flimsy excuse (the prohibition of adoption) in order to exonerate himself.

But embarrassment is relative. We may see this incident as casting Muhammad in a bad light, but what constitutes a negative depiction is not necessarily constant from age to age and culture to culture. Consider the story of Muhammad's marriage to Aisha, the daughter of his close companion and first successor, Abu Bakr. Whereas the Qur'anic text that refers elliptically to Muhammad's marriage to Zaynab provides an elaborate explanation for the whole incident, the earliest records about Muhammad's dalliance with Aisha state events without apology. A hadith collected by Bukhari notes: "The Prophet wrote the (marriage contract) with Aisha while she was six years old and consummated his marriage with her while she was nine years old and she remained with him for nine years (i.e., till his death)."[5]

Aisha herself betrayed nervousness, but no one else seemed particularly concerned:

> The Prophet engaged me when I was a girl of six (years). We went to Medina and stayed at the home of Bani al-Harith bin Khazraj. Then I got ill and my hair fell down. Later on my hair grew (again) and my mother, Umm Ruman, came to me while I was playing in a swing with some of my girl friends. She called me, and I went to her, not knowing what she wanted to do to me. She caught me by the hand and made me stand at the door of the house. I was breathless then, and when my breathing became all right, she took some water and rubbed my face and head with it. Then she took me into the house. There in the house I saw some Ansari women who said, "Best wishes and Allah's blessing and

good luck." Then she entrusted me to them and they prepared me (for the marriage). Unexpectedly Allah's Apostle came to me in the forenoon and my mother handed me over to him, and at that time I was a girl of nine years of age.[6]

The earliest Islamic sources offer no hint that anyone around Muhammad had a problem with this marriage. Bukhari reports matter-of-factly, and more than once, that she was nine when the marriage was consummated. Nothing in the accounts of this marriage can compare with the evident embarrassment attending Muhammad's marriage to Zaynab. In fact, the Qur'an takes child marriage for granted in its directives about divorce. When speaking about the waiting period required to determine if a woman is pregnant, it says: "As for your women who have despaired of further menstruating, if you are in doubt, their period shall be three months, and those who have not menstruated as yet" (65:4). The last part, "and those who have not menstruated as yet," has been understood in Islamic tradition not as a non sequitur or incomplete thought but as a specification that the waiting period for divorce should be three months for prepubescent girls as well. This passage suggests that in the time and place the stories about Muhammad and Aisha began to be told, few people, if any, had any particular problem with a fifty-four-year-old man consummating a marriage with a nine-year-old girl; it was a cultural norm, and that was that.

Other elements of Muhammad's career that jar modern sensibilities seem to have caused no embarrassment for the authors of the earliest Islamic texts. Far from recoiling from their warrior prophet, one hadith has him boast, "I have been made victorious with terror."[7] Another hadith tells of how Muhammad, enraged by a tribe that murdered a shepherd and drove away his camels, had the culprits captured and ordered their eyes put out with heated pieces of iron and their hands and feet amputated. (The latter punishment accords with the Qur'an's directive that the hands and feet of those who make war against Allah and his messenger be amputated on opposite sides

[5:33].) Then he left the tribesmen in the desert without water. All this was justified, according to a companion of Muhammad who is quoted in the hadith, because "those people committed theft and murder, became infidels after embracing Islam and fought against Allah and His Apostle."[8] As brutal as this episode appears to modern eyes, to those who invented it, it demonstrated Muhammad's strength and fearlessness in the face of injustice. It also supported punishments that are still part of Islamic law, including amputation for theft (cf. Qur'an 5:38) and the death penalty for apostasy (cf. 4:89).

Similarly, hadiths portray Muhammad's polygamy as a sign not of libertinism but of his unmatched virility. The prophet is reported as saying: "Gabriel brought a kettle from which I ate and I was given the power of sexual intercourse equal to forty men."[9] Other hadiths have Aisha saying, "I used to wash the traces of Janaba (semen) from the clothes of the Prophet and he used to go for prayers while traces of water were still on it (water spots were still visible)."[10] This is odd—how and why did the semen get on his clothes in the first place?—but apparently it is meant to indicate his divinely assisted virility.

Other hadiths appear merely curious to modern readers. That is largely because the controversies that gave rise to these traditions have long since faded, and also because a great deal of folk material and superstition appears to have made its way into the Hadith. For example, in one hadith Muhammad is made to say that Muslims should blow their noses three times upon waking, for Satan sleeps in the bridge of one's nose at night.[11] He also said that if someone is troubled by a nightmare, "he should spit on his left side and should seek refuge with Allah from its evil, for then it will not harm him."[12] He claimed that "yawning is from Satan and if anyone of you yawns, he should check his yawning as much as possible, for if anyone of you (during the act of yawning) should say: 'Ha,' Satan will laugh at him."[13] He advised the Muslims that "when you hear the crowing of a cock, ask for Allah's Blessings for (its crowing indicates that) it has seen an angel. And when you hear the braying of a donkey, seek refuge with Allah from Satan for (its braying indicates) that it has seen a Satan.' "[14] He counseled: "If a housefly falls in the drink of anyone of you, he should dip it (in the drink), for one of its wings has a disease and the other has the cure for the disease.' "[15] Muhammad even announced a startling biological discovery: "A non-Muslim eats in seven intestines whereas a Muslim eats in one intestine."[16]

The Hadith contain a great deal of this sort of thing. We cannot know with certainty the derivation of such material, but it seems unlikely that it was added in the heat of some sectarian or dynastic battle. It is much more likely that everything considered wise or useful or just good to know was attributed to the prophet of Islam.

These maxims and pearls of folk wisdom did not cause the early Muslims any embarrassment. The story of Zaynab did—or so it seems.

## Why the Zaynab Story Was Composed

The story of Muhammad's marriage to his former daughter-in-law appears to betray embarrassment about, and provide a justification for, a negative episode in Muhammad's life. But it may actually be something else altogether.

The Qur'an's allusive and fragmented reference to the incident concludes with the affirmation that "Muhammad is not the father of any one of your men, but the Messenger of God, and the Seal of the Prophets; God has knowledge of everything" (33:40). What does that affirmation have to do with Muhammad's marriage to his daughter-in-law? Possibly nothing—the Qur'an is remarkably decontextualized, veering from topic to topic within many of its suras, often without any discernable logical connection between the subjects treated. Thus the appearance of this affirmation of Muhammad as "the Seal of the Prophets" may have nothing to do with the Zaynab incident. Then again, when considered in light of a central tenet of Islamic theology, the assertion that Muhammad is "the Seal of the Prophets" appears to have *everything* to do with the story of his marriage to Zaynab.

In the Qur'an, the prophets are all related to one another, and it appears that the prophetic office is handed down from father to son, like an inheritance or a genetic predisposition. Speaking of Abraham, Allah says:

And We gave to him Isaac and Jacob—each one We guided; and Noah We guided before; and of his seed David and Solomon, Job and Joseph, Moses and Aaron—even so We recompense the good-doers—Zachariah and John, Jesus and Elias; each was of the righteous; Ishmael and Elisha, Jonah and Lot—each one We preferred above all beings. (6:84–86)

Thus "David and Solomon, Job and Joseph, Moses and Aaron" and the rest were "of his seed"—that is, Abraham's. These prophets were all relatives, and presumably they received their prophetic spirit as something of an inheritance. This view is reinforced by the Qur'an's confusion of Miriam the sister of Moses and Aaron with Mary the mother of Jesus—the name of each is the same in Arabic: *Maryam*. This makes Jesus Moses' nephew. While Islamic tradition has Muhammad saying that the appellation "sister of Aaron" for Mary in the Qur'an (19:28) was merely an honorific and not an expression of an actual blood relationship, the Qur'an also has Mary being born of the wife of Imran, the father of Moses (3:36).

If, therefore, Muhammad had a son who survived into adulthood—he is said to have had as many as five sons, all of whom died before reaching puberty—the son would have been a prophet as well, and Muhammad would not have been the last prophet, "the Seal of the Prophets."[17] Cornell University professor David S. Powers, a scholar of Islamic history and law, has written an extraordinarily well-researched and well-reasoned book-length examination of the Zaynab incident and its historical and theological status. In it Powers notes that "as the Last Prophet, Muhammad could not have a son who reached puberty; otherwise, as Muqatil states, that son would have been a prophet."[18] Muqatil ibn Sulayman (d. 767) was an early commentator on the Qur'an.

Suddenly, then, the presence of Muhammad's adopted son takes on immense importance to Islamic theology. Powers explains:

> The logic of this argument applies not only to Muhammad's natural sons, none of whom reached puberty, but also to his adopted son Zayd, who did. By virtue of his status as Muhammad's adult son, Zayd b. Muhammad was a member of the Abrahamic family to which the mantle of prophecy had been entrusted as an exclusive possession. Similarly, Muhammad's grandson, Usama b. Zayd b. Muhammad, was also a member of this family. In theory, the mantle of prophecy might have passed from Muhammad to Zayd, and from Zayd to Usama.[19]

Indeed, something very like this developed among the Shiites, who differed from the Sunnis in maintaining that the leader of the Islamic community had to be a member of Muhammad's household. In the absence of a son, the authority fell to Ali ibn Abi Talib, by virtue of his being Muhammad's son-in-law, the husband of his daughter Fatima. By that point, then, Zayd's claim to be Muhammad's son must have already been repudiated. Powers observes:

> The Muslim community had no choice but to construct its foundation narrative in such a way as to marginalize both Zayd and Usama. However, Muhammad's repudiation of Zayd did not fully eliminate the threat to the theological doctrine of the finality of prophecy. This is because at the time of Zayd's repudiation in 5 A.H. [A.D. 626], he was already a grown man. The fact that the Prophet had an adult son named Zayd b. Muhammad conflicted with the assertion in v. 40 that "Muhammad is not the father of any of your men." For the sake of theological consistency, it was important to demonstrate that the *man* who had been Muhammad's *son* failed to outlive the Prophet. Like Muhammad's repudiation of Zayd, the death of the Beloved of the Messenger of God some time prior to the year 11/632 was a theological imperative.[20]

Sure enough, Islamic tradition holds that Zayd died in the Battle of Muta in the year 629—three years before Muhammad himself.

Thus in order to ensure the centrality of Muhammad in Islamic tradition, and to establish a religious orthodoxy that held the empire together, stories had to be invented emphasizing that Muhammad had neither natural nor adopted sons. This was because a son of Muhammad could potentially become a rallying figure for a rival political faction, as Ali became for the Shiites. Even Aisha said: "Had Zayd outlived Muhammad, he would have appointed him as his successor."[21] So Zayd had to die before Muhammad, and Usama had to be seen as having no reasonable claim to leadership. A delegitimization of adoption had the added benefit of striking at Islam's chief spiritual rival, Christianity, with its doctrine of Gentiles as adopted sons of God.

To our twenty-first-century Western sensibilities, then, the traditional account of Muhammad's marriage to the wife of his adopted son at first appears to construct a cover for that action by delegitimizing adoption, saying (as in Qur'an 33:4) that adopted sons are not to be considered actual sons. But a closer examination of the story, based on what we know of early Islamic history and theology, suggests that the pronouncements on adoption were not a convenient justification for Muhammad's marriage to Zaynab but rather were the very point the story was meant to illustrate. In short, this incident no longer appears to be an embarrassment that Muslims felt compelled to explain away; it seems fundamental to Islam's theological claims.

## Zayd and Usama: Historical Figures?

This explanation has the advantage over the canonical Islamic account in that it does what the mainstream version does not and cannot do: It explains how Qur'an 33:40, which affirms that Muhammad is not the father of any of the Muslims but rather is the Seal of the Prophets, relates to the story of Zaynab, even in the fragmentary form in which it is told in the Qur'an.

This exposition raises other questions, however. Although it explains why the Zaynab story may have been invented to serve various theological and political imperatives, it seems to take for granted that Zayd himself was a historical figure, known in the early Muslim community—and that he was known to have been Muhammad's adopted son. It apparently assumes that Zayd and his son, Usama, had been known and were remembered, and that their existence, or at least their nonprophetic status, had to be explained.

In other words, the story of Zaynab may not have been constructed to explain away Muhammad's lechery, but if it was constructed to dismiss Zayd or Usama's claims to succeed the prophet, this suggests that the story deals with real historical figures, not myths. And if Usama and Zayd were real, wouldn't Muhammad be also? Is it possible that the mysterious Arab prophet who appears in the earliest documents of the Arab conquest, apparently preaching some form of monotheism and kinship with the Jews and Christians, was indeed Muhammad?

At the very least, the figure of Usama must be considered in this context. Zayd may have conveniently died before Muhammad did, but Usama did not. Usama shows up in several hadiths. For example, Islamic tradition indicates that in the last year of his life, Muhammad appointed Usama as commander of an expedition to Syria. This was an unpopular choice among the Muslims, goes the story, but Muhammad defended Usama: "I have been informed that you spoke about Usama. (Let it be known that) he is the most beloved of all people to me."[22] Abu Bakr, Muhammad's successor, later sent Usama on a raid, from which he returned with captives and booty.[23]

All this, however, depends on the Hadith, which, as we have seen, were subject to rampant forgery for political reasons. There is no contemporary indication that Zayd or Usama existed at all. Given the theological imperative to establish Muhammad as the final prophet, there would have been ample reason to invent them. If Zayd and Usama did exist, most of what we know about them appears to be legend that was attached to shadowy historical personages whose actual deeds had been largely forgotten.

Giving Muhammad a son whom he adopted and then repudiated decades later in obedience to divine revelation reinforced the Qur'an's point that one should obey not human beings but Allah alone (33:37). Having Usama appear in the early Muslim community, but not as a contender for the leadership, reinforced the point that Muhammad had no sons of any kind, and thus the prophetic line ended with his death.

## Zayd's Death and the Battle of Muta

Similarly, what we know of Zayd bin Haritha, formerly known as Zayd bin Muhammad, depends entirely on much later accounts. There are no contemporary records of the Battle of Muta that Islamic tradition tells us took the life of Zayd in 629. The first known reference to the battle in a non-Muslim source is found nearly two centuries later in the writings of a Byzantine chronicler, Theophanes the Confessor (760–818). Theophanes places the battle *after* Muhammad's death: "Mouamed, who had died earlier, had appointed four emirs to fight those members of the Arab nation who were Christian." According to Theophanes, the local Byzantine ruler, "on learning this from a certain Koraishite called Koutabas, who was in his pay, gathered all the soldiers of the desert guard and, after ascertaining from the Saracens the day and hour when they were intending to attack, himself attacked them at a village called Mothous, and killed three emirs and the bulk of their army."[24]

Muslim historians such as Ibn Ishaq and al-Waqidi (748–822) also write of this battle but tell a much different story. According to Ibn Ishaq, Muhammad was still alive and sent out the expedition personally with specific instructions about who was to be in command: "The apostle sent his expedition to Muta in Jumada'l-Ula in the year 8 [629] and put Zayd b. Haritha in command; if Zayd were slain then Jafar b. Abi Talib was to take command, and if he were killed then Abdullah b. Rawaha."[25] Sure enough, the men were slain in exactly that order: "When fighting began Zayd b. Haritha fought holding the apostle's standard, until he died from loss of blood among the spears of the enemy. Then Jafar took it and fought with it until when the battle hemmed him in he jumped off his roan and hamstrung her and fought till he was killed." And finally Abdullah "seized his sword and died fighting."[26]

Waqidi offers additional detail about the battle. Powers explains just how different his account is from that of Theophanes: "Waqidi and Theophanes disagree about . . . the casus belli, the *identity* of the Byzantine military commander, the *size* of the opposing armies, the *reason* for the Muslim defeat, and the *number* of Muslims who were killed. The discrepancies are so striking that one is justified in asking if these two historians are talking about the same battle."[27]

Waqidi's account is also encrusted with legend. He recounts that during the battle, Muhammad, who was back in Medina in the mosque, received visions of what was happening and relayed the news to other Muslims. The accuracy of these visions of course provided yet more indication that he was indeed a prophet of Allah. Muhammad reported to the assembled Muslims that before the battle, Satan tried to tempt Zayd with worldly pleasures, but that Zayd responded contemptuously: "Now that belief has been firmly established in the hearts of the Believers, you are enticing me with the pleasures of this world!"[28] When Zayd was killed, Muhammad told the people in the mosque to ask Allah to forgive him, "for he has entered the garden, running." According to al-Waqidi, Muhammad then reported that Satan tried to tempt Jafar as well, and that Jafar gave him the same pious answer as Zayd had. When Jafar was killed, he sprouted wings and entered the garden flying. Abdullah then took up the standard and was killed. Muhammad said that he entered the garden stumbling—which puzzled Muhammad's audience, until the prophet of Islam explained that Abdullah could not enter the garden as gracefully or enthusiastically because he had had a great desire for life.[29] After all, the Qur'an takes for granted that those who are the "friends" of Allah will "long for death": "You of Jewry, if you assert that you are the friends of God, apart from other men, then do you long for death, if you speak truly" (62:6).

With Ibn Ishaq and al-Waqidi, it does not seem that we are dealing with straightforward historical records. Raising doubts are the serious discrepancies from the non-Muslim historical accounts and the legendary character of al-Waqidi's story. (And here again, if Muhammad was such a miracle worker and seer, why do the critics of the prophet complain in the Qur'an that he has worked no wonders?) Add to this the report that the three commanders whom Muhammad designated died in the order in which he designated them; commanding generals can only wish that battles would unfold in such an orderly manner. There may have been a battle at Muta, but what actually happened there is lost in mists of time and cannot be reconstructed from Theophanes, Ibn Ishaq, or al-Waqidi.

Whether or not there was a battle between the Muslims and the Byzantines at Muta at some time in the late 620s or early 630s, the Muslim accounts of it that include the martyrdom of Zayd have no historical value. Like so many other elements of the canonical account of early Islam, they may have been invented to emphasize a political and theological point—in this case, that "Muhammad is not the father of any of your men" and hence is "the Seal of the Prophets."

## Muhammad Bewitched

Other tales that appear to show Muhammad in a less than flattering light have even less to recommend their historicity. Apparently difficult to explain is why anyone would have invented the hadiths in which Muhammad fell under the influence of magic spells. One spell made him think he had had sexual relations with his wives when he actually had not. In one such hadith, Aisha recalls Muhammad telling her about this spell:

O Aisha! Allah has instructed me regarding a matter about which I had asked Him. There came to me two men, one of them sat near my feet and the other near my head. The one near my feet, asked the one near my head (pointing at me), "What is wrong with this man?" The latter replied, "He is under the effect of magic." The first one asked, "Who had worked magic on him?" The other replied, "Lubaid bin Asam." The first one asked, "What material (did he use)?" The other replied, "The skin of the pollen of a male date tree with a comb and the hair stuck to it, kept under a stone in the well of Dharwan."

Muhammad then went to a well and found that it was "the same well which was shown to me in the dream": "The tops of its date-palm trees look like the heads of the devils, and its water looks like the henna infusion." He ordered that the date palm trees be cut down and that the brackish water be drained, which presumably ended the magic spell's power over him.

Aisha then asked him, "O Allah's Apostle! Won't you disclose (the magic object)?" Muhammad refused: "Allah has cured me and I hate to circulate the evil among the people." The hadith ends with Aisha explaining that the magician who cast this spell on Muhammad, Lubaid bin Asam, "was a man from Bani Zuraiq, an ally of the Jews."[30]

In another version of the story, one of Muhammad's companions explains that this magic, which was "worked on Allah's Apostle so that he used to think that he had sexual relations with his wives while he actually had not," was in fact "the hardest kind of magic."[31] This version explains that Lubaid, or Labid, was not only "an ally of the Jews" but also a hypocrite.[32]

Upon a first reading, it may appear odd that Allah's prophet could fall under a magic spell, but the intentions of the story are clear: once again to demonize the Jews (who are the "strongest in enmity to the believer," according to Qur'an 5:82) and to show that even the "hardest kind of magic" could not ultimately prevail over Muhammad, for Allah would give him the information he needed to defeat it. The atmosphere here is more redolent of folk tales than of soberly recounted history. Muhammad is cast as the victor over even the unseen forces of darkness that superstitious men of a prescientific era feared and dreaded. In this, as in his warrior's might and sexual prowess, he is a worthy prophet, a strong man in a wild and untamed time.

## Don't Bother Muhammad at Home

One passage of the Qur'an, however, reads like a plea from a star who is tired of his adoring but persistent followers:

> O believers, enter not the houses of the Prophet, except leave is given you for a meal, without watching for its hour. But when you are invited, then enter; and when you have had the meal, disperse, neither lingering for idle talk; that is hurtful to the Prophet, and he is ashamed before you; but God is not ashamed before the truth. And when you ask his wives for any object, ask them from behind a curtain; that is cleaner for your hearts and theirs. It is not for you to hurt God's Messenger, neither to marry his wives after him, ever; surely that would be, in God's sight, a monstrous thing. (33:53)

Such a passage seems to reflect the experience of a leader whose followers were annoying him by barging into his home at inconvenient times—but that leader was not necessarily Muhammad. It could just as easily have originated with the annoyance of a later ruler; by means of this directive, this leader could have invoked the example of Muhammad to get petitioners and hangers-on out of his house.

In all these apparent difficulties, we do not see indications of authentic historical material about Muhammad. In every case we encounter material that appears designed to reinforce Muhammad's status as a prophet and an altogether exceptional human being. Moreover, the hadiths that detail Muhammad's personal habits reflect the interest of one party or another in portraying such behavior as exemplary; as we have seen, such stories could easily be—and often were—invented. Nothing in these accounts is inconsistent with the possibility that Muhammad was fashioned as a hero and prophet beginning toward the end of the seventh century and with increasing industry during the eighth and ninth centuries.

We have already reviewed some of the many reasons to question the veracity of the canonical account of Islam's origins and Muhammad's life. But perhaps no evidence is more important to consider than the numerous curious facts about the perfect book, the pure Arabic Scripture, the book that Muslims believe Allah delivered to Muhammad through the angel Gabriel in pristine form, and that contains everything a human being needs to understand this world and his place in it: the Qur'an.

## 6

## The Unchanging Qur'an Changes

### The Qur'an: Muhammad's Book?

The Qur'an is Muhammad's foremost legacy and the primary source for knowledge of Islamic doctrine and (to a lesser degree) history.

According to the Qur'an, the sole author of the Muslim holy book is Allah, who delivered the book piecemeal but in perfect form through the angel Gabriel to Muhammad: "It is We Who have sent down the Qur'an to thee by stages" (76:23).[1] Allah taunts the unbelievers with this fact: "It is surely a noble Koran in a hidden Book none but the purified shall touch, a sending down from the Lord of all Being. What, do you hold this discourse in disdain, and do you make it your living to cry lies?" (56:77–82).

Those who do not accept this claim generally assume that it was Muhammad who wrote the Qur'an. Certainly the book gives an immediate impression of originating from a single author, what with its repetitions, its stylistic tics (such as ending verses with a tagline such as "Allah is Mighty, Wise," which appears with slight variations forty times in the Qur'an), and its overall unity of message (despite numerous contradictions on particulars).

For many, both Muslim and non-Muslim, the Qur'an itself is the principal indication that the canonical story of Islam's origins is essentially true. After all, if Muhammad never existed, or did little

or nothing of what he is thought to have done, then where did the
Qur'an come from? If Muhammad was not its author or conduit,
then someone else must have been, for it speaks with a unified voice
and bears the imprint of a singular personality—or so it is generally
assumed.

For Muslims, the Qur'an is a perfect copy of the perfect, eternal book—the Mother of the Book (*umm al-kitab*)—that has existed
forever with Allah in Paradise. The Qur'an testifies this of itself: "By
the Clear Book, behold, We have made it an Arabic Koran; haply you
will understand; and behold, it is in the Essence of the Book [*umm
al-kitab*], with Us; sublime indeed, wise" (43:2–4). It contains, quite
simply, the truth: "These are the signs [*ayats*, "signs" or "verses"] of
the Book; and that which has been sent down to thee from thy Lord
is the truth, but most men do not believe" (13:1). Muslims throughout history have regarded the Qur'an as the unquestioned, unques-
tionable word of Allah, the supreme guide to human behavior, the
inexhaustible fount of knowledge, wisdom, and insight into the inner
workings of this world and the next.

What's more, Muslims believe that the Qur'an's text as it stands
today is the same as it was when the caliph Uthman compiled and
published the standard canonical text. Nothing has been changed,
nothing has been added, nothing has been lost. "The text of the
Qur'an is entirely reliable," says the modern-day Turkish Muslim
political and educational leader Fethullah Gülen. "It has been as it is,
unaltered, unedited, not tampered with in any way, since the time of
its revelation."[2] This view has been the standard in the Islamic world
since at least the tenth century. The Mutazilites, alone among Muslims, believed the Qur'an to be a human creation, not a perfect copy
of an eternal divine book. But by the tenth century, this idea was
generally regarded as a heresy. The Mutazilites, facing persecution,
eventually died out, along with the idea that the text of the Qur'an
was ever subject to human vagaries.

And so the nineteenth-century non-Muslim historian William
Muir asserted that the Qur'anic text had been preserved so carefully

that "there are no variations of importance—we might almost say no variations at all—to be found in the innumerable copies scattered throughout the vast bounds of the Empire of Islam."[3] The twentieth-century Qur'an commentator and politician Syed Abul Ala Maududi said that the Qur'an "exists exactly as it had been revealed to the Prophet; not a word—nay, not a dot of it—has been changed. It is available in its original text and the Word of God has now been preserved for all times to come."[4]

This claim is a commonplace of Muslim apologetic literature. Yet today's Qur'ans are based on a text that can be traced back to medieval Islamic tradition but no further. The standard text, published in Cairo in 1924, is based on Islamic traditions about the text of the Qur'an that date at their earliest from more than a century after Muhammad is supposed to have lived.[5] The lack of variation to which Gülen and so many other Islamic spokesmen refer reflects the fact that most Qur'ans today depend on the same medieval sources, not on anything close to an original seventh-century manuscript. And even that consistency breaks down on closer inspection. So, too, does the claim that the Qur'anic text has never been changed since the various suras were delivered to Muhammad through the angel Gabriel. Even Islamic tradition shows this contention to be highly questionable, with indications that some of the Qur'an was lost and other parts were added to or otherwise changed.

There is little dispute, however, about the Islamic account that the Qur'an originated with Muhammad. For most people who consider the question at all, what is at issue is whether Muhammad was really reciting revelations from Allah or passing off warmed-over biblical stories and other material as the divine voice. But an examination of the records—including early Islamic tradition itself—indicates that the canonical text of the Qur'an cannot be attributed to Muhammad alone.

## Flexible Revelations

Even the canonical Islamic accounts of how Muhammad received revelations suggest a less-than-heavenly origin to many Qur'anic verses. The hadiths concerning the circumstances of Qur'anic revelations sometimes betray a certain improvisational quality. Since, as we have seen, these stories are almost certainly not actual historical accounts, the question must be raised as to why they may have been invented. The answer to this lies in the evolving nature of Islamic tradition itself: These stories were developed as the particular characteristics of Islam were coming to the fore. Islam began to take shape as a religion different from—indeed, opposed to—Judaism and Christianity. Central to it was the figure of the prophet Muhammad, and tales of his exploits began to be circulated among the subjects of the Arabian Empire.

But if the founding figure of the new religion was to have received a perfect new scripture from the supreme God, why not have the stories of its delivery emphasize its perfection and flawless transmission? To be sure, many hadiths emphasize just those things. If, however, Islam and the Qur'an were evolving during the eighth and ninth centuries, as it appears from the historical evidence, that ongoing evolution had to be explained somehow. The hadiths would thus need to convince the faithful that although they had never heard of these sayings of Muhammad before, they were authentic and ancient tradition.

The best way to explain and justify this considerable theological flux would have been to make revision, and even forgetfulness, part of the new divine revelations from the beginning. And so it was done.

One hadith, for example, relates how Muhammad revised a revelation he had just received from Allah because of a question a blind man posed to him. The revelation concerned the value of fighting jihad: "Such believers as sit at home are not the equals of those who struggle in the path of God [*mujahidun fi sabil Allah*] with their possessions and their selves." According to the hadith, Muhammad called for one of his scribes, Zayd ibn Thabit, so he could dictate the revelation. But when the prophet began to dictate, a blind man, Amr bin Umm Maktum, interrupted him, calling out, "O Allah's apostle! What is your order for me, as I am a blind man?" Would Amr be considered a lesser Muslim for being unable to participate in jihad warfare because of his disability? Hearing the question, Muhammad dictated the new revelation with a caveat: "Such believers as sit at home—unless they have an injury—are not the equals of those who struggle in the path of God with their possessions and their selves" (Qur'an 4:95).[6]

Another hadith relates how Muhammad was traveling with Umar, who later became caliph, when Umar asked a question of his prophet. Muhammad, however, did not answer. Umar repeated his question twice but still received no answer. This greatly disquieted Umar: "I feared that a piece of Qur'an was being sent down about me. It was not long before I heard a crier calling for me, and I said that I feared that a piece of Qur'an had been sent down about me."[7] A portion of the Qur'an—sura 48—did indeed come to Muhammad, so the hadith goes, but Umar was not rebuked or even mentioned in it. Still, Umar clearly had the idea that Qur'anic revelation—the revelation of the perfect and eternal book—could be altered by his questioning or by his behavior. This would indicate either that Umar had a place in Allah's eternal plan for the Qur'anic revelation or that it was not perfect and eternal at all but could be altered as circumstances warranted. And that may have been the purpose this hadith served: to explain the variants that such alterations created.

Another trace of the alterations to the Qur'an comes from the thirteenth-century Muslim historian Ibn al-Athir. He stated that one of Muhammad's secretaries, Abdullah ibn Sa'd ibn Abi Sarh, "used to record the revelation for the Prophet" in Medina but then left Islam and returned to Mecca, where he noted that Muhammad was remarkably cavalier about the revelations he received: "I used to orient Muhammad wherever I willed; he dictated to me 'All-Powerful All-Wise' and I suggested 'All Knowing All-Wise' so he would say: 'Yes, it is all the same.' "[8]

The ninth-century Muslim historian al-Waqidi records that Abdullah ibn Sa'd said to the Meccans: "It was only a Christian slave who was teaching him (Muhammad); I used to write to him and change whatever I wanted."[9] In line with this, another thirteenth-century Islamic scholar, Abdullah al-Baydawi, recorded in a hadith that Abdullah ibn Sa'd used to mock Muhammad's claim to have received revelations: "'To me it has been revealed,' when naught has been revealed to him." This secretary to the prophet repudiated Islam when he became convinced that divine intervention was not responsible for the Qur'an. Muhammad was once dictating Qur'an 23:14 to Abdullah: "We created man of an extraction of clay, then We set him, a drop, in a receptacle secure, then We created of the drop a clot, then We created of the clot a tissue, then We created of the tissue bones, then We garmented the bones in flesh; thereafter We produced him as another creature." Hearing this, Abdullah exclaimed, "So blessed be God, the fairest of creators!" Muhammad responded: "Write it down; for thus it has been revealed"—which is to say that Abdullah's exclamation became part of the Qur'anic revelation.

Abdullah was disillusioned: "If Muhammad is truthful then I receive the revelation as much as he does, and if he is a liar, what I said is a good as what he said."[10] Muslim scholars, of course, describe Abdullah as a disgruntled former employee, fabricating stories about the former boss he had come to dislike. But if the entire scenario of Muhammad's receiving and dictating revelations was an ahistorical invention of the later Muslim community, such stories may have helped explain why variants existed in the Qur'an and Hadith. Hadiths may have been composed at a time when some people in the community remembered earlier formulations that had been discarded. If, however, the revered prophet of Islam could be shown as having freely altered the revelations he had received from Allah, then clearly alterations to the texts and teachings of the religion could not be condemned outright.

## Muhammad's Forgetfulness

In line with the apparent necessity to justify variability and change within Islamic tradition, many hadiths record that even Muhammad himself forgot parts of what Allah had revealed to him. One recounts that "Allah's Messenger heard a man reciting the Qur'an at night, and said, 'May Allah bestow His Mercy on him, as he has reminded me of such-and-such verses of such-and-such *sura*, which I was caused to forget.'"[11]

As might be expected in confessional literature, this is represented as being all part of Allah's plan. A hadith has Muhammad himself say so: "It is a bad thing that some of you say, 'I have forgotten such and such Verse of the Qur'an,' for indeed, he has been caused (by Allah) to forget it. So you must keep on reciting the Qur'an because it escapes from the hearts of men faster than camels do when they are released from their tying ropes."[12] Even in the Qur'an itself, Allah tells his prophet: "We shall make thee recite, to forget not save what God wills; surely He knows what is spoken aloud and what is hidden" (87:6–7).

Thus if Muhammad has forgotten part of what Allah revealed, it is no cause for concern: "None of Our revelations do We abrogate or cause to be forgotten, but We substitute something better or similar: knowest thou not that Allah Hath power over all things?" (2:106).[13] Allah even complains that this process makes some doubt the veracity of his prophet: "And when We exchange a verse in the place of another verse—and God knows very well what He is sending down— they say, 'Thou art a mere forger!' Nay, but the most of them have no knowledge" (16:101). If religious authorities in the Umayyad or Abbasid caliphates were busy substituting one revelation for another, such a statement from Allah himself would be exceedingly useful.

Elsewhere the Qur'an seems to address concerns about variant versions of its contents: "And say, 'Surely I am a manifest warner.' So We sent it down to the partitioners, who have broken the Koran into fragments" (15:89–91). Some hadiths record that Muhammad himself was unconcerned with variations that early on began to appear in

how Muslims were reciting his revelations—implying that if Muhammad did not worry over such matters, why should his followers?

Ubayy bin Kab, whom a hadith had Muhammad praising as "the
best reader (of the Qur'an) among my people," is made to recall his
shock at Muhammad's lack of concern about these variations. The
strange incident began, according to the hadith, when Ubayy heard
variant readings of the Qur'an recited in the mosque: "I was in the
mosque when a man entered and prayed and recited (the Qur'an) in a
style to which I objected. Then another man entered (the mosque) and
recited in a style different from that of his companion." Ubayy decided
to appeal to Muhammad himself: "When we had finished the prayer,
we all went to Allah's Messenger (may peace be upon him) and said
to him: This man recited in a style to which I objected, and the other
entered and recited in a style different from that of his companion."

But according to the hadith, Muhammad "expressed approval
of their affairs"—that is, of their way of reciting the Qur'an. Ubayy
was troubled, recalling, "And there occurred in my mind a sort of
denial which did not occur even during the Days of Ignorance [before
the revelation of the Qur'an]." His reaction annoyed Muhammad:
"When the Messenger of Allah (may peace be upon him) saw how I
was affected (by a wrong idea), he struck my chest, whereupon I broke
into sweating and felt as though I were looking at Allah with fear."
Muhammad explained that the variants, which he represented simply
as differences in the Arabic dialect used for recitation, were all parts
of Allah's plan: "He (the Holy Prophet) said to me: Ubayy, a message
was sent to me to recite the Qur'an in one dialect, and I replied: Make
(things) easy for my people. It was conveyed to me for the second
time that it should be recited in two dialects. I again replied to him:
Make affairs easy for my people. It was again conveyed to me for the
third time to recite in seven dialects."[14]

If variants and changes existed and had to be explained, this was
as good an attempt to do so as any.

In another hadith, Umar is made to recall: "I heard Hisham bin
Hakim reciting *Surat Al-Furqan* [sura 25 of the Qur'an] during the

lifetime of Allah's Messenger and I listened to his recitation and noticed that he recited in several different ways which Allah's Messenger had not taught me." Umar, according to the story, was incensed enough to treat Hisham roughly: "I was about to jump over him during his *Salat* (prayer), but I controlled my temper, and when he had completed his *Salat* (prayer), I put his upper garment around his neck and seized him by it and said, 'Who taught you this *Surah* which I heard you reciting?'"

Hisham's response was as surprising to Umar as Muhammad's casual reaction to the variants had been to Ubayy: "He replied, 'Allah's Messenger taught it to me.' I said, 'You have told a lie, for Allah's Messenger has taught it to me in a different way from yours.' So, I dragged him to Allah's Messenger and said (to Allah's Messenger), 'I heard this person reciting *Surat Al-Furqan* in a way which you haven't taught me!'"

Muhammad, according to the hadith, backed up Hisham, commanding, "Release him, (O 'Umar!) Recite, O Hisham!" The prophet explained: "It was revealed in this way." Then he turned to Umar and told him to recite as well. Again Muhammad said, "It was revealed in this way. This Qur'an has been revealed to be recited in seven different ways, so recite of it whichever (way) is easier for you (or read as much of it as may be easy for you)."[15]

On another occasion, Muhammad is made to elaborate on this odd explanation for the variants: Gabriel, he explained, "recited the Qur'an to me in one way. Then I requested him (to read it in another way), and continued asking him to recite it in other ways, and he recited it in several ways till he ultimately recited it in seven different ways."[16]

*"Recited in seven different ways."* Yet if the canonical Islamic stories of his life are accurate, Muhammad recited the Qur'an in only one way. What's more, it is unlikely that Ubayy and Umar would have been depicted as becoming so enraged over these variants if the only difference was a matter of dialect—that is, a shift in the pronunciation of the words.

How could variants have arisen if Muhammad received revelations from Allah in a perfect fashion, which would apparently involve his total recall of what Gabriel delivered to him? Did the perfect book exist in variant readings? And if not, then how did the perfect earthly copy of that book, the Qur'an, come to have such variants?

## Haphazard Collection

Even Islamic tradition implies that the Qur'an was altered after it first appeared among the believers. According to the Hadith, during Muhammad's lifetime, his companions would memorize various portions of the Qur'an. Some had some portions committed to memory, others had others. Some of it, but not all of it, was written down. But not long after Muhammad died, the traditions say, some of those who had memorized portions of the Qur'an died in the Battle of Yamama. Parts of the Qur'an died with them, according to a hadith: "Many (of the passages) of the Qur'an that were sent down were known by those who died on the day of Yamama . . . but they were not known (by those who) survived them, nor were they written down, nor had [the first three caliphs] Abu Bakr, Umar or Uthman (by that time) collected the Qur'an, nor were they found with even one (person) after them."[17]

No contemporary historical evidence establishes that there ever was a Battle of Yamama or that anyone who had memorized portions of the Qur'an died there. As we have seen, no mention of the Qur'an is made until nearly a century after this battle is supposed to have taken place. So the traditions regarding the Battle of Yamama, and the collection of the Qur'an that followed from it, probably emerged in a context in which the holy book was undergoing editing and alteration, such that variant formulations and differences in content had to be explained.

Early Islamic sources repeatedly attest to the loss of sections of the Qur'an. One hadith has an elderly Muslim recalling a passage from sura 98 that said: "The religion with Allah is *al-hanifiyya* (the Upright Way) rather than that of the Jews or the Christians, and those who do good will not go unrewarded." But it was gone.[18]

Likewise vanished, according to another hadith, was the section that mandated the stoning of adulterers. Umar declared:

> I am afraid that after a long time has passed, people may say, "We do not find the Verses of the Rajam (stoning to death) in the Holy Book." And consequently they may go astray by leaving an obligation that Allah has revealed. Lo! I confirm that the penalty of Rajam be inflicted on him who commits illegal sexual intercourse, if he is already married and the crime is proved by witnesses or pregnancy or confession. . . . Surely Allah's Apostle carried out the penalty of Rajam, and so did we after him.[19]

Sura 33 of the Qur'an, according to another hadith, was originally 127 verses longer than it is in the canonical text. In this hadith, Muhammad's wife Aisha is made to say: "Surat al-Ahzab [that is, sura 33] used to be recited in the time of the Prophet with two hundred verses, but when Uthman wrote out the codices he was unable to procure more of it than what there is today."[20] Aisha asserted that the sura originally included a verse mandating stoning: "The fornicators among the married men (ash-shaikh) and married women (ash-shaikhah), stone them as an exemplary punishment from Allah, and Allah is Mighty and Wise."[21]

Still another hadith records an occasion on which a venerable Muslim in the city of Basra reminisced about a lost sura of the Qur'an: "We used to recite a surah which resembled in length and severity to (Surah) Bara'at."[22] Surah Bara'at (Surat al-Bara'a), more commonly known as Surat at-Tauba (Repentance), is the Qur'an's ninth sura, and it contains the book's fiercest exhortations to jihad warfare (9:5, 9:123, etc.), including jihad against Jews and Christians (9:29). But the old man could recall little of the lost sura: "I have, however, forgotten it with the exception of this which I remember out of it: 'If there were two valleys full of riches, for the son of Adam, he would long for a third valley, and nothing would fill the stomach of the son of Adam but dust.' We used to recite a sura similar to one of the *Musabihat*, and I no longer remember it, but this much I have indeed preserved: 'O you who truly believe, why do you preach that which you do not practise?' [Qur'an 61:2] (and) 'that is inscribed on your necks as a witness and you will be examined about it on the Day of Resurrection [Qur'an 17:13].'"²³ Significantly, the only two verses of this sura that this man is made to recall are both found elsewhere in the Qur'an; they could have been added into the Qur'anic text after these hadiths were produced to assert their divine origin.

Other hadiths have the caliph Abu Bakr, seeing the loss of sections of the Qur'an as a looming crisis that threatened the still-nascent Muslim community, ordering one of Muhammad's secretaries to collect the various portions of the holy book to keep it from being lost. The scribe he summoned was Zayd ibn Thabit, the same one featured in the story of Muhammad and the blind man. This hadith has Zayd explain the way he recorded the prophet's revelations and helped him communicate with the local Jewish leaders: "The Messenger of God ordered me to study for him the script of the Jews [*kitab al-yahud*, which can also be translated as "Book of the Jews"], and he said to me, 'I do not trust the Jews with regard to my correspondence' [i.e., correspondence with the Jews, written in their script]. Not even half a month passed until I used to write for him, and they wrote to him, I would read their letter."²⁴

Zayd was chosen to collect the Qur'an, this hadith explains, because he had already memorized the entire book. Of course, if Zayd really had memorized the entire Qur'an, Abu Bakr would not have needed him to track down various people who had retained particular sections of the Qur'an and collect what he found; Zayd could have simply written it down.

In any case, the hadith recounts that Zayd refused the caliph's request: Muhammad himself had never tried to collect the Qur'an together, so why should they do what the "good example" (Qur'an

33:21) had not done? In response, Abu Bakr and Umar, who would soon succeed him as caliph, insisted that collecting the Qur'an was a matter of necessity—thus advancing a justification for this religious innovation under the guise of traditionalism. Zayd reluctantly agreed to undertake the project: "By Allah! If they had ordered me to shift one of the mountains, it would not have been heavier for me than this ordering me to collect the Qur'an."

Nonetheless, a hadith depicts him going to work conscientiously: "I started locating Qur'anic material and collecting it from parchments, scapula, leaf-stalks of date palms and from the memories of men (who knew it by heart). I found with Khuzaima two Verses of Surat-at-Tauba which I had not found with anybody else."[25] Khuzaima was an early Muslim who accosted Zayd when he heard his version of sura 9 recited and informed him: "I see you have overlooked (two) verses and have not written them."[26] Zayd duly added them.

If Khuzaima hadn't been present, apparently those two verses (9:128–29) would not have been included in the Qur'an. That loss would not have been significant to Islamic doctrine or devotions, but it does bear witness to how the Hadith explain and obliquely justify what must have been evident to many ninth-century believers: that their religion and even their holy book were going through extensive changes.

The process of collecting the Qur'an was random and disorganized enough for one Muslim to warn in a hadith: "Let none of you say, 'I have acquired the whole of the Qur'an.' How does he know what all of it is when much of the Qur'an has disappeared? Rather let him say, 'I have acquired what has survived.'"[27] This hardly conforms with confident pronouncements that the Qur'an "has been as it is, unaltered, unedited, not tampered with in any way, since the time of its revelation."

Even Aisha, Muhammad's favorite wife, known by the honorific Mother of the Believers, is made to testify indirectly to the haphazard quality of the Qur'an's collection. She recalled that "amongst what was sent down of the Qur'an was 'ten known sucklings make haram'—then it was abrogated by 'five known sucklings.' When the

Messenger of Allah, may Allah bless him and grant him peace, died, it was what is now recited of the Qur'an."[28] In another version, while discussing "fosterage which (makes marriage) unlawful," Aisha said: "There was revealed in the Holy Qur'an ten clear sucklings, and then five clear (sucklings)."[29] Here Aisha referred to the Islamic doctrine that an unmarried male and female may lawfully be alone together—in, for example, a workplace environment—only if she becomes his foster mother by suckling him a specified number of times. According to Aisha's word in these hadiths, this doctrine was originally in the Qur'an itself.

Another hadith has Aisha ordering one of her servants, Yunus, to write out a copy of the Qur'an. She instructed him: "When you reach this ayat ['sign,' or verse of the Qur'an] let me know, 'Guard the prayers carefully and the middle prayer and stand obedient to Allah'" (Qur'an 2:238). When Yunus reached that point, Aisha dictated an amended version of the verse to him: "Guard the prayers carefully and the middle prayer and the asr prayer [the 'afternoon' prayer] and stand obedient to Allah." Aisha explained: "I heard it from the Messenger of Allah, may Allah bless him and grant him peace."[30]

## Signs that the Text Has Been Altered

Islamic tradition does not provide the only evidence that changes were made to the wording of the eternal book of Allah. Although manuscript evidence is scarce, on close scrutiny the text of the Qur'an offers telling indications that it has been altered. This evidence makes it extraordinarily unlikely that the text was the product of one man, whether a historical person named Muhammad or someone else; rather, it indicates that the text has undergone extensive revision, consistent with the likelihood that it was developed over time by a series of people.

The pioneering Qur'anic scholar Richard Bell (1876–1952) closely examined the Qur'anic text and identified numerous signs that the text had been changed. Lack of continuity and inherent contradictions are two of the most common indications. One curious passage Bell highlighted comes in a polemic against the Jews and Christians (2:116–21):

116. And they say, "God has taken to Him a son." Glory be to Him! Nay, to Him belongs all that is in the heavens and the earth; all obey His will—

117. The Creator of the heavens and the earth; And when He decrees a thing, He but says to it "Be," and it is.

118. And they that know not say: "Why does God not speak to us?, Why does a sign not come to us?" So spoke those before them as these men say; their hearts are much alike. Yet We have made clear the signs unto a people who are sure.

119. We have sent thee with the truth, good tidings to bear, and warning. Thou shalt not be questioned touching the inhabitants of Hell.

120. Never will the Jews be satisfied with thee, neither the Christians, not till thou followest their religion. Say: "God's guidance is the true guidance." If thou followest their caprices, after the knowledge that has come to thee, thou shalt have against God neither protector nor helper.

121. Those to whom We have given the Book and who recite it with true recitation, they believe in it; and whoso disbelieves in it, they shall be the losers.

Bell points out that all the polemical assertions in verses 116 and 117 answer the claim in verse 120, that the Jews and Christians will never be satisfied with the Muslim believers until they convert to their religions. He suggests that these verses were inserted later and were originally intended to follow verse 120.[31] It also appears that verses 118 and 119 introduce some other argument, against those who demand miracles of the Muslim prophet, whose only miracles are the verses of the Qur'an themselves. As presented in the Qur'an we know today, these verses unaccountably interrupt the polemic against the People of the Book. The passage reads much more logically in this order:

120. Never will the Jews be satisfied with thee, neither the Christians, not till thou followest their religion. Say: "God's guidance is the true guidance." If thou followest their caprices, after the knowledge that has come to thee, thou shalt have against God neither protector nor helper.

116. And they say, "God has taken to Him a son." Glory be to Him! Nay, to Him belongs all that is in the heavens and the earth; all obey His will—

117. The Creator of the heavens and the earth; And when He decrees a thing, He but says to it "Be," and it is.

121. Those to whom We have given the Book and who recite it with true recitation, they believe in it; and whoso disbelieves in it, they shall be the losers.

Bell also sees considerable manipulation of the text in this passage from sura 4:

23. Forbidden to you are your mothers, and your daughters, and your sisters, and your father's sisters, and your mother's sisters, and your brother's daughters and your sister's daughters, and your foster-mothers, and your foster-sisters, and your mothers-in-law, and your step-daughters who are under your protection, born of your women unto whom you have gone in—but if you have not gone in unto them, then it is no sin for you—and the wives of your sons who spring from your own loins. And (it is forbidden to you) that you should have two sisters together, except what has already happened in the past. Lo! Allah is ever Forgiving, Merciful.

24. And all married women (are forbidden to you) save those captives whom your right hands possess. It is a decree of Allah for you. Lawful to you are all beyond those men-

tioned, so that you seek them with your wealth in honest wedlock, not debauchery. And those of whom you seek content by marrying them, give them their portions as a duty. And there is no sin for you in what you do by mutual agreement after the duty has been done. Lo! Allah is ever Knower, Wise.

25. And whoever is not able to afford to marry free, believing women, let them marry from the believing maids whom your right hands possess. Allah knows best your faith. You proceed one from another; so wed them by permission of their folk, and give them their portions in kindness, they being honest, not debauched nor of loose conduct. And if when they are honorably married they commit lewdness, they shall incur the half of the punishment prescribed for free women. This is for him among you who fears to commit sin. But to have patience would be better for you. Allah is Forgiving, Merciful.

26. Allah would explain to you and guide you by the examples of those who were before you, and would turn to you in mercy. Allah is Knower, Wise.[32]

Bell posits that "the marriage laws in Sura IV are a clear case of alternative continuations"—that is, an instance in which an editor simply tacked on his addition to an already complete passage, doing nothing to address the resulting contradictions. The first verse above, says Bell, "lays down the forbidden degrees of relationship, and reproduces the Mosaic list with some adaptation to Arab custom." This was deliberate, Bell argues, as indicated by verse 26: "Allah would explain to you and guide you by the examples of those who were before you." But, Bell continues, "at a later time . . . some relaxation appeared necessary." Thus verse 25 was added, "allowing marriage with slaves," and finally verse 24, which "gives ample liberty."

Bell points out that the similar endings of verse 24 ("Allah is ever Knower, Wise"), the first part of verse 25 ("Allah knows best your faith"), and the latter part of verse 25 ("Allah is Knower, Wise") provide evidence that "substitutions have been made."[33] Repeating whole phrases as taglines may have been an attempt to make sense out of what would otherwise be the most awkward of rhyme schemes—an attempt to make poetry out of prosaic, didactic material.[34]

Of course, many passages in the Qur'an can be adduced in which such recurring taglines are the only unifying aspect. The Qur'an, as we have seen, is remarkably devoid of context.[35] Islamic spokesmen in the West frequently argue that those who point out the book's violent and hateful passages are taking them out of context, but there is hardly any context to begin with. Nonetheless, when one encounters discussions of a subject that is interrupted and then resumed, it is not unreasonable to suspect that the textual integrity of the passage has been compromised. Such interruptions appear fairly often in the Qur'an. Another example is Qur'an 2:221–242. For seventeen straight verses this passage discusses women, marriage, and divorce, but suddenly verses 238 and 239 interrupt the discussion to exhort the Muslims to maintain regular prayers and instruct them on how to maintain prayers while in fear of an enemy. Then, just as suddenly, the passage returns to the subject of divorce. Those two intervening verses, 238 and 239, have nothing to do with what came either before or after.

In short, both close analysis of Quran'ic passages and Islamic tradition itself raise serious doubts about the textual integrity of the Qur'an. But when it comes to critical evaluation of the Qur'an, there are much larger questions.

# 7

## The Non-Arabic Arabic Qur'an

### A Book in Pure and Clear Arabic
### (with Some Non-Arabic Thrown In)

The twentieth-century translator of the Qur'an Muhammad Marmaduke Pickthall, an English convert to Islam, once declared that the Qur'an in Arabic was an "inimitable symphony, the very sounds of which move men to tears and ecstasy."[1] Pickthall would not have dared to claim the same about any translation of the Muslim holy book, including his own English translation. For Muslims, the Arabic of the Qur'an is essential, such that in any other language, the book may contain the meaning of the Qur'an but is no longer truly the Qur'an.

This belief stems from the Qur'an itself, which insists on its Arabic character so often that Islamic theologians have quite understandably understood Arabic to be part of the Qur'an's very essence. The Qur'an says that it is written in "Arabic, pure and clear" (16:103).[2] It is an "Arabic judgment" (13:37). It is "the revelation of the Lord of all Being" that was "brought down by the Faithful Spirit upon thy heart, that thou mayest be one of the warners, in a clear, Arabic tongue" (26:192–195). Allah says that he has "sent it down as an Arabic Qur'an, in order that you may learn wisdom" (12:1).[3] It is "a Qur'an in Arabic, that you may be able to understand" (43:3).[4]

The Qur'an is not only a guide to understanding but is also

intended for those Arabic speakers who already grasp its message: It is "a Book whose signs have been distinguished as an Arabic Koran for a people having knowledge" (41:3). Allah even explains that if he had sent down the Qur'an in any other language, people would have complained: "Had We sent this as a Qur'an in a language other than Arabic, they would have said: 'Why are not its verses explained in detail? What! Not in Arabic and its Messenger an Arab?'" (41:44).[5] It is, quite simply, an "Arabic Qur'an" (12:2; 20:113; 39:28; 41:3; 42:7).

Islamic tradition reinforces this point. In one hadith, an early Muslim, al-Hasan, recounts of another early Muslim: "I heard Abu Ubaida say that whoever pretends that there is in the Qur'an anything other than the Arabic tongue has made a serious charge against God, and he quoted the verse 'Verily we have made it an Arabic Qur'an.'"[6] Ibn Kathir, author of a renowned medieval commentary on the Qur'an that is still widely read by Muslims, elaborated the orthodox view: "The Arabic language is the most eloquent, plain, deep and expressive of the meanings that might arise in one's mind. Therefore, the most honorable Book was revealed in the most honorable language, to the most honorable Prophet and Messenger, delivered by the most honorable angel, in the most honorable land on earth, and its revelation started during the most honorable month of the year, Ramadan. Therefore, the Qur'an is perfect in every respect."[7]

There is only one problem with the widespread assertion that the Qur'an was written in Arabic: It doesn't seem to be true. Even the most cursory examination of the evidence indicates that "the most honorable Book" in its original form was not actually "in the most honorable language" at all.

## Thou Doth Protest Too Much, Methinks

The very fact that the Qur'an asserts so many times that it was handed down in Arabic raises questions. Why would a clear and easily understandable book need to assert more than once that it was clear and easy to understand? Why would an Arabic book need to insist again and again that it was in Arabic? The various authors of the Greek New Testament never feel the need to assert the fact that they're writing in Greek; they're simply doing so. This is a point that they take for granted.

Of course, the New Testament doesn't make the claims about Greek that the Qur'an makes about Arabic. Greek in Christianity is not the language of God; it has no more significance than any other language. But that in itself is part of the mystery of the Qur'anic claims: Why did they need to be made at all? Why was there such anxiety about the Arabic character of the Qur'an that it had to be repeated so many times? This peculiar insistence on the Arabic character of the Qur'an even became part of Islamic theology, which affirms that Arabic is the language of Allah and that the deity who created every human being and presumably understands every human tongue will not accept prayers or recitations of the Qur'an in any other language.

When the Qur'an repeatedly insists that it is written in Arabic, it is not unreasonable to conclude that someone, somewhere was saying that it wasn't in Arabic at all. A point needs emphasis only when it is controverted. As the nineteenth-century man of letters John Henry Cardinal Newman wrote in a vastly different context, "No doctrine is defined till it is violated."[8] In other words, the assertion of a religious doctrine, in an environment involving a competition of religious ideas, doesn't generally take place *except* as a response to the contrary proposition. The Qur'an thus may insist so repeatedly on its Arabic essence because that was precisely the aspect of it that others challenged.

The Qur'an is highly polemical in nature. It answers the theological claims of Judaism and Christianity and responds to the arguments of the unbelievers and hypocrites against Muhammad's prophetic claims and its own divine origins. On practically every page there is a denunciation of the unbelievers; many of these contain reports of what those unbelievers are saying against Muhammad and Islam, and explanations of why their charges are false. It would not be unusual if it also took on challenges to its Arabic origins.

## Muhammad's Non-Arabic Sources

The Qur'an itself tells us of challenges to claims of the book's Arabic origins. According to the Qur'an, Muhammad's detractors charged the prophet of Islam with getting material from non-Arabic sources and then passing off what he received as divine revelation. The Qur'an responds furiously to those who deride the prophet for listening intently—perhaps to the Jewish and Christian teachers whose teachings ended up as part of Qur'anic revelation: "And some of them hurt the Prophet, saying, 'He is an ear!'" Allah tells Muhammad how to respond to those who make fun of him in this way: "Say: 'An ear of good for you; he believes in God, and believes the believers, and he is a mercy to the believers among you. Those who hurt God's Messenger—for them awaits a painful chastisement'" (9:61).

Muhammad's foes apparently charged him with getting material from a non-Arabic speaker as well: "We know indeed that they say, 'It is a man that teaches him.' The tongue of him they wickedly point to is notably foreign, while this is Arabic, pure and clear" (16:103).[9] This mysterious foreigner has often been identified as one of Muhammad's early companions, Salman the Persian. The Arabic word translated as "foreign" in this Qur'an verse is *ajami*, which means "Persian" or "Iranian," or is more generalized as "foreigner." Ibn Ishaq identifies the foreigner of Qur'an 16:103 as "Jabr the Christian, slave of the B. al-Hadrami" and teacher of Muhammad.[10]

Another *ajami* identified in Islamic tradition is Abu Fukayha Yasar. The Qur'anic scholar Muqatil ibn Sulayman (d. 767) says Yasar was "a Jew, not an Arab," who spoke Greek."[11] The modern-day Islamic scholar Claude Gilliot observes that it is more likely he spoke Aramaic, of which Syriac is a dialect.[12] Muqatil also recounts accusations from Muhammad's opponent an-Nasr ibn al-Harith that mention both Jabr and Yasar: "This Qur'an is naught but lies that Muhammad himself has forged. . . . Those who help him are Addas, a slave of Huwaytib b. Abd al-Uzza, Yasar, a servant of Amr b. al-Hadrami, and Jabr who was a Jew, and then became a Muslim. . . .

This Qur'an is only a tale of the Ancients, like the tales of Rustam and Isfandiyar. These three [were] teaching Muhammad at dawn and in the evening."[13]

This accusation recalls the criticism to which the Qur'an heatedly responds: "The unbelievers say, 'This is naught but a calumny he has forged, and other folk have helped him to it.' So they have committed wrong and falsehood. They say, 'Fairy-tales of the ancients that he has had written down, so that they are recited to him at the dawn and in the evening'" (25:4–5).

The Hadith offer yet another candidate for the man who was "notably foreign": Waraqa bin Naufal, the uncle of Muhammad's first wife, Khadija. Islamic tradition holds that after Muhammad's confusing and terrifying first encounter with the angel Gabriel, it was Waraqa who told Muhammad that he had been called to be a prophet. According to one hadith, Waraqa, like Abu Fukayha Yasar, was a Jew. The hadith says that "during the [pre-Islamic] Period of Ignorance [Waraqa] became a Christian and used to write the writing with Hebrew letters. He would write from the Gospel in Hebrew as much as Allah wished him to write."[14]

Even Khadija herself, according to the Persian Muslim Bal'ami (d. 974), "had read the ancient writings and knew the history of the prophets, and also the name of Gabriel."[15]

Why would the Qur'an acknowledge critics who accused the book of having non-Arabic origins? And why would hadiths tell us of various people of foreign tongue instructing Muhammad? If the Qur'an arose long after Muhammad is supposed to have lived, as appears to have been the case, then the editors of the Qur'an would have been working with non-Arabic material and rendering it into Arabic. In that case, they would have needed to explain the non-Arabic elements in the Qur'an.

Those non-Arabic elements are certainly present.

## Non-Arabic Sources

The Qur'an's dependence on non-Arabic Jewish and Christian sources for much of its theological and cultural milieu is well known. These sources include not only the Bible but other material as well. In the Qur'an's story of the creation and fall of Adam and Eve (2:30–39, 7:11–25, 15:28–42, 20:115–126, and 38:71–85), Allah creates Adam and then orders the angels to prostrate themselves before him (2:34, 7:11, 15:29, 18:50, 20:116). Satan refuses, saying: "I am better than he; Thou createdst me of fire, and him Thou createdst of clay" (7:12, 38:76; cf. 15:33, 17:61). Allah thereupon curses Satan (38:77–78) and banishes him from Paradise (7:13, 15:34). The order to the angels and Satan's refusal is not in the Bible but is found in Jewish apocryphal and rabbinic literature.[16]

Similarly, in the Qur'anic account of Cain and Abel (5:30–35) comes the celebrated Qur'anic prohibition on the murder of innocents: "Therefore We prescribed for the Children of Israel that whoso slays a soul not to retaliate for a soul slain, nor for corruption done in the land, shall be as if he had slain mankind altogether; and whoso gives life to a soul, shall be as if he had given life to mankind altogether" (5:32). This may also be taken from Jewish tradition, from the *Mishnah Sanhedrin*, which states: "As regards Cain who killed his brother, the Lord addressing him does not say, 'The voice of thy brother's blood crieth out,' but 'the voice of his bloods,' meaning not his blood alone, but that of his descendants; and this to show that since Adam was created alone, so he that kills an Israelite is, by the plural here used, counted as if he had killed the world at large; and he who saves a single Israelite is counted as if he had saved the whole world."[17]

The Qur'anic account of Solomon and the Queen of Sheba (27:16–44) contains material that was likely derived from another Jewish source, the Targum of Esther. The historian W. St. Clair Tisdall notes that "the story of Balkis, Queen of Saba, as told at length in the Koran, corresponds so closely with what we find in the II. Targum of the Book of Esther, that it was evidently taken from it, as heard by Mohammed from some Jewish source. . . . In respect of the Queen of Saba, her visit to Solomon, the letter sent by him to her, etc., there is a marvellous resemblance between the two, excepting this, indeed, that in place of the Lapwing of the Koran, the Targum Speaks of a Red-cock,—Not a very vital difference after all!" [18]

There are Christian influences in the Qur'an also. The story of the "companions of the Cave and of the Inscription" (18:9–26) is an Islamic version of the Christian account of the Seven Sleepers of Ephesus, which was well known in Eastern Christianity at the time that Islam was taking shape. And when the Qur'an writes of the child Jesus fashioning clay birds and then bringing them to life (Qur'an 3:49), it recounts something that is recorded in the second-century Infancy Gospel of Thomas. [19]

All this dependence on non-Arabic sources indicates that the Qur'an in its original form was something quite different from what Muslims have always taken it to be, and that its very character as an Arabic book is the product of later development, not a feature of the original text.

In fact, there is evidence that the Qur'an was not originally an Arabic book at all.

## Incomprehensible

One element of that evidence is the Qur'an's manifest lack of clarity, despite its boasts to the contrary. Many words in this self-proclaimed clear Arabic book are neither clear nor Arabic. Philologist Gerd-R. Puin explains: "The Koran claims for itself that it is *'mubeen,'* or 'clear.' But if you look at it, you will notice that every fifth sentence or so simply doesn't make sense. Many Muslims—and Orientalists—will tell you otherwise, of course, but the fact is that a fifth of the Koranic text is *just incomprehensible.* This is what has caused the traditional anxiety regarding translation. If the Koran is not comprehensible—

if it can't even be understood in Arabic—then it's not translatable. People fear that. And since the Koran claims repeatedly to be clear but obviously is not—as even speakers of Arabic will tell you—there is a contradiction. Something else must be going on."[20]

Islamic apologists have been sanguine about the incomprehensible sections of the Qur'an: Allah knows what they mean, and their very presence indicates that the book was written by someone whose understanding is beyond that of ordinary mortals. The Qur'an itself acknowledges that portions of the book cannot be understood and warns Muslims not to waste their time trying: "It is He who sent down upon thee the Book, wherein are verses clear that are the Essence of the Book, and others ambiguous. As for those in whose hearts is swerving, they follow the ambiguous part, desiring dissension, and desiring its interpretation; and none knows its interpretation, save only God. And those firmly rooted in knowledge say, 'We believe in it; all is from our Lord'; yet none remembers, but man possessed of minds" (3:7).

Perhaps such passages were placed in the book to explain the anomalies created by the rendering of considerable material that was not originally Arabic into Arabic.

Theodor Nöldeke, the great nineteenth-century scholar of Islam, explains what makes so much of the Qur'an incomprehensible:

> On the whole, while many parts of the Qur'an undoubtedly have considerable rhetorical power, even over an unbelieving reader, the book, aesthetically considered, is by no means a first-rate performance. . . . Let us look at some of the more extended narratives. It has already been noticed how vehement and abrupt they are where they ought to be characterized by epic repose. Indispensable links, both in expression and in the sequence of events, are often omitted, so that to understand these histories is sometimes far easier for us than for those who learned them first, because we know most of them from better sources. Along with this, there is a great deal of superfluous verbiage; and

nowhere do we find a steady advance in the narration. Contrast, in these respects, "the most beautiful tale," the history of Joseph (xii.), and its glaring improprieties, with the story in Genesis, so admirably executed in spite of some slight discrepancies. Similar faults are found in the non-narrative portions of the Qur'an. The connection of ideas is extremely loose, and even the syntax betrays great awkwardness. Anacolutha are of frequent occurrence, and cannot be explained as conscious literary devices. Many sentences begin with a "when" or "on the day when," which seem to hover in the air, so that the commentators are driven to supply a "think of this" or some ellipsis. Again, there is no great literary skill evinced in the frequent and needless harping on the same words and phrases; in xviii., for example, "till that" (*hatta idha*) occurs no fewer than eight times. Muhammad, in short, is not in any sense a master of style.[21]

Muhammad, or whatever committee that may have finalized the Qur'anic text in his name.

Whole phrases of this "pure and clear" book are unclear. In A. J. Arberry's elegant and often audaciously literal Qur'an (audacious in its reproduction in English of the Arabic original's grammatical infelicities and linguistic oddities), Qur'an 2:29 reads this way: "It is He who created for you all that is in the earth, then He lifted Himself to heaven and levelled them seven heavens; and He has knowledge of everything." The contemporary Islamic scholar Ibn Warraq points out that "the plural pronoun 'them' in this verse has resisted all explanation."[22] Many translators smooth over the difficulty by reducing the "them" to an "it"; Pickthall, for example, renders this verse as "He it is Who created for you all that is in the earth. Then turned He to the heaven, and fashioned it as seven heavens. And He is knower of all things." But in the Arabic, the first "heaven" is singular and yet the pronoun is unaccountably plural. To what, then, does the "them" refer? Any answer would be pure conjecture.

## Nonce Words

There is more that makes the Qur'an incomprehensible. A number of words in the Qur'an simply don't make any sense: Not only are they not Arabic words, but they also have no meaning in any known language. Islamic scholars who have translated the Qur'an into other languages for the purposes of proselytizing and to aid non-Arabic-speaking Muslims have generally agreed on the meaning of these words; often, however, this agreement is simply a matter of convention, without any grounding in linguistic analysis. And sometimes there is no agreement at all. For example, the historian and Qur'anic scholar Muhammad ibn Jarir at-Tabari (839–923) details three different definitions, supported by twenty-seven witnesses through different chains of transmission, circulating among Islamic authorities for the word *kalala* in Qur'an 4:12. It is not clear, in a passage that is foundational for Islamic law regarding inheritance, whether this word refers to the person who has died or to his heirs—a crucial distinction.[23]

Some words have no clear referent. In Qur'an 2:62 and 5:69, salvation is promised to those who believe in the Qur'an, as well as to Jews, Christians, and Sabians. Muslim exegetes identify the Sabians as the followers of the Israelite King David. The word *Sabians* means "Baptizers."[24] The Qur'an identifies David as a prophet, and Allah gives him the book of Psalms (4:163). The Sabians are thus supposed to be followers of David and readers of the Psalms for whom baptism was a central ritual. But the only Sabians of whom something is known historically, the Sabians of Harran, did not practice baptism or notably revere the Psalms. There is no record independent of Islamic literature of any group of Sabians that actually did do those things. Thus the actual recipient of the Qur'anic promise of salvation remains unclear.[25]

The Qur'an also coins such terms as *Sijjin*, which appears in 83:7–9: "Nay, the Book of the libertines is in Sijjin; and what shall teach thee what is Sijjin? A book inscribed." *Sijjin* is not an Arabic word; nor is it a recognizable word from any other language. Even this brief Qur'an passage is bewildering, as Sijjin is first identified as the place where the "Book of the libertines"—apparently the record of the evil deeds of the damned—is stored (it is "in Sijjin") and then, almost immediately afterward, as that record itself (Sijjin is "a book inscribed").[26] Perhaps Sijjin is a larger written record of which the "Book of the libertines" is only a part—but that is just the sort of intellectual contortions that the Qur'an forces the attentive reader into.

A similar word is *sijill* in Qur'an 21:104: "On the day when We shall roll up heaven as a *sijill*." Arberry translates *sijill* as a "scroll . . . rolled for the writings." Pickthall translates the word as "a written scroll," and that is the accepted understanding today—perhaps owing to its similarity to *Sijjin*, which the Qur'an identifies as "a book inscribed." But *sijill* could also be a proper name, or something else altogether.[27] Arthur Jeffery, author of the important book *The Foreign Vocabulary of the Qur'an*, notes that the meaning of *sijill* was "unknown to the early interpreters of the Qur'an." He adds, "Some took it to be the name of an Angel, or of the Prophet's amanuensis."[28] The fourteenth-century Islamic scholar Ibn Kathir reflects the confusion in his commentary on the passage:

What is meant by *Sijill* is book. As-Suddi said concerning this Ayah: "*As-Sijill* is an angel who is entrusted with the records; when a person dies, his Book (of deeds) is taken up to *As-Sijill*, and he rolls it up and puts it away until the Day of Resurrection." But the correct view as narrated from Ibn Abbas is that *as-Sijill* refers to the record (of deeds). This was also reported from him by Ali bin Abi Talhah and Al-Awfi. This was also stated by Mujahid, Qatadah and others. This was the view favored by Ibn Jarir, because this usage is well-known in the (Arabic) language.[29]

The parenthetical "Arabic" was added by the English translator. According to Jeffery, however, *sijill* is not an Arabic word at all. The term is derived from Greek *sigillon,* meaning an "imperial edict." Jeffery notes that the first Arabic use appears to be in this very passage of the Qur'an.[30]

Equally puzzling is the term *Allahu as-samad,* which is found in Qur'an 112:2. Mainstream twentieth-century Muslim translators of the Qur'an render this term alternately as "God, the Everlasting Refuge" (Arberry), "Allah, the Eternal, Absolute" (Abdullah Yusuf Ali), and "Allah, the eternally Besought of all!" (Pickthall). But no one is sure what *as-samad* really means; it is another Qur'anic nonce word that has puzzled scholars through the ages. It is commonly translated as "eternal," but that is a matter of convention more than of any actual discernment of its meaning. Tabari offers a variety of meanings for the word, including "the one who is not hollow, who does not eat and drink," and "the one from whom nothing comes out," the latter being a familiar Qur'anic designation of Allah as the one who does not beget and is not begotten.[31] After examining the available evidence, the Yale philologist and historian Franz Rosenthal concludes that *as-samad* may be "an ancient Northwest Semitic religious term, which may no longer have been properly understood by Muhammad himself"[32]—or by whoever actually compiled the Qur'an.

Another mysterious Qur'anic word is *al-kawthar,* the title of sura 108. The first verse of that sura is "Lo! We have given thee *al-kawthar*"; the word, unknown outside of this phrase, is commonly rendered as "abundance," "bounty," or "plenty." But this, too, is a matter of convention. The popular Qur'an commentary known as the *Tafsir al-Jalalayn* explains that "*Kawthar* is a river in the Garden from which the Basin of his Community is watered. *Kawthar* means immense good, in the form of Prophethood, Qur'an, intercession and other things."[33] Other Muslim scholars, however, are not so sure. The Qur'anic scholar al-Qurtubi (d. 1273) offers seventeen different interpretations of *al-kawthar*; al-Qurtubi's contemporary Ibn an-Naqib (d. 1298) offers twenty-six.[34] The multiplicity of explanations testifies to the fact that no one really knew what the word meant at all; everyone was simply hazarding his best guess.

There is also an abundance of non-Arabic words in this most self-consciously Arabic book. Many Islamic exegetes have understood that the Qur'an contains no non-Arabic words at all, since the Qur'an is in "Arabic, pure and clear" (16:103), and Allah has explained that he would not have "sent this as a Qur'an in a language other than Arabic" (41:44).[35] The renowned Islamic jurist ash-Shafii, for instance, argues that "the Book of God is in the Arabic language without being mixed with any (foreign words)."[36]

Yet this position is impossible to sustain. As both Muslim and non-Muslim scholars have noted, the Qur'an is full of non-Arabic loanwords.

## A Syriac Religious Universe

Since the Qur'an frequently retells biblical stories and refers to biblical prophets, one might expect the Qur'anic names for those prophets to be informed by Hebrew usage. But the Jews in the Near East no longer spoke Hebrew. Rather, they spoke Aramaic, Greek, and other languages. And the names in the Qur'an consistently show signs of having been derived from Syriac, the dialect of Aramaic that was the primary literary language in Arabia and the surrounding regions when Muhammad is supposed to have lived.

Syriac, also known as Syro-Aramaic, "is the branch of Aramaic in the Near East originally spoken in Edessa and the surrounding area in Northwest Mesopotamia and predominant as a written language from Christianization to the origin of the Koran," explains the modern scholar Christoph Luxenberg. "For more than a millennium Aramaic was the lingua franca in the entire Middle Eastern region before being gradually displaced by Arabic beginning in the 7th century."[37]

Alphonse Mingana (1878–1937), the pioneering Assyrian historian of early Islam, explains that "the proper names of biblical personages found in the Qur'an are used in their Syriac form. Such names include those of Solomon, Pharaoh, Isaac, Ishmael, Jacob,

Noah, Zachariah and Mary."[38] In fact, "there is not a single biblical name with an exclusively Hebrew pronunciation in the whole of the Qur'an," and "the Jewish influence on the religious vocabulary of the Qur'an is indeed negligible."[39]

Nor is the Syriac influence restricted to names. "Almost all the religious terms in the Qur'an," Mingana notes, "are derived from Syriac."[40] These include words that have come to be closely identified with Islam itself, including *Allah*; *ayah* ("sign," in the sense of a divine manifestation, or verse of the Qur'an); *kafir* ("unbeliever"); *salat* ("prayer"); *nafs* ("soul"); *jannah* ("Paradise"); *taghut* ("infidelity"); and *masih* ("Christ").[41] The Qur'anic word for Christians is *nasara*; according to Mingana, "there is no other language besides Syriac in which the word 'Christians' is expressed by the word *nasara* or anything near it. . . . There is no doubt whatever that in the Persian Empire, and to some extent also in the Roman Empire, the Christians were called by non-Christians *nasraye* (the *Nasara* of the Qur'an), and that the Prophet took the word from the Syrians."[42]

Other Qur'anic words were common in Syriac but rare in Arabic before the composition of the Qur'an. These include *rahman* ("compassionate"), which forms part of the Qur'anic invocation *bismilla ar-rahman ar-rahim* ("In the name of Allah, the compassionate, the merciful").

Even the word *Qur'an* itself may come from the Syriac, in which language it refers to a liturgical reading from scripture, a lectionary.[43]

The Qur'an also features traces of Syriac sentence constructions. Mingana notes that Qur'an 2:79, which is generally translated as "Then are you the very persons who kill yourselves," is "very peculiar" in the Arabic: "The use of demonstrative pronouns without the relative pronouns, when followed by a verb the action of which they tend to corroborate, is Syriac and not Arabic." Among many other such examples, he cites Qur'an 62:11, usually given as "And if any of your wives escape from you to the unbelievers." But in Arabic, Mingana says, the word interpreted as "wives," *shai*, is not "applied to a human being"; this usage "betrays the Syriac *middaim*, which is applied to reasonable beings." Because of the "insurmountable difficulty" this usage poses, Muslim scholars have resorted to "worthless compromises."[44]

The Syriac influence is not restricted simply to word usage and sentence construction. The Qur'an in sura 18 (verses 83–101) tells the curious story of Dhul-Qarnayn, "the one with two horns," who traveled to "the setting-place of the sun," where "he found it setting in a muddy spring" (18:84–86), and then journeyed on "till, when he reached the rising-place of the sun, he found it rising on a people for whom We had appointed no shelter therefrom" (18:90).[45] Who was this mysterious traveler? Islamic tradition has identified him frequently, albeit not unanimously, as Alexander the Great. The Alexander legend circulated in many languages, but none had any presence in Arabia at the time of Muhammad except the Syriac. As a result, after eliminating other possibilities, Mingana declares that "we have only the Syrians left from whom the Prophet, or the editor of the Qur'an, could have derived his information."[46]

It is not outside the realm of possibility, of course, that these Syriac words were circulating in seventh-century Arabia. But in view of the Qur'an's self-conscious insistence that it is an Arabic book, they provide additional evidence that the Qur'an originated in circumstances quite different from the standard Islamic picture of a lone prophet huddled in a cave on Mount Hira, where he encountered the angel Gabriel.

## Not Just the Religious Vocabulary But the Cultural Vocabulary Also

And there is more evidence. Arthur Jeffery wrote in 1938 that "not only the greater part of the religious vocabulary, but also most of the cultural vocabulary of the Quran is of non-Arabic origin."[47]

That is a staggering claim to make about a book that presents itself as having been delivered by an Arabian prophet for Arabic speakers. Yet Jeffery notes an anomaly: Despite the fact that the Qur'an is supposed to have originated in Arabia, it breathes very little of the air of that time and place: "From the fact that Muhammad was an Arab, brought up in the midst of Arabian paganism and practising its rites himself until well on into manhood, one would naturally have expected to find that Islam had its roots deep down in this old Arabian paganism. It comes, therefore, as no little surprise, to find how little of the religious life of this Arabian paganism is reflected in the pages of the Qur'an."[48]

One explanation for this odd absence may be that the Qur'an didn't originate in the milieu of Arabian paganism, or in Arabia at all.

To examine the "cultural vocabulary" of the Qur'an, consider one of the most notable non-Arabic words in the book: *jizya*. This word appears in the Qur'an only once, but it became extremely significant in the Muslim world. Qur'an 9:29 says: "Fight those who believe not in Allah nor the Last Day, nor hold that forbidden which hath been forbidden by Allah and His Messenger, nor acknowledge the religion of Truth, (even if they are) of the People of the Book, until they pay the Jizya with willing submission, and feel themselves subdued."[49]

The jizya was a poll tax the Islamic state levied on the *dhimmis*, or the People of the Book (primarily Jews and Christians), as a symbol of their submission and subservience. In Islamic law this payment was (and is) the cornerstone of the humiliating and discriminatory regulations meant to deprive those who rejected Muhammad's prophetic claim. "The subject peoples," according to a classic manual of Islamic law, must "pay the non-Muslim poll tax (jizya)"—but that is by no means all. They "are distinguished from Muslims in dress, wearing a wide cloth belt (zunnar); are not greeted with 'as-Salamu 'alaykum' [the traditional Muslim greeting, "Peace be with you"]; must keep to the side of the street; may not build higher than or as high as the Muslims' buildings, though if they acquire a tall house, it is not razed; are forbidden to openly display wine or pork . . . recite the Torah or Evangel aloud, or make public display of their funerals or feastdays; and are forbidden to build new churches."⁵⁰ If they violated these terms, they could lawfully be killed or sold into slavery.

But there are problems with the Qur'anic passage from which such Islamic laws supposedly derive. The People of the Book, in the translation of Qur'an 9:29 by Abdullah Yusuf Ali, must be made to pay "the Jizya with willing submission, and feel themselves subdued" (*al-jizyata 'an yadin wa-humma saghirun*). Although *saghirun* clearly means "subdued," or "humbled" or "lowly," the words *al-jizya* and *'an yadin* do not appear anywhere else in the Qur'an, and their meaning is not entirely clear. Of *jizya*, Jeffery notes a Syriac word from which the Arabic one may be derived. He says that the word "looks very much like an interpolation in the Qur'an reflecting later usage. In later Islam, *jizya* was the technical term for the poll-tax imposed on the Dhimmis, i.e., members of protected communities."⁵¹ *'An yadin*, meanwhile, can be understood in different ways. Ali renders it as "with willing submission," but it could also mean "out of hand," in the sense not only of submission but also of direct, in-person payment. The thirteenth-century Qur'anic commentator al-Baydawi explains: "Out of hand, indicating the condition of those who pay the tribute. Out of a hand that gives willingly, in this way indicating that they submit obediently; or out of their hand, meaning that they pay the tribute with their own hands, instead of sending it through others; no one is allowed to use a proxy in this case."⁵² There are many other possible understandings of this text. The great scholar Franz Rosenthal observes that *'an yadin* has "completely defied interpretation. All post-Qur'anic occurrences of it are based upon the Qur'an."⁵³

What's more, although the Islamic law regarding the *dhimmis* was elaborated from supposed commands of the Muslim prophet, the regulations centered on the *jizya* were not codified in so specific a form until several centuries after Muhammad's time.⁵⁴ So the term *jizya* could have been elaborated in later Islam—when the great corpus of Islamic law was being formulated and codified—but read back into a much earlier setting and incorporated into the Qur'an. And the strong evidence of Syriac linguistic influence suggests that when it was elaborated, it could have been done in a Syriac environment, farther north than the Arabian setting the Qur'an so self-consciously insists on.

## A Text Converted to Arabic

It may be, then, that the Qur'an's foreign derivation is one of the primary reasons the book takes pains to establish itself as an Arabic text. One reason for the Qur'an's Arabic protestations, other than the charges that Muhammad was listening to a nonnative speaker of Arabic, may be that the Qur'an was not originally written in Arabic at all but was eventually rendered in Arabic as the new religion was being developed. Because the empire that it was designed to buttress was an Arabic one, it was essential that the new holy book be in Arabic. The political imperative was to provide the new and growing empire with a religious culture distinct from that of the Byzantines and Persians—one that would provide for the loyalty, cohesiveness, and unity of the newly conquered domains.

To provide the new religion with its own holy book, its developers turned to existing sources.

# 8

## What the Qur'an May Have Been

### A Clue

What, then, was the Qur'an in its original form?

One clue comes from Qur'an 25:1: "Blessed is He Who has revealed unto His slave the Criterion (of right and wrong), that he may be a warner to the peoples."[1] The word that Muhammad Marmaduke Pickthall here translates as "the Criterion (of right and wrong)" is *al-furqan*, which is also the name of the sura as a whole. Islamic tradition generally identifies the Criterion, *al-furqan*, as the Qur'an, and Muhammad as the "warner to the peoples." The mainstream Qur'an commentary known as the *Tafsir al-Jalalayn* says that the Qur'an is "called thus [*al-furqan*] because it has discriminated (*faraqa*) between truth and falsehood"[2] If the *furqan* is that which discriminates between truth and falsehood, then it is the criterion by which one distinguishes one from the other.[3]

In Syriac, *furqan* means "redemption" or "salvation." And warner, *nadhir*, is a word that is constructed from three consonants—*n, dh,* and *r*—that in Hebrew, Aramaic, and Syriac all have the principal meaning of "to vow." The particular form *nadhir* is a verbal adjective meaning "vowed," "votive gift," or "sacrifice."

Accordingly, a more precise, albeit less traditionally Islamic, translation of Qur'an 25:1 would be "Blessed is He who sent down the redemption on His servant that he might be a sacrifice for the peoples."

161

This is a Christian statement: It is Jesus Christ who was sent down (John 1:1, 1:14) to be a sacrifice (Ephesians 5:1; Hebrews 10:10–14) for the redemption (Ephesians 1:7) of all people (I John 2:2).[4]

Of course, it may appear preposterous on its face that the Qur'an, which contains so much polemical material attacking orthodox Christianity, would make a Christian statement. But as we have seen, the early historical records contain elements that seem equally odd when compared with the canonical account of Islam's origins. These records, including official Arab inscriptions and coins bearing crosses, show that the Arab conquerors, though generally hostile to the concepts of the divinity and redemption of Christ, had a much freer attitude toward Christian symbols than mature Islam would later display. The Arab attitude toward Christianity and Judaism in this era appears to have been far more fluid and in many ways more welcoming than it would ultimately become in Islam.

Moreover, on close examination, the Qur'an itself betrays evidence of having been adapted from a Christian text.

## Ambiguous Text

To move toward a fuller answer to the question of what the Qur'an may have been originally, one must know a bit about how the Arabic alphabet works. Like Hebrew, Arabic does not have letters for short vowels (it does for long ones). Nor does it have letters for certain consonants. Many Arabic letters are identical to one another in appearance except for their diacritical marks—that is, the dots that appear above or below the character. In fact, twenty-two of the twenty-eight letters in the Arabic alphabet in some or all forms depend on diacritical marks to distinguish them from at least one other letter.

The Arabic letter *ra* (ر), for example, is identical to the letter *zay* (ز), except that the *zay* carries a dot above it. The letter *sin* (س) looks exactly the same as *shin* (ش), except that the latter features three dots above the character. One symbol could be three different letters: *ba*

(ب) with a dot under it, *ta* (ت) with two dots above it, and *tha* (ث) with three dots above it; *nun* (ن) is also quite similar in form. Obviously, these similarities can make for enormous differences in meaning.

As such, diacritical marks are essential to being able to make sense of the Qur'an or any other Arabic text. Unfortunately, the earliest manuscripts of the Qur'an do not contain most diacritical marks. A scholar of hadiths named Abu Nasr Yahya ibn Abi Kathir al-Yamami (d. 749) recalled: "The Qur'an was kept free [of diacritical marks] in *mushaf* [the original copies]. The first thing people have introduced in it is the dotting at the letter *ba* (ب) and the letter *ta* (ت), maintaining that there is no sin in this, for this illuminates the Qur'an."[5] Abu Nasr did not say when these marks began to be introduced, but the fragments of Qur'anic manuscripts that many scholars date to the first century of the Arabian conquests have only rudimentary diacritical marks. Some manuscripts distinguish one set of identical letters from another—*ta* (ت) from *ba* (ب), or *fa* (ف) from *qaf* (ق)—but they

---

### What's in a Mark?

Arabic letters that can be confused with one another if the diacritical marks are not present:

> *ba* ١.٠    *ta* ٠٠٠    *tha* ث    *nun* ن
> *jim* ج    *ha* ح    *kha* خ
> *dal* د    *dhal* ذ
> *ra* ر    *zay* ز
> *sin* س    *shin* ش
> *sad* ص    *dad* ض
> *ta* ط    *za* ظ
> *ayn* ع    *ghayn* غ
> *fa* ف    *qaf* ق
> *nun* ـن (medial form)    *ya* ـيـ (medial form)

leave the other sets of identical letters indistinguishable. Nor are all the earliest manuscripts consistent in the sets of identical letters they choose to distinguish from one another.[6]

An Islamic scholar writing late in the tenth century recounted a story in which the confusion of two sets of letters—*zay* (ز) for *ra* (ر), and *ta* (ت) for *ba* (ب)—came into play. A young man named Hamza began reciting the Qur'an's second sura, which begins, "This is the Book with no doubt in it" (2:2). "No doubt in it" in Arabic is *la raiba fihi*, but this unfortunate young man read out *la zaita fihi*, or "no oil in it," so that the book, instead of being beyond question, was oil-free. (Hamza was thereafter known as *az-Zayyat*, or "the dealer in oil.")

Hamza may simply have slipped up or been making a joke. But because the earliest extant manuscripts of the Qur'an contain none of the marks that would have enabled him to distinguish a *ra* from a *zay* and a *ba* from a *ta*, it is entirely possible that he was doing the best he could with a highly ambiguous text.

The implications of this confusion are enormous. Hamza's error could have been committed even by those Islamic scholars who added in the diacritical marks that now form the canonical text of the Qur'an. It is entirely possible that what is taken for one word in that canonical text may originally have been another word altogether.

Diacritical marks may have been purposefully omitted. The Qur'an begins, after all, by proclaiming itself to be "a guidance unto those who ward off evil" (2:2); it may be that that guidance was a secret given only to the initiated. If the Qur'an's instructions were to be denied anyone outside a select circle, it would explain why there is virtually no mention of the Qur'an, much less quotation of it, in the coinage and inscriptions of the Arabian conquerors. Even as the conquerors grew entrenched, some saw the introduction of diacritical marks and vowel points as an unlawful *bida*, "innovation." Hence the caliph al-Mamun (813–833) forbade either one to be introduced into the Qur'anic text, confusion be damned.[7]

Nonetheless, the diacritical marks were ultimately introduced without causing any major conflict. Thereafter the text was largely frozen in meaning. That canonical text, however, is the one in which, as the philologist Gerd-R. Puin notes, "every fifth sentence or so simply doesn't make sense." Consequently, some scholars speculate that perhaps the diacritical marks themselves caused the incoherence of the Qur'an. If these marks were added incorrectly or with some polemical or dogmatic objective in mind, it may be that by stripping them out and applying different ones, we can discover the true meaning of difficult and borderline nonsensical Qur'anic passages.

It is by no means an arbitrary practice to strip out diacritical marks and reevaluate the Qur'anic text: The Qur'an contains numerous indications of a non-Arabic derivation, or at the very least considerable non-Arabic influence. As we have seen, even the word *Qur'an* itself may be a Syriac word for a lectionary.[8] Furthermore, Muhammad's first biographer, Ibn Ishaq, uses language that otherwise, according to scholar Alfred Guillaume, appears only in a "Palestinian Syriac Lectionary of the Gospels which will conclusively prove that the Arabic writer had a Syriac text before him."[9]

Some Qur'anic passages that are puzzling or contain odd locutions become clear once the canonical diacritical marks are stripped out and the text reread in light of the Syriac language. The Qur'anic account of Abraham's near-sacrifice of his son contains this verse, in Abdullah Yusuf Ali's rendering: "So when they had both submitted their wills (to Allah), and he had laid him prostrate on his forehead (for sacrifice) . . ." (37:103). Pickthall renders the same verse as: "Then, when they had both surrendered (to Allah), and he had flung him down upon his face . . ." The passage translated as "laid him prostrate on his forehead" or "flung him down upon his face" is *wa-tallahu li'l jabin*. But this is the only time the word *jabin* appears in the Qur'an. Although Muslim scholars interpret the word to mean "forehead" or "face," the philologist Christoph Luxenberg reads *jabin* as a corruption of the Syriac *habbin*, firewood. The *j* in *jabin* (ج) and the *h* in *habbin* (ح) differ by only one dot. Luxenberg reads *wa-tallahu* not as "laid him" or "flung him" but, in light of the Syriac *tla*, "bind." Thus he renders the verse in a way that is much more consonant with the biblical account: "He bound him to the firewood."[10]

## A Christian Lectionary

Numerous scholars have noted traces of a Christian text underlying the Qur'an. In line with the meaning of the Syriac word *Qur'an*, that Christian text may have been a lectionary. The Qur'anic scholar Erwin Gräf declares that the Qur'an, "according to the etymological meaning of the word, is originally and really a liturgical text designed for cultic recitation and also actually used in the private and public service. This suggests that the liturgy or liturgical poetry, and indeed the Christian liturgy, which comprises the Judaic liturgy, decisively stimulated and influenced Mohammed."[11]

Similarly, the German philologist Günter Lüling posits that "the text of the Koran as transmitted by Muslim Orthodoxy contains, hidden behind it as a ground layer and considerably scattered throughout it (together about one-third of the whole Koran text), an originally pre-Islamic Christian text."[12] Earlier Qur'anic scholars such as Alois Sprenger and Tor Andrae have also identified a Christian substratum to the Qur'an.[13]

Luxenberg states that if *Qur'an* "really means *lectionary*, then one can assume that the Koran intended itself first of all to be understood as nothing more than a liturgical book with selected texts from the *Scriptures* (the Old and New Testament) and not at all as a substitute for the *Scriptures* themselves, i.e. as an independent *Scripture*."[14]

But what, then, of passages in which the Qur'an seems to refer to itself as exactly that, an independent scripture? Consider, for example, Qur'an 12:1–2, which Abdullah Yusuf Ali renders this way: "These are the symbols (or Verses) of the perspicuous Book. We have sent it down as an Arabic Qur'an, in order that ye may learn wisdom." Referring to Syriac to elucidate the Arabic, Luxenberg translates the passage in this way: "This is the written copy of the elucidated Scripture: We have sent it down as an Arabic lectionary so that you may understand it."[15]

Luxenberg explains the implications: "It is thus not surprising that Jesus (*Isa*) is cited 25 times in the Koran and that he is there referred to as the Messiah (*al-Masih*) eleven times. Thus it is only logical to see other Syro-Christian passages being a part of this foundation which constitutes the origin of the Koran."[16]

Luxenberg is among the scholars who have pioneered the critical examination of the *rasm*—that is, the basic form of the Qur'anic text without diacritical marks. Because diacritical marks are not found in the earliest Qur'an manuscripts, these scholars posit that the Qur'an originally had a meaning quite different from that of the now-standard Arabic text. Luxenberg notes that many of the Qur'an's linguistic peculiarities vanish when one strips out the Arabic diacritical marks, which were added later, and reads the book as a Syriac document. He even contends that Syriac was the original language of the Arab conquerors; although other scholars dispute this claim, it is plausible given that Syriac was the chief literary language of the Middle East from the fourth to the eighth centuries.

By referring to the Syriac and examining the *rasm*, Luxenberg solves the difficulties of a passage that has perplexed readers of the Qur'an for centuries. Just as Mary gives birth to Jesus in the Qur'anic account, there is this: "Then (one) cried unto her from below her, saying: Grieve not! Thy Lord hath placed a rivulet beneath thee" (19:24). It is unclear from the text who is speaking (the newborn Jesus or someone else?) and what the nature of this rivulet is. Luxenberg, however, finds that this passage has nothing to do with rivulets. Rather, it refers to Mary's delivering a Virgin Birth. In Luxenberg's philological reconstruction, the infant Jesus (who speaks elsewhere in the Qur'an) tells Mary: "Do not be sad, your Lord has made your delivery legitimate."[17]

## Raisins, Not Virgins

Luxenberg's investigations won international attention for his reinterpretation of Qur'anic passages referring to the virgins of Paradise (44:51–57, 52:17–24, 56:27–40). These passages are among the most famous in the entire Qur'an, promising "perfect . . . spotless virgins, chastely amorous" (56:35–37) to the inhabitants of Paradise. Most notably, after the 9/11 terrorist attacks many news stories focused on the Qur'anic promise of virgins in Paradise as the reward for Islamic martyrs.

The Arabic word *hur*, which is usually translated as "virgins," is central to the canonical understanding of these passages (it appears in 44:54 and 52:20). But *hur* does not actually mean "virgins," as even Arabic philologists acknowledge. Rather, it is the plural form of an Arabic feminine adjective that means simply "white." Qur'an commentators and Arabic scholars often explain that it actually means "white-eyed," an expression that Qur'an translators have taken as an expression of the beauty of these virgins, translating it as "large-eyed," "wide-eyed," "with lustrous eyes," and similar expressions. Luxenberg argues that this interpretation not only contradicts Arabic usage but doesn't even make sense as a sign of beauty:

> When one describes the beauty of eyes, it is said as a rule, and not just in Arabic, "beautiful *black*, beautiful *brown* and beautiful *blue* eyes," but never "beautiful *white* eyes," unless of course one is *blind*. For instance, in the Koran it is also said of Jacob that from all his crying over his son Joseph his eyes have become "white" (Sura 12:84), i.e. they have been *blinded*. The further explanation given by the Arabic commentators that the white particularly emphasizes the beauty of (big) *black* eyes is only an invented makeshift explanation.[18]

According to Islamic tradition, *hur* is the equivalent of *houri*, which does mean virgin, but Luxenberg argues that this is a clear misreading of the text. For starters, the idea of the virgins contradicts the Qur'an's promise that the blessed will enter Paradise with their wives (43:70), unless the earthly wives are supposed to watch in rage and sorrow as their husbands cavort with the heavenly virgins.[19] And a closer philological analysis indicates that the Qur'an does not offer such a contradictory promise. After examining the *rasm*, the other contexts in which *hur* appears in the Qur'an, and the contemporary usage of the word *houris*, Luxenberg concludes that the famous passages refer not to virgins but instead to white raisins, or grapes.

Yes, fruit. Strange as that may seem, given all the attention paid to the Qur'an's supposed promises of virgins in Paradise, white raisins were a prized delicacy in that region. As such, Luxenberg suggests, they actually make a more fitting symbol of the reward of Paradise than the promise of sexual favors from virgins. Luxenberg shows that the Arabic word for "Paradise" can be traced to the Syriac word for "garden," which stands to reason, given the common identification of the garden of Adam and Eve with Paradise. Luxenberg further demonstrates that metaphorical references to bunches of grapes are consonant with Christian homiletics expatiating on the refreshments that greeted the blessed in Heaven. He specifically cites the fourth-century hymns "on Paradise" of St. Ephraem the Syrian (306–373), which refer to "the grapevines of Paradise." The fact that the Syriac word Ephraem used for "grapevine" was feminine, Luxenberg explains, "led the Arabic exegetes of the Koran to this fateful assumption" that the Qur'anic text referred to sexual playthings in Paradise.[20]

Similarly misleading is the standard translation of the famous Qur'anic passages regarding the boys of Paradise ("Immortal youths shall go about them; when thou seest them, thou supposest them scattered pearls" [76:19]; "and there go round them youths, their own, as if they were hidden pearls" [52:24]; "immortal youths going round about them" [56:17]). Luxenberg shows that these passages refer not to boys but, again, to grapes—the refreshment of the blessed. For example, he renders Qur'an 76:19 as: "Iced fruits pass around among them; to see them, you would think they were loose pearls."[21]

This imagery, too, harks back to the hymns of Ephraem the Syrian, in which the symbols of Paradise include not white grapes and iced fruits but also wine. Luxenberg concludes: "Through the philologically based misinterpretation, until now, of both the *huris* or *virgins of Paradise* and the *youths of Paradise*, one can gauge the extent to which the Koranic exegesis has become estranged vis-à-vis the original Christian symbolism of the wine of Paradise."[22]

Luxenberg also looks at the Qur'anic verses (44:54 and 52:20) in which, according to the typical understanding, Allah promises that virgins will be given in marriage to the blessed. He suggests that the word understood to mean "marriage," *zawwagnahum*, could be a misreading of *rawwahnahum*, which refers to giving rest to the departed in heaven, for without diacritical marks, the differing letters, such as the *r* and the *z*, are interchangeable. Here again, then, the verses would have nothing to do with virgins. Instead, they would be prayers for God to grant eternal rest to the souls of the deceased. Such prayers are part of Christian memorial observances. Other evidence supports Luxenberg's position. For instance, ancient North African inscriptions use *r-ww-H*, the root of *rawwahnahum*, in exactly this Christian liturgical context of praying for God to give eternal rest to the souls of the departed.[23]

All this evidence reinforces the possibility that Arabic exegetes of the Qur'an were working with what was originally a Christian text.

## The Last Supper

The Qur'an's Christian substratum can be seen in what Islamic tradition regards as chronologically the Qur'an's very first segment. In what now stands as sura 96, the angel Gabriel appears before Muhammad in the cave on Mount Hira and exhorts him to "Recite!":

1. Recite: In the name of thy Lord who created,
2. Created Man of a blood-clot.

3. Recite: And thy Lord is the Most Generous,
4. who taught by the Pen,
5. taught man that he knew not.
6. No indeed; surely Man waxes insolent,
7. for he thinks himself self-sufficient.
8. Surely unto thy Lord is the Returning.
9. What thinkest thou? He who forbids
10. a servant when he prays—
11. What thinkest thou? If he were upon guidance
12. or bade to godfearing—
13. What thinkest thou? If he cries lies, and turns away—
14. Did he not know that God sees?
15. No indeed; surely, if he gives not over, We shall seize him by the forelock,
16. A lying, sinful forelock.
17. So let him call on his concourse!
18. We shall call on the guards of Hell.
19. No indeed; do thou not obey him, and bow thyself, and draw nigh.

This text is, in the words of the contemporary Islamic scholar Ibn Rawandi, "for the most part, incoherent nonsense" that "makes a mockery of the Koran's description of itself as 'clear Arabic language.'"[24] For example, the word *kalla*, "no indeed," occurs three times in sura 96. In verses 6, 15, and 19. According to Ibn Rawandi, "its first appearance at XCVI.6 is senseless, since it cannot be a negation of the preceding section no matter how those verses are interpreted."[25] The Qur'an translator Rudi Paret draws out that senselessness in his rendering of verses 4–6: "[He] who has taught the use of the writing cane has taught unto man what he didn't know. Not at all! Man is really rebellious . . ."[26]

The sura shows signs of editing, appearing to be in two parts. Verses 1–8 fit in with the traditional Muslim setting, in which Gabriel approached Muhammad on Mount Hira. But then the subject abruptly and unaccountably changes in verses 9–19, denouncing some unnamed person who prevents a "servant" (or "slave," as many other translations have it) from praying.

Günter Lüling explains this sudden shift by suggesting that the text of sura 96 was originally a strophic Christian hymn that had been reworked to fit it into an Islamic setting. In Lüling's reconstruction, based on an original reading of the Arabic text, "Recite in the name of your Lord" becomes "Invoke the Name of your Lord." Lüling translates the Arabic verb *iqra* as "invoke" rather than "recite," pointing out that the Arab philologist Abu Ubaida (d. 818), author of *Strange Matters of Hadith* (*Gharib al-Hadith*), explained that the verb *qara'a*—"to recite," with *iqra* as its imperative form—meant the same thing as the verb *dakara*: "invoke, laud, praise."[27] Ibn Rawandi supports Lüling's argument, noting that "understanding '*iqra*' as 'invoke,' rather than 'read' or 'recite,' becomes plausible when it is realized that in the ancient world reading was invariably reading aloud, so that the distinction between reading and invoking would not have been what it is today." Thus to "recite" would mean essentially the same thing as "invoke": to proclaim aloud.[28]

The entire phrase "Invoke the Name of your Lord" recalls the common Hebrew phrase *qara' be shem Yahwe*, "Invoke the name of the Lord" (cf. Genesis 4:25–26). It also recalls Psalm 130, known in Latin as *De profundis*, "out of the depths I call to you," in which "to call to God," *qeraatiikha* in Hebrew, is rendered in Latin as *Clamavi ad te Domine*, which obviously means "to pray to God."

In Lüling's reconstruction, the digressive "He who forbids a servant when he prays" becomes a confession of God's faithfulness: "Have you ever seen that He denies a servant when he prays?" The warning questions, "What thinkest thou? If he cries lies, and turns away—Did he not know that God sees?" become "Have you ever seen that He betrayed and turned away? Have you not learned that God sees?" The odd "So let him call on his concourse! We shall call on the guards of Hell" Lüling renders as an exhortation to call on the members of the heavenly court: "So call for His High Council! You will then call up the High Angelship!"[29]

Lüling's reconstruction of sura 96 as a Christian hymn exhorting the pious to call on God's name and assuring them of his faithfulness makes more sense than the cryptic, abrupt, and decontextualized canonical text of sura 96.

Examining the Syriac substratum, Luxenberg goes even further. He agrees with Lüling that *iqra* is more accurately rendered "invoke" rather than "recite." But he contends that the sura does not simply fit into a Christian liturgical context but actually calls its followers to participate in that Christian liturgical service. Luxenberg writes that "the lexicological and syntactical analysis of this sura, examined under its Syriac connection, has revealed—contrary to the confusion which has reigned in its Arabic reading up to now—a clear and coherent composition in which the faithful is entreated to pray and participate in the liturgical service that the Koran designates as the Eucharist, corresponding to *iqtarib*, taken from the Syriac liturgical term *etqarrab*, which signifies 'take part in a liturgical service' as well as 'to receive the Eucharist.' "[30]

Specifically, he renders the segment of the sura's last verse not as "bow thyself, and draw nigh," but as a call to participate in the Eucharistic celebration: "Return to your religious practices and take part in the offering (= Eucharist)."[31] Luxenberg explains that the word *iqtarib*, normally translated as "draw nigh," is "in fact Arabic only in form and corresponds in reality to the liturgical Syriac term *el qarra / ethqarrab*, meaning 'to take part in the offering (Eucharistic)' as well as 'to receive the Eucharist.' "[32]

In Qur'an 5:114–115, Jesus prays: " 'O God, our Lord, send down upon us a Table out of heaven, that shall be for us a festival, the first and last of us, and a sign from Thee. And provide for us; Thou art the best of providers.' God said: 'Verily I do send it down on you; whoso of you hereafter disbelieves, verily I shall chastise him with a chastisement wherewith I chastise no other being.' " This has long been seen as a vestige of the Christian doctrine of the Eucharist, but Luxenberg sees it as much more than a mere vestige. Jesus' prayer in Qur'an 5:114 asks Allah that this table from heaven be "a feast (*'id*) for us and a sign (*ayah*) from thee." Notes Luxenberg: "The Arabic word *'id*, borrowed from the Syriac, has been, in conformity with its Arabic meaning, correctly translated by 'celebration' [or 'feast,' in the liturgical sense]."

Luxenberg is not alone. In fact, in the words of the scholar of Islam and Jesuit priest Samir Khalil Samir, "according to unanimous scholarly opinion [the Arabic word *'id*] is a borrowing from the Syriac *'ida*, which signifies 'Feast' or 'liturgical festival.' "[33] Noting that this verse is the only place in the Qur'an where the word *'id* appears, Samir concludes: "This *ma'ida* [table] is thus defined by two terms: *'id* and *aya*, a 'Feast' or 'liturgical festival' and a 'sign.' Is this not the most appropriate definition of the Eucharist of Christians, which is a festive celebration and a sacramental sign? Even more, it seems evident that in this passage we are dealing with a rather faithful description of Christian faith, otherwise not shared by Muslims." [34]

Luxenberg adds even more:

> The table being laid out, one could have thought, in fact, that the passage was talking about "having a celebration." However, the same writing or script transcribed in Syriac and pronounced *'yadda* has the meaning "liturgy." Thus one must understand this verse as follows: "Lord our God, send us down from the sky a Last Supper which would be a liturgy for the first and last of us." In his reply, God says . . . 'I am going to send it down to you. Whoever is then impious among you will receive from me a torment the like of which I will not inflict on anyone else in the world.'"[35]

"For the first and last of us" in 5:114 is *li-awwalina wa-akhirina*, another phrase found nowhere else in the Qur'an; literally it means "all, nobody excluded." Samir relates this to the Christian liturgical phrase regarding the Body and Blood of Christ, "which is offered for you and for many for the remission of sins."[36] Thus this brief and mysterious Qur'an passage likely contains yet another hint of Christian Eucharistic theology.

Accordingly, Luxenberg concludes: "Islam was not impressed by this divine injunction with its threats of the most severe punishments, not having grasped its significance. If the Muslim exegetes had understood these passages as the Koran intended them, there would have been a liturgy of the Last Supper in Islam."[37]

## A Christian Confession of Faith

One Qur'anic passage that shows obvious signs of editing is sura 74, reproduced here in its entirety in order to demonstrate an obvious anomaly in the verse structure and rhythm (even in English translation):

1. O thou shrouded in thy mantle,
2. arise, and warn!
3. Thy Lord magnify,
4. thy robes purify,
5. and defilement flee!
6. Give not, thinking to gain greater
7. and be patient unto thy Lord.
8. For when the Trump is sounded
9. that day will be a harsh day,
10. for the unbelievers not easy.
11. Leave Me with him whom I created alone,
12. and appointed for him ample wealth
13. and sons standing before him,
14. and made all things smooth for him;
15. then he is eager that I should do more.
16. Nay! He is forward unto Our signs;
17. and I shall constrain him to a hard ascent.
18. Lo! He reflected, and determined—
19. death seize him, how he determined!
20. Again, death seize him, how he determined!

21. Then he beheld,

22. then he frowned, and scowled,

23. then he retreated, and waxed proud.

24. He said, "This is naught but a trumped-up sorcery;

25. this is nothing but mortal speech."

26. I shall surely roast him in Sakar;

27. and what will teach thee what is Sakar?

28. It spares not, neither leaves alone

29. scorching the flesh;

30. over it are nineteen.

31. We have appointed only angels to be masters of the Fire, and their number We have appointed only as a trial for the unbelievers; that those who were given the Book may have certainty, and that those who believe may increase in belief, and that those who were given the Book and those who believe may not be in doubt; and that those in whose hearts there is sickness, and the unbelievers, may say, "What did God intend by this as a similitude?" So God leads astray whomsoever He will, and He guides whomsoever He will; and none knows the hosts of thy Lord but He. And it is naught but a Reminder to mortals.

32. Nay! By the moon

33. and the night when it retreats

34. and the dawn when it is white,

35. surely it is one of the greatest things

36. as a warner to mortals,

37. to whoever of you desires to go forward or lag behind.

38. Every soul shall be pledged for what it has earned,

39. save the Companions of the Right;

40. in Gardens they will question

41. concerning the sinners,

42. "What thrusted you into Sakar?"

43. They shall say, "We were not of those who prayed,

44. and we fed not the needy,

45. and we plunged along with the plungers,

46. and we cried lies to the Day of Doom,

47. till the Certain came to us."

48. Then the intercession of the intercessors shall not profit them.

49. What ails them, that they turn away from the Reminder,

50. as if they were startled asses

51. fleeing before a lion?

52. Nay, every man of them desires to be given scrolls unrolled.

53. No indeed; but they do not fear the Hereafter.

54. No indeed; surely it is a Reminder;

55. So whoever wills shall remember it.

56. And they will not remember, except that God wills; He is worthy to be feared, worthy to forgive.

Even in English, the lengthy, discursive verse 31 does not appear to be an original part of this passage. It looks immediately as if it has been added to the sura from another source—possibly some other sura of the Qur'an itself. It breaks the flow of the clipped, spare verses of the rest. The verse sounds more like the prosaic ruminations of what Islamic tradition considers to be the Qur'an's chronologically later passages than the vivid poetic visions of those traditionally held to be the chronologically early suras.

Lüling observes that Qur'an 74:1–30 "is composed in a very homogeneous form, in that every verse has the same rhythmic style and approximate length of, on average, three to four words (indicating its having originally been a strophic text)." Even Muslim scholars acknowledge that the sura was edited, he points out: "Islamic Koran scholarship has . . . classified this over-length-verse 74.31 as a late insertion into an earlier text." According to those scholars, the editing took place during Muhammad's life, originating "in the Medinan period of the Prophet's activities as against his earlier Meccan period."[38] But the very fact that Islamic scholars admit that changes were made to the perfect book is significant.

The last line of the "homogeneous" section, verse 30, could be a fragment of what was originally a longer (and clearer) statement. Neither this verse nor any other states explicitly what there are "nineteen" of, or what these nineteen are exactly "over." Apparently they are above "Sakar," which is often translated as "the burning." Accordingly, the Qur'an commentator Ibn Kathir explains that the nineteen are "the first of the guardians of Hell. They are magnificent in (their appearance) and harsh in their character."[39] While this interpretation is plausible, the cryptic nature of the verse has led many Islamic theologians and apologists to speculate about the mystical significance of the number nineteen.

To shed some light on this puzzling sura, Lüling looks closely at verses 11–17. In the traditional rendering, this passage is full of questionable material. Like Qur'an 96:9–19, it denounces an anonymous miscreant. Of whom is Allah, the sole creator and judge of all things, demanding that he be left alone to deal with? Again by examining the *rasm* and noting grammatical and other anomalies in the Arabic, Lüling smoothes out the difficulties and presents a reconstruction that makes more sense than the standard Qur'anic text. This reconstruction reveals the text as a Christological confession:

11. He has created me and the one He has created as a unique being.
12. And He has made him a property obedient to His will.
13. And He has testified to him by witnesses.
14. And He paved for him the way.
15. Then he desired that he might be increased.
16. Not at all that he was rebellious against His commandments.
17. So finally He has made him step through death up to the heights.[40]

Among other emendations, Lüling reads *dharni*, the contextually bizarre imperative in 74:11 to "leave me alone" or "dismiss me," as *dharaani*, "He has created me." And so, he argues, this passage begins to become clear as a Christian confession of faith—but not one reflecting the theology of the Byzantine Empire or the Church of Constantinople. Rather, it is a rejection of Trinitarian Christology.

For centuries the Byzantine Empire had been convulsed by controversy over the nature of Christ. Once the emperor Constantine converted to Christianity and issued the Edict of Milan decriminalizing Christianity in 313, the rapidly growing new faith became important for the unity of the empire. Constantine sought to safeguard that unity by calling the first ecumenical council—that is, a meeting of all the bishops in the empire—to settle the question of the nature of Christ. This council met at Nicaea in 325.

At Nicaea the theology of Arius, a priest of the Church of Alexandria, was anathematized, and Arius himself was defrocked and excommunicated. Arius taught that Christ was not coeternal with God, as the victorious party taught, but was a created being, albeit an exalted one. After the council, Arians still wielded considerable influence within the empire; they came close on more than one occasion to becoming the dominant form of Christianity and reversing the decision of Nicaea. Their power waned, however, and eventually the political and social restrictions that the empire imposed on them became so onerous that they left its domains for points east: Syria and Arabia.[41]

The Arians were by no means the first or only Christian group to view Christ as created. The Jewish Christian Ebionites viewed Jesus as the Messiah but not in any sense divine. Their influence spread to Syria and the surrounding areas in the centuries immediately before the advent of Islam.[42] The Pseudo-Clementine Homilies, three Christian writings falsely attributed to St. Clement of Rome that actually appear to be fourth-century Jewish Christian texts, declare that "our Lord neither asserted that there were gods except the Creator of all, nor did He proclaim Himself to be God, but He with reason pronounced blessed him who called Him the Son of that God who has arranged the universe." They reject the idea that "he who comes from God is God."[43]

Thus it is entirely possible that the Christian substratum of the Qur'an reflects a Christology that views Christ as a created being.

In Lüling's reconstruction of this passage, God created Jesus Christ as a unique being, "a property obedient to His will." Jesus is not, in other words, the coeternal Son of God who existed for all eternity and became man. Lüling presents sura 74 as the product of a Christian group that rejected the high Christology of the great Church of Constantinople and maintained that Jesus was nothing more than a servant of God and His messenger. In his reconstruction, the entire sura 74 becomes a Christian hymn recounting Christ's descent into hell and affirming him as a created being.

As for the obviously interpolated verse 31, Lüling explains it as a later Islamic commentary on a pre-Islamic Christian text that was reworked and Islamized in verses 1–30.[44] Whereas Qur'an commentators assert that verse 31 was added during the Medinan period of Muhammad's career, Lüling argues that "this traditional [Meccan/Medinan] division must be given up in favour of the contrast 'pre-Islamic Christian strophic texts' and 'Islamic texts.'"[45]

According to Lüling, 74:31 is an Islamic commentary on the cryptic 74:30, "over it are nineteen." The added verse is designed to affirm that the "nineteen" are the angels who are the guardians of hell, but there follows the odd warning that Allah has made this number "as a trial for the unbelievers; that those who were given the Book may have certainty, and that those who believe may increase in belief, and that those who were given the Book and those who believe may not be in doubt." Lüling takes this strange warning as an indication that the Qur'an's explanation of "over it are nineteen" in 74:30 was controversial at the time it was written. He concludes that 74:31 is "not merely a sober commentary on that immediately preceding verse, but it is the emphatic reminder, most urgently put forward, to endorse the belief that these enigmatic words of verse 74.30 'on it are nineteen' should actually mean 'on it (the hellfire) are 19 (angels) appointed (as custodians).' This urgent reminder is combined with threats against those who were unwilling to believe in this interpretation, obviously because they rejected this 'simile' (*matal* as the text of verse 31 calls it itself) as inappropriate or even as wrong."[46]

And they rejected it as wrong, and had to be threatened with becoming one of those whom Allah led astray, because "most probably they still knew the original meaning of this pre-Islamic Christian hymn in general, and therefore also the original meaning of verse 74.30 in particular, within its pre-Islamic Christian context. The Islamic interpretation, on which the inserted commentary verse 74.31 insists with intimidating warnings, represents indeed no biblical or other religious topos or well-known simile, so that from our point of view, based on the pre-Islamic hymnody so far uncovered in the Koran, this Islamic interpretation of 74.30 is nothing but the reinterpretation of an original Christian strophic text—which at that time of early Islam a lot of people still knew and tried to defend."[47]

### Hanifs—Pagans or Monotheists?

The Qur'an's Christology, both in the canonical Islamic text and in the pre-Islamic Christian substratum that many scholars see in the book, is defiantly anti-Trinitarian. The Qur'an rejects the idea that Jesus is the Son of God and above all denounces those who take Christ to be part of the Godhead: "Say, 'He is God, One, God the Everlasting Refuge, who has not begotten, and has not been begotten, and equal to Him is not any one'" (112:1–4). The phrase "equal to Him is not any one" may be a denial of the orthodox Christology holding the Son of God to be equal to the Father, and the assertion that God neither begets nor was begotten is clearly a response to the orthodox Christian designation of Christ as the "only begotten Son of God."

Lüling sees traces of the Christian controversies over the nature of Christ in the Qur'an's denunciations of those who associate partners with Allah. To Lüling, the Muslim charge that the pagan Quraysh of Mecca were *mushrikun*, those who associated others with Allah in worship, indicates that the Quraysh had actually converted to Trinitarian Christianity. As the Islamic faith began to develop as a distinct religion, it decisively rejected this faith in Christ. Once

Islam's hard-line monotheism became more firmly established, the Qur'an needed to be reinterpreted to fit the new religion's developing theology.[48]

The Qur'an also speaks of *hanifs*, those who held to pre-Islamic monotheism. Qur'an 3:67 speaks of them gently, referring to the faith adhered to by the patriarch Abraham and the prophets. As Islamic tradition explains it, this verse makes clear that Abraham and his followers were not idol worshippers. But the term *hanif* is cognate with *hanpe*, or "pagan"—this is the word used for "pagan" in the Syriac rendering of the Bible, the Peshitta. The medieval Christian apologist al-Kindi (not to be confused with the Muslim Arab philosopher of the same name) writes that "Abraham used to worship the idol, i.e., the one named al-Uzza in Harran, as a *hanif*, as you agree, O you *hanif*. . . . He abandoned *al-hanifiyya*, which is the worship of idols, and became a monotheist. . . . Therefore we find *al-hanifiyya* in God's revealed scriptures as a name for the worship of idols."[49] Al-Kindi's reliability has been questioned, but the point here is not his assertions but his usage of the word *hanif* to refer to an idol worshipper rather than to a pre-Islamic monotheist.

It is odd that the Qur'an, according to Islamic tradition, uses the word *hanif* to refer to a pre-Islamic monotheist, whereas for the Peshitta and al-Kindi the term suggests a pagan. The discrepancy may suggest an intermediate step between pagan idolatry and the development of a full-blown Islam featuring Muhammad and his Qur'an: In this interim stage, some of the idolatrous *hanifs* may have embraced a vague monotheism that identified itself with, or considered itself akin to, Judaism and Christianity. Such *hanifs* would have endorsed a creedal statement such as Lüling's version of Qur'an 74:11–17, with its strong emphasis on Jesus Christ as a created being and messenger of God, not as God become man. As we have seen, the first decades of the Arab conquest show the conquerors holding not to Islam as we know it but to a vague creed with ties to some form of Christianity and Judaism. Perhaps this was the very embodiment of *al-hanifiyya*: arising out of Arab paganism, embracing monotheism, and then being overwhelmed by the development of the specific faith of Islam.

## Christmas in the Qur'an

There is a great deal more in the Qur'an that suggests the presence of an originally Christian substratum. Luxenberg explains: "It is not just on the level of simple isolated words but also at the level of syntax that the Arab commentators have misunderstood the Koranic text, to the extent of misinterpreting entire suras. Thus the Arab exegetes saw in the title of Sura 108 (*al-Kawthar*), among other things, the name of a river in Paradise reserved exclusively for the Prophet or Muslims, and in the subsequent text the reprobation of an opponent of the Prophet who must have despised the latter for having been deprived of children. However the Syriac reading of this sura calls to mind the First Epistle of St Peter, Chapter 5 verses 8–9, according to which—and in accordance with the introduction to the compline of the Roman service—the faithful are exhorted to persevere in their prayers by which their adversary, Satan, is routed."[50]

Many of the Quran's more obscure passages begin to make sense when read in light of its having a foundation in Christian theology. For example, there is an enigmatic sura on the Night of Power, *al-Qadr* ("Power"): "Behold, We sent it down on the Night of Power; and what shall teach thee what is the Night of Power? The Night of Power is better than a thousand months; in it the angels and the Spirit descend, by the leave of their Lord, upon every command. Peace it is, till the rising of dawn" (97:1–5). Muslims associate the Night of Power with the first appearance of Gabriel to Muhammad and the first revelation of the Qur'an; they commemorate this night during the fasting month of Ramadan. But the Qur'an makes no explicit connection between the Night of Power and the revelation of the Qur'an. The book doesn't explain what the Night of Power is, except to say it is the night on which the angels (not just one angel) and the Spirit descend and proclaim Peace.

In light of the Qur'an's Syriac Christian roots, there is another plausible interpretation—that sura 97 refers to Christmas.

The Qur'anic scholar Richard Bell saw in the night, angels, Spirit, and peace of the sura a hint of the Nativity even without a detailed philological examination: "The origin of the idea of the Night of Power is unexplained. The only other passage in the Quran which has any bearing on it is XLIV, 2a,3. In some ways what is here said of it suggests that some account of the Eve of the Nativity may have given rise to it."[51]

Luxenberg points out that because the Night of Power is associated with the revelation of the Qur'an, Muslims undertake vigils during Ramadan. "However," he notes, "with regard to the history of religions this fact is all the more remarkable since Islam does not have a nocturnal liturgy (apart from the *tarawih*, prayers offered during the nights of Ramadan). There is thus every reason to think that these vigils corresponded originally to a Christian liturgical practice connected to the birth of Jesus Christ, and which was later adopted by Islam, but re-interpreted by Islamic theology to mean the descent of the Koran."[52]

A close textual analysis supports this argument. *Al-qadr*, the Arabic word for "power," also means "fate" or "destiny." Luxenberg observes that the Syriac *qaaf-daal-raa*—the *q-d-r* root of the Arabic word *al-qadr*—has three meanings, designating "i) the birth (meaning the moment of birth); ii) the star under which one is born and which determines the fate of the newly born; iii) The Nativity, or Christmas." He continues: "Thus defined, the term *al-qadr*, 'destiny,' is related to the star of birth, which the Koranic *al qadr* applies, in the context of this sura, to the Star of Christmas. As a result, a connection is found to be established with Matthew II.2, 'Saying, Where is he that is born King of the Jews? For we have seen his star in the East and are come to worship him.'"[53] Then the verse "the Night of Power is better than a thousand months" (97:4) would be rendered "Christmas night is better than a thousand vigils."[54]

The Qur'an concludes the Night of Power passage with "Peace it is, till the rising of dawn" (97:5). Luxenberg notes that this verse "sends us back to the hymn of the Angels cited by Luke II.14: 'Glory to God in the highest and on earth peace, good will toward men.' This chant of the Angels has always constituted the principal theme of the Syriac vigils of the Nativity which lasts into Christmas night, with all sorts of hymns, more than all the other vigils." Indeed, in the Syriac Orthodox Church, the Divine Liturgy of the Nativity was traditionally celebrated at dawn, after a nightlong vigil—"Peace it is, till the rising of dawn." [55]

In addition, the thirteenth-century Arabic lexicon *Lisan al-Arab* (*The Language of the Arabs*) quotes the ninth-century Arab philologist al-Asmai referring to a winter night that "lasts so long that all the stars appear during it. It is also the night of the birth of Jesus—on our Prophet and on him blessing and well-being—and the Christians honour it and hold vigils during it." [56]

In time, however, this connection was forgotten, such that, says Luxenberg, "the Muslims of today are no longer aware that the night that they celebrate and honour with so much fervour is in reality the night of Christmas." [57]

## Who Is Responsible?

Clearly the text of the Qur'an has been worked over. Even Islamic scholars acknowledge that diacritical marks were added to the Arabic, and that other additions were made after the revelation of the Qur'an. And as we have seen, a host of other evidence indicates that much of the text was reworked from Christian source material.

But who would have taken this Christian text and adulterated it, and why? If a new religious text or even a new religion had to be constructed, why not start from scratch rather than rework existing material? The answers to these questions are elusive, although a number of clues enable us to piece together a coherent narrative. In order to do that, we must first examine the history of the Qur'an after it was supposedly collected and distributed by the caliph Uthman.

# 9

---

# Who Collected the Qur'an?

## After Zayd, Still No Qur'an

According to the canonical account of the Qur'an's origins, Muhammad's first successor as leader of the Islamic community, Abu Bakr, commanded the prophet's secretary Zayd ibn Thabit to collect the Qur'an. But once Zayd had finished his task, his Qur'an was not, as one might have expected, distributed among the Muslims. One hadith holds that there weren't even any copies made of it. The original was kept in the home of Abu Bakr and then in the home of his successor, Umar, and then in that of Umar's daughter Hafsa, one of Muhammad's wives.[1]

Years later, in the early 650s, the story goes, a Muslim named Hudhaifa bin al-Yaman approached the caliph Uthman (644–656) about the Qur'an. This was, of course, long after the Battle of Yamama in 632, which Islamic tradition identifies as the first impetus for collecting and standardizing the Qur'anic text. Hudhaifa was concerned about variations in the Qur'an among the Muslims in Syria and Iraq, so he appealed to the caliph to save the situation: "O chief of the Believers! Save this nation before they differ about the Book (Quran) as Jews and the Christians did before."

Uthman responded, according to Islamic tradition, by asking Hafsa to "send us the manuscripts of the Qur'an so that we may compile the Qur'anic materials in perfect copies and return the manuscripts to you." Hafsa sent what she had—presumably Zayd ibn Thabit's Qur'an, but apparently more than just that. Uthman then turned to Zayd, along with three other Muslims, Abdullah ibn Az-Zubair, Said ibn al-As, and Abdur Rahman bin Harith bin Hisham, to make copies. He told Abdullah, Said, and Abdur Rahman: "In case you disagree with Zaid bin Thabit on any point in the Qur'an, then write it in the dialect of Quraish, the Qur'an was revealed in their tongue." This order demonstrates that there were disagreements among the various manuscripts that Uthman now wanted standardized.

It also reveals another curiosity: The Quraysh were the Arabs of Mecca; Muhammad was of the Quraysh. It is very strange, then, that Uthman would have needed to issue an explicit order to harmonize the diverging Qur'anic traditions in accord with the Qurashi dialect. If Muhammad were really the source of it all, presumably it would have been in the Qurashi dialect. Of course, some of the material may have been altered in transmission—or it may have not been written in the Quraysh's dialect of Arabic in the first place. Maybe, given the Qur'an's numerous non-Arabic features, it even originated elsewhere, outside of Arabia altogether.

In any case, while standardizing the Qur'an, Zayd ibn Thabit was saved once more by Khuzaima. When Zayd was collecting the Qur'an for Abu Bakr, Khuzaima pointed out two verses that the scribe had overlooked. Now Khuzaima recalled still another portion that otherwise would have been omitted. A hadith has Zayd recall: "When we collected the fragmentary manuscripts of the Qur'an into copies, I missed one of the Verses of *Surat Al-Ahzab* [sura 33] which I used to hear Allah's Messenger reciting. Finally, I did not find it with anybody except Khuzaima Al-Ansari, whose witness was considered by Allah's Messenger equal to the witness of two men. (And that verse was): 'Among the Believers are men who have been true in their covenant with Allah . . .' (33.23)."[2] That separate reports exist depicting Khuzaima saving a portion of the Qur'an that would otherwise have been lost—a different portion in each case—is yet another indication that these reports are themselves the product of legendary elaboration, not scrupulous historical reportage.

Once his commission's work was done, around the year 653, Uthman is supposed to have sent back Hafsa's manuscripts and distributed the final version to all the Islamic provinces. He ordered any other Qur'anic material already in the provinces to be burned. The canonical Islamic accounts say that Hafsa's manuscripts were spared, but the governor of Medina, Marwan ibn al-Hakam, who was later to become caliph, is supposed to have burned them, too, after Hafsa died in 665.[3]

## The Qur'an and the Battle of Siffin

If Uthman really distributed copies of a standardized Qur'an throughout the Islamic provinces, the contents of the book would have become generally known among Muslims. Sure enough, Islamic tradition has it that the Qur'an was widely copied and universally known only four years after Uthman completed his task, when the Battle of Siffin is supposed to have occurred. The battle, in a village on the banks of the Euphrates River in Syria, pitted two rival claimants for the caliphate against each other: Ali ibn Abi Talib and Muawiya ibn Abi Sufyan.

According to Islamic accounts of the battle, the hostilities began when Muawiya brought a Syrian force to contest Ali's having been chosen to succeed Uthman, who had just been murdered. Addressing the Syrians, Ali invoked the Qur'an: "I have given you time so that you might revert to the truth and turn to it in repentance. I have argued against you with the Book of God and have called you to it, but you have not turned away from oppression or responded to truth."[4] On the eve of battle, he told his own men: "Tomorrow you will meet the enemy, so lengthen the night standing in prayer, make abundant recitation of the Qur'an, and ask God for help and steadfastness."[5] One of his commanders exhorted his men in a similar way: "Fight the crude tyrants and do not fear them. How can you fear them when you have in your hands the Book of God in purity and reverence?"[6]

The battle was hotly contested and protracted. Finally, when it looked as if victory was in sight for Ali, one of Muawiya's commanders, Amr ibn al-As, offered his chief a plan: "What if I put something to you," he said to Muawiya, "that can only increase our unity and their division?" When Muawiya agreed, Amr suggested: "We will raise the *masahif* and say, 'their contents are to be authoritative in our dispute.'"[7] *Al-mushaf*, with its plural *al-masahif*, has been taken in Islamic tradition to refer to a codex of the Qur'an. Muawiya agreed, so his men raised up copies of the Qur'an on their lances and called out to Ali's men: "This is the Book of God between us and you." Ali's pious Muslims responded: "We respond to the Book of God, and we turn in repentance to it."

Amr's plan was a canny one, for Ali had charged that Muawiya's forces were "men without religion and without *qur'an*."[8] He told his men that Muawiya was trying to trick them, but they were impressed by the enemy's maneuver: "If we are called to the Book of God, we are bound to respond." Ali did his best to parry this, but finally two of his men approached him with a warning: "Ali, respond to the Book of God when you are called to it. Otherwise we shall indeed deliver you up entirely to the enemy or do what we did with Ibn 'Affan"—that is, Uthman, who had recently been murdered. "It is our duty," they continued, "to act in accordance with what is in the Book of God. We have accepted it and, by God, if you do not do what we tell you, we will do what we say."[9]

Ultimately, Ali had to relent. He called to his men and told them, "We have agreed to make the Qur'an an authority (*hukm*) between us and them."[10] One of his commanders, Al-Ash'ath, reported to him that "the men all seem satisfied and pleased to respond to the enemy's summons regarding the authority of the Qur'an."[11]

In subsequent truce talks, the two sides reportedly drew up a document in which they mutually agreed to "refer to the Book of

God, from its opening to its close," and "effect what it lays down and eliminate what it does away with."[12]

Thus the entire episode centered on the Qur'an, according to Islamic accounts. But such accounts date from at least two centuries after the event. One of the most detailed and compelling narratives of the battle comes from the Muslim historian Tabari. But Tabari died in 923, 266 years after the Battle of Siffin. His proximity to the events he was writing about would be comparable to that of a writer today publishing one of the first accounts of the War of the Austrian Succession—except Tabari was working in a primarily oral culture, without benefit of any significant written records.

The early records offer nothing to indicate that Ali and Muawiya settled their differences by recourse to the Book of Allah. In fact, as we have seen, the records left behind by the Arab conquerors—the coins they issued, their official inscriptions on public buildings—include no mention of the Qur'an. Thus it is extremely unlikely that Muawiya's partisans raised up copies of the Qur'an on their lances, or that they had copies of the Qur'an at all. In a culture in which every copy of a book had to be painstakingly written out by hand, it is difficult to imagine that these warriors would have had that many copies of the Qur'an on hand so soon after Uthman standardized the text. It is equally difficult to believe that everyone involved—the partisans of Ali and of Muawiya and others as well—would be so familiar with the Qur'an's contents at this early date, in a culture where literacy could not be taken for granted. And even if they somehow managed to secure all these copies of the Qur'an, would they really have risked losing or damaging the "Book of God" in the heat of battle?

Tabari's account of the Battle of Siffin makes for a good story. But it does not hold up as reliable history.

The canonical version of the early Islamic conquests holds that the conquerors stormed out of Arabia with the Qur'an in their hands and Muhammad as their inspiration. At the same time, Islamic tradition situates the collection of the Qur'an during the reign of the caliph Uthman—some two decades after the Arab conquests began.

That means that even according to the canonical account, most, if not all, of the early conquerors could have had only part of the Qur'an with them, if they had any of it at all. It is undeniable that throughout the Middle Ages, at the apex of the great Islamic Empires, Arab and Muslim armies had the words of the Qur'an on their lips as they conquered huge expanses of territory. But in what are generally understood as the earliest days of Islam, when they conquered Syria in 637, Armenia and Egypt in 639, North Africa beginning in the early 650s, and probably Cyprus in 654, there was no Qur'an for them to brandish. Nor is it even certain that they had one for many years after that. Recall that the Qur'an makes no appearance in the surviving documents and artifacts of the Muslims until around six decades after the Arab conquests began.

And when the Qur'an finally emerged, it may have been considerably different from the Qur'an that Muslims revere today.

## Textual Variants and Uncertainty in the Qur'an

The standard Qur'anic text that circulates today is supposed to be based on the version Uthman distributed, but there is no direct evidence of that. Only fragments of Qur'an manuscripts date back to the seventh century. And these fragments mostly do not contain diacritical marks, so it is impossible to confirm that they were written as the Qur'an in the first place, rather than as some other document that was adapted as part of the Qur'an.[13] There is also no telling what textual alterations might have been made before the time of the earliest surviving manuscripts.[14] Historian John Gilchrist notes that the "Samarqand and Topkapi codices are obviously two of the oldest sizeable manuscripts of the Qur'an surviving, but their origin cannot be taken back earlier than the second century of Islam. It must be concluded that no such manuscripts of an earlier date have survived. The oldest manuscripts of the Qur'an still in existence date from not earlier than about one hundred years after Muhammad's death."[15] No complete extant copy of the Qur'an dates from the first century of the Arabian conquests.[16]

Beyond the fact that the text Uthman supposedly collected does not survive, there is also no mention of the Qur'an as such in the available literature until early in the eighth century. What's more, although Uthman supposedly burned other versions of the Qur'an, some variant readings in the Qur'anic text have survived to the present day. To be sure, none of the extant variants is large, but even the smallest is enough to debunk the Islamic apologetic argument that Fethullah Gülen articulated, that the Qur'anic text is reliable because it remains "unaltered, unedited, not tampered with in any way, since the time of its revelation."

The variants begin with the Qur'an's very first sura, the *Fatiha*, or "Opening." This sura is the most common prayer in Islam; a pious Muslim who prays five times a day will repeat it seventeen times daily. As a prayer and a liturgical text, it may have been added to the Qur'an later. According to hadiths, Abdullah ibn Masud, one of Muhammad's companions, did not have this sura in his version of the Qur'an, and other early Islamic authorities expressed reservations about its inclusion also.[17] The sura does not fit in with the rest of the Qur'an, in that it is in the voice of the believer offering prayer and praise to Allah, not Allah addressing Muhammad. Islamic orthodoxy has it that Allah is the speaker in every part of the Qur'an; so with the *Fatiha*, the believer must accept that the deity is explaining how he should be prayed to, without explaining directly that that is what he is doing.

Not only was there early uncertainty about whether the *Fatiha* should be in the Qur'an, but there are also variations in its text. One version of the prayer that circulates among the Shiites says to Allah, "Thou dost direct to the path of the Upright One," rather than the canonical "Show us the Straight Path" (1:6). The historian Arthur Jeffery found in Cairo a manual of Islamic law of the Shafii school that contained the same variant, along with other departures from the canonical text.[18]

## Hafs, Warsh, and Other Variants

The edition of the Qur'an published in Cairo in 1924 has won wide acceptance as an accurate reflection of the Uthmanic text. But little known even among Muslims is the existence of an entirely separate and officially sanctioned manuscript tradition. The Warsh tradition of the Qur'anic text predominates in western and northwest Africa; the Cairo Qur'an represents the more common Hafs tradition.

Most of the differences between the Hafs and Warsh traditions are ones of orthography, some of which can be significant. There are also several instances of small but unmistakable divergences in meaning. In Qur'an 2:125, for example, the Hafs text has Allah commanding the Muslims: "Take the station of Abraham as a place of prayer." The Warsh tradition, however, has no imperative, saying merely: "They have taken the station of Abraham as a place of prayer."[19] In Qur'an 3:13, Allah recalls of the Battle of Badr that there was "one army fighting in the way of Allah, and another disbelieving, whom they saw as twice their number, clearly, with their very eyes." At least so goes the Hafs text. In the Warsh, the pronoun is different, so that the text reads "whom you saw" rather than "whom they saw."[20] In the Hafs Qur'an, sura 3:146 asks, "And with how many a prophet have there been a number of devoted men who fought?" The Warsh question is significantly different: "And with how many a prophet have there been a number of devoted men who were killed?"[21]

In recent decades, numerous other Qur'ans have been published that differ markedly in orthography from the Cairo text.[22] In 1998 the King Fahd Complex for the Printing of the Holy Qur'an released an edition. In this Saudi edition, the *Fatiha* calls Allah "Master of the Day of Judgment" (1:4). The word *malik* means "master" with a long *alif* (a). With a short *alif*, however, the word means "king." "King of the Day of Judgment" is exactly how some other texts of the Qur'an render this verse, including a text published in Istanbul in 1993.[23]

At least one variant in modern Qur'ans involves a flat contradiction. The Hafs tradition presents Qur'an 3:158 this way: "And if you die, or are slain, lo, it is certainly to Allah that you are gathered." On the other hand, a Qur'an published in Tehran in 1978 asserts: "And if you die, or are slain, lo, it is not to Allah that you are gathered."[24]

None of these divergences in meaning (even the contradiction) is so significant as to affect Islamic doctrine or practice. But the very existence of discrepancies, like the many hints of a Christian Syriac substratum, suggests that the Qur'an is the product of many hands and that its text was at one point considerably more fluid than Islamic orthodoxy acknowledges. In an examination of Islam's origins, this fluidity becomes a matter of no small significance. Like so much else about the accepted story of how Islam began, the standard Islamic account of how the Qur'an came about falters in the face of the facts.

Once it becomes clear that the Qur'an was not a single unified text in every time and place in which it was distributed, the responsible historian has no choice but to look for alternative explanations for the Qur'an's origins.

## The First Mention of the Qur'an

If the canonical stories about Zayd ibn Thabit and Uthman were true, one would expect to see references to the Qur'an in other records. But no such references are to be found in the historical records of the mid-seventh century. As we have seen, the coinage of the early caliphate and the edifices that survive from that period bear no Qur'anic inscriptions, quotes, or references of any kind. And although the Arab invaders poured through the Middle East and North Africa, the peoples they conquered seemed to have no idea that the conquerors, whom they called "Hagarians," "Saracens," "Muhajirun" or "Ishmaelites," had a holy book at all. Christian and Jewish writers of the period never made even the smallest reference to such a book.

Not until the early part of the eighth century did mentions of the Qur'an begin to appear in the polemical literature of non-Muslims and Muslims alike. The first reference to the Qur'an by a non-Muslim

occurred around the year 710—eighty years after the book was supposedly completed and sixty years after it was supposedly collected
and distributed. During a debate with an Arab noble, a Christian
monk in the Middle East cited the Qur'an by name. The monk wrote,
"I think that for you, too, not all your laws and commandments are
in the Qur'an which Muhammad taught you; rather there are some
which he taught you from the Qur'an, and some are in *surat albaqrah*
and in *gygy* and in *twrh*."[25]

By this point Arab armies had conquered a huge expanse of territory, stretching from North Africa, across the Levant, Syria, and Iraq,
and into Persia, and yet those eight decades of conquest had produced
scarcely a mention of the book that supposedly inspired them. And
when the Qur'an finally was mentioned, it appears that the book was
not even in the form we now know. *Surat albaqrah* (or *al-Baqara*) is
"the chapter of the Cow," which is the second, and longest, sura of
the Qur'an. The eighth-century monk thus quite clearly knew of a
Qur'an that didn't contain this sura; he considered *surat albaqrah* to
be a stand-alone book, along with *gygy* (the Injil, or Gospel) and *twrh*
(the Torah). It is unlikely that the monk simply made an error: Who
ever mistakes a chapter of a book for a separate book? If the Qur'an's
largest sura was not present in the Muslim holy book by the early
eighth century, it could not have been added by Muhammad, Zayd
ibn Thabit, or Uthman.

There is other evidence that the "chapter of the Cow" existed as
a separate book and was added to the Qur'an only at a later date. As
noted, John of Damascus, writing around 730, referred to the "text
of the Cow" (as well as the "text of the Woman" and the "text of
the Camel of God"), giving the impression that it existed as a stand-
alone text. Even Islamic tradition points to the "chapter of the Cow"
as a separate book. The Islamic chronicler Qatada ibn Diama (d. 735)
made one of the earliest references to any part of the Qur'an by a
Muslim. He recorded that during the Battle of Hunayn in 630, during the lifetime of Muhammad, Muhammad's uncle al-Abbas rallied
the troops by crying out, "O companions of the chapter of the Cow

[*ya ashab surat al-Baqara*]!"[26] Qatada ibn Diama did not have al-Abbas saying, "O companion of the Qur'an," but instead fixed on one sura of the Muslim holy book, albeit its longest and arguably most important one. This suggests that even by Qatada's time, the Qur'an was not yet fixed in its present form.

## Abd al-Malik and Hajjaj ibn Yusuf: Collectors of the Qur'an?

In light of all this evidence, the Islamic traditions pointing to the caliph Abd al-Malik and his associate Hajjaj ibn Yusuf as collectors of the Qur'an take on new significance. Abd al-Malik, who reigned from 685 to 705, claimed to have been responsible for the collection of the Qur'an when he said: "I fear death in the month of Ramadan—in it I was born, in it I was weaned, in it I have collected the Qur'an (*jama'tul-Qur'ana*), and in it I was elected caliph."[27] Remember, too, the hadiths that record Hajjaj ibn Yusuf as collecting and editing the Qur'an during Abd al-Malik's caliphate.

From the historical records available to us, it makes sense that the Qur'an was not collected until Abd al-Malik's reign. If Uthman had indeed collected the standard book and sent copies to all the Muslim provinces in the 650s, it is inexplicable that the Muslims would have made no reference to it for decades thereafter. The first Qur'anic references, as we have seen, did not appear until the time of Abd al Malik and his Dome of the Rock Inscriptions. And even then, it is not certain whether the inscriptions were quoting the Qur'an or the Qur'an was quoting the inscriptions.

Among the hadiths pointing to Hajjaj ibn Yusuf as a collector of the Qur'an, one cites a Muslim recalling: "I heard al-Hajjaj b. Yusuf say, in a speech delivered from the pulpit (*minbar*), 'compose the Qur'an as Gabriel composed it: the writings that include the mention of the cow, and the writings that include mention of women, and the writings that include mention of the family of 'Imran.'"[28] The Cow is sura 2 in the standard text of the Qur'an; Women is sura 4; and the Family of Imran is sura 3. This hadith thus suggests that the Qur'an had not yet been collected at the time of Abd al-Malik and Hajjaj. The fact that Hajjaj mentioned the suras out of their canonical order adds to that impression, for one who knew Hajjaj well recalled: "When I heard al-Hajjaj reading, I realized that he had long studied the Qur'an."[29] Hajjaj is even said to have altered eleven words of the Qur'anic text.[30]

Hadiths show Hajjaj throwing himself into the work of collecting the Qur'an. One reports him as taking to the task with an incandescent ferocity; in the hadith, he pronounced that if he heard anyone reading from the Qur'an of Abdullah ibn Masud, "I will kill him, and I will even rub his *mushaf* with a side of pork."[31] On occasion he even dared to boast about his work. When Muhammad died, the prophet's slave Umm Ayman (who had been his daughter-in-law, as the wife of his former adopted son, Zayd) cried disconsolately: "I know well that God's Messenger has left for something better than this lowly world. I am crying because the inspiration has stopped." When Hajjaj heard about what Umm Ayman had said, he responded: "Umm Ayman lied: I only work by inspiration."[32] Such a statement is placed in the context of Hajjaj's work on the Qur'an. Of course, the Abbasids, who replaced the Umayyads, are known to have fabricated numerous hadiths portraying their rivals in a bad light. So this hadith may have been an invention of Hajjaj's enemies, along with Hajjaj's more famous, or notorious, statement to Abd al-Malik that Allah's caliph was more important to him than his prophet.[33] Even if that is the case, however, it testifies to Hajjaj's fame as the editor of the Qur'an—if not its actual author.

Like Uthman, Hajjaj is said to have sent official copies of his revised Qur'an to all the Muslim provinces. The jurist Malik ibn Anas (d. 795) said that al-Hajjaj "sent the *mushaf* [the codex of the Qur'an] to the capitals. He sent a large one to Medina. He was the first to send the *mushaf* to the cities."[34] Also like Uthman in the canonical account, Hajjaj ordered all variants burned. The original copy that Uthman approved did not survive, even according to Islamic tradition. A hadith holds that when Hajjaj's *mushaf* arrived in Medina, Uthman's family indignantly asked that it be compared with the Qur'an of their illustrious forbear, saying, "Get out the *mushaf* of Uthman b. Affan, so that we may read it."[35] Someone asked Malik ibn Anas what had happened to it; Malik answered, "It has disappeared."[36] It was said to have been destroyed on the same day Uthman was assassinated.[37]

Coming from hadiths, the information about Hajjaj and the collection of the Qur'an has no more presumption of authenticity than the reports in any other hadith. But it is easy to understand why Hajjaj and Abd al-Malik, if they were collecting and editing the Qur'an, would have ascribed their work to Uthman, so as to give it a patina of authority and authenticity. It is much harder to understand why any Muslim would have invented hadiths saying that Abd al-Malik and Hajjaj did this work if Uthman had already done it decades earlier and the standardized Qur'an had been available throughout the Islamic world all that time.

In any case, hadiths are not the only sources for the claim that Abd al-Malik and Hajjaj collected the Qur'an. Another indication appears in polemical letters that the iconoclastic Byzantine emperor Leo III the Isaurian (717–741) purportedly wrote to the caliph Umar II (717–720). No text of these letters survives that goes back earlier than the late eighth century, so it cannot be said with certainty that Leo III actually wrote them, at least in the form in which they have come down to us.[38] Nonetheless, the letters offer evidence that the Qur'an was widely believed to be Hajjaj's work:

It was 'Umar, Abu Turab and Salman the Persian who composed that ("your *P'ourkan*" [or *Furqan*]), even though the rumour has got around among you that God sent it down from the heavens. . . . As for your [Book], you have already given us examples of such falsifications and one knows among others of a certain Hajjaj, named by you as governor of Persia, who had men gather your ancient books, which he replaced by others composed by himself according to his taste and which he disseminated everywhere in your nation, because it was easier by far to undertake such a task among a people speaking a single language. From this destruction, nonetheless, there escaped a few of the works of Abu Turab, for Hajjaj could not make them disappear completely.[39]

Abu Turab, "Father of the Soil," was a title of Ali ibn Abi Talib—earned by his many prayers, which involved prostrations that resulted in a permanent mark on his forehead.

The Christian al-Kindi, who wrote between 813 and 833—well before the most authoritative Hadith collections came together—asserted that Hajjaj "gathered together every single copy" of the Qur'an he could find "and caused to be omitted from the text a great many passages. Among these, they say, were verses revealed concerning the House of Umayyah with names of certain persons, and concerning the House of Abbas also with names." Then Hajjaj "called in and destroyed all the preceding copies, even as Uthman had done before him."[40]

Al-Kindi contended that the text of the Qur'an had been altered, noting that "the enmity subsisting between Ali and Abu Bakr, Umar and Uthman is well known; now each of these entered in the text whatever favored his own claims, and left out what was otherwise. How, then, can we distinguish between the genuine and the counterfeit?"[41] He continued: "And what about the losses caused by Hajjaj? . . . How can we make an arbiter as to the Book of God a man who never ceased to play into the hands of the Umayyads whenever he found opportunity?"[42]

How indeed? The answer to al-Kindi's question is not clear. What can be determined is that the dominant Qur'anic text today appears to derive from Hajjaj, not Uthman.

## Shaky Foundations

Even if the Dome of the Rock inscriptions are taken at face value as a declaration of the Islamic faith as we know it today, it is exceedingly strange that they are the first clear declaration of Islamic faith. Dating from 691, they were written six decades after the Arab conquests began. Meanwhile, the textual variants in the Qur'an are striking enough simply for existing; after all, if the Qur'an was standardized and distributed early on, and the alternate copies burned, variants should not have emerged. Similarly, if it was well established that Uthman collected the Qur'an, and if a common Qur'an was in widespread use among the early Arab conquerors, there is no clear reason why alternative explanations for the origins of the book would have been invented.

All this and, as we have seen, much more demonstrates that the canonical account of the origins of Islam is far shakier than most people realize.

# 10

## Making Sense of It All

### The Canonical Story

In broad outline, the accepted story of Islam's origins is well known. It begins with an Arabian merchant of the Quraysh tribe of Mecca, known to the world as Muhammad, a name that means the "praised one." He rejected the polytheism of his tribe and was given to frequent prayer in the hills and caves outside Mecca. In the year 610, when he was forty, he was praying in a cave on Mount Hira, about two miles from Mecca, when he was suddenly confronted by the angel Gabriel, who commanded him to *recite*.

For the next twenty-three years, until his death in 632, Muhammad did just that: He recited the messages he received from Gabriel, presenting them to his followers as the pure and unadulterated word of the supreme and only God. Many of his followers memorized portions. The Arabia in which Islam was born was an oral culture that respected poetic achievement, and thus the prodigious feats of memory required to memorize lengthy suras were not so unusual. After Muhammad's death, the revelations he had received were collected together into the Qur'an, or "Recitation," from the accounts of those who had memorized them or written them down.

Muhammad began his career simply as a preacher of religious ideas. But his uncompromising monotheism cut directly against the entrenched polytheism of the Quraysh—and against their lucrative business in the Ka'ba, the shrine that attracted pilgrims from all over Arabia. The Quraysh scoffed at the preacher, his words of Allah, and his prophetic pretensions. Tensions steadily increased until finally Muhammad fled from Mecca after learning of a plot afoot to assassinate him. In 622 he and the Muslims left Mecca and settled in the city of Yathrib. This was the *hijra*, or flight, which marks the beginning of the Islamic calendar (years are given as "A.H.," after the Hijra). Because of this momentous migration, Yathrib came to be known as the *Madinat an-Nabi*, or the City of the Prophet—Medina.

Once the Muslims were in Medina, the revelations Muhammad received began to change in character. In addition to warning of the impending judgment of Allah, he called the believers to take up arms in the defense of the new community and ultimately to fight offensive wars against nonbelievers. Muhammad himself led the Muslims into battle against the Quraysh and other pagan Arab tribes. This series of battles forms the backbone of Islamic salvation history, illustrating the core point that obedience to Allah brings success in this world as well as the next, and that the converse is also true: Disobedience will bring earthly disaster as well as hellfire.

After Muhammad died, his teachings lived on. Muslim warriors, energized by the prophet's exhortations to jihad and his example in unifying Arabia, embarked on a series of conquests unprecedented in their breadth and swiftness: Syria and the Holy Land by 637, Armenia and Egypt in 639, Cyprus in 654, and North Africa in the 650s and 660s. By 674 the Muslims were besieging Constantinople, the capital of the Byzantine Empire. A century after the death of their warrior prophet, they controlled a vast empire stretching across the Middle East and North Africa. Even as the Islamic Empire's political fortunes waned, its cultural and religious grip did not loosen: Now fourteen hundred years after its birth, Islam has receded from only a handful of areas it conquered.

And it all depends on the words and example of Muhammad, the last prophet.

Muslims around the globe, who number more than a billion,

are not the only ones who take this account for granted; even non-Muslims generally accept the broad contours of this narrative, which has been told and retold for centuries.

By now, however, it is clear that, aside from the Arab conquests themselves, virtually none of the standard account could have happened as stated.

## A Revisionist Scenario

After the investigations of the preceding chapters, here is what we know about the traditional account of Muhammad's life and the early days of Islam:

◈ No record of Muhammad's reported death in 632 appears until more than a century after that date.

◈ A Christian account apparently dating from the mid-630s speaks of an Arab prophet "armed with a sword" who seems to be still alive.

◈ The early accounts written by the people the Arabs conquered never mention Islam, Muhammad, or the Qur'an. They call the conquerors "Ishmaelites," "Saracens," "Muhajirun," and "Hagarians," but never "Muslims."[1]

◈ The Arab conquerors, in their coins and inscriptions, don't mention Islam or the Qur'an for the first six decades of their conquests. Mentions of "Muhammad" are non-specific and on at least two occasions are accompanied by a cross. The word can be used not only as a proper name but also as an honorific.

◈ The Qur'an, even by the canonical Muslim account, was not distributed in its present form until the 650s. Contradicting that standard account is the fact that neither the Arabians nor the Christians and Jews in the region mention the Qur'an until the early eighth century.

◈ During the reign of the caliph Muawiya (661–680), the Arabs constructed at least one public building whose inscription was headed by a cross.

◈ We begin hearing about Muhammad, the prophet of Islam, and about Islam itself in the 690s, during the reign of the caliph Abd al-Malik. Coins and inscriptions reflecting Islamic beliefs begin to appear at this time also.

◈ Around the same time, Arabic became the predominant written language of the Arabian Empire, supplanting Syriac and Greek.

◈ Abd al-Malik claimed, in a passing remark in one hadith, to have collected the Qur'an, contradicting Islamic tradition that the collection was the work of the caliph Uthman forty years earlier.

◈ Multiple hadiths report that Hajjaj ibn Yusuf, governor of Iraq during the reign of Abd al-Malik, edited the Qur'an and distributed his new edition to the various Arab-controlled provinces—again, something Uthman is supposed to have done decades earlier.

◈ Even some Islamic traditions maintain that certain common Islamic practices, such as the recitation of the Qur'an during mosque prayers, date from orders of Hajjaj ibn Yusuf, not to the earliest period of Islamic history.

◈ In the middle of the eighth century, the Abbasid dynasty supplanted the Umayyad line of Abd al-Malik. The Abbasids charged the Umayyads with impiety on a large scale. In the Abbasid period, biographical material about Muhammad began to proliferate. The first complete biography of the prophet of Islam finally appeared during this era—at least 125 years after the traditional date of his death.

◈ The biographical material that emerged situates Muhammad in an area of Arabia that never was the center for trade and pilgrimage that the canonical Islamic account of Islam's origins depends on it to be.

In short, the lack of confirming detail in the historical record, the late development of biographical material about the Islamic prophet, the atmosphere of political and religious factionalism in which that material developed, and much more suggest that the Muhammad of Islamic tradition did not exist, or if he did, he was substantially different from how that tradition portrays him.

How to make sense of all this? If the Arab forces who conquered so much territory beginning in the 630s were not energized by the teachings of a new prophet and the divine word he delivered, how did the Islamic character of their empire arise at all? If Muhammad did not exist, why was it ever considered necessary to invent him?

Any answer to these questions will of necessity be conjectural—but in light of the facts above, so is the canonical account of Islam's origins.

## The Creation of the Hero

The immutable fact in this entire discussion is the Arab Empire. The Arab conquests (whatever may have precipitated them) and the empire they produced are a matter of historical record. Some historians have minimized the martial aspect of the Arab conquests, contending that the Byzantines were exhausted after their protracted wars with the Persians and simply withdrew from the area, leaving a vacuum that the Arabs filled.[2] That may be true to a degree,[3] but in any case, the result was the same: The Arabs built a mighty empire.

Every empire of the day was anchored in a political theology. The Romans conquered many nations and unified them by means of the worship of the Greco-Roman gods. This Greco-Roman paganism was later supplanted by Christianity. The Christological controversies of the early Church threatened to tear the empire asunder, so much so that the newly Christian emperors felt compelled to get involved in ecclesiastical affairs. They called the first ecumenical councils primarily to secure unity within the empire, and the Christology of the first four councils became so closely identified with the empire in the East that to oppose one was essentially to oppose the other. Many of the Christian groups whom the ecumenical councils deemed heretical left the empire.

The realm of political theology, then, offers the most plausible explanation for the creation of Islam, Muhammad, and the Qur'an. The Arab Empire controlled and needed to unify huge expanses of territory where different religions predominated. Arabia, Syria, and other lands the Arabs first conquered were home to many of the Christian groups, such as Nestorians and Jacobites, that had fled the Byzantine Empire after the ecumenical councils judged their views heretical. Persia, meanwhile, was home to Zoroastrians. These monotheists had an imperial theology—that is, a conviction that a common religion would unify an empire of diverse nationalities—akin to that of the Romans and to some degree even based on it. This influence was understandable, given that the Persian emperor Chosroes had spent time in Constantinople and was married to two Christian women.[4]

But at first, the Arab Empire did not have a compelling political theology to compete with those it supplanted and to solidify its conquests. The earliest Arab rulers appear to have been adherents of Hagarism, a monotheistic religion centered around Abraham and Ishmael.[5] They frowned upon the Christian doctrines of the Trinity and the divinity of Christ—hence Muawiya's letter to the Byzantine emperor Constantine, calling on him to "renounce this Jesus and convert to the great God whom I serve, the God of our father Abraham."

This umbrella monotheistic movement saw itself as encompassing the true forms of the two great previous monotheistic movements, Judaism and Christianity. Traces of this perspective appear in the Qur'an, such as when Allah scolds the Jews and Christians for fighting over Abraham, who was neither a Jew nor a Christian but a Muslim *hanif*—in the Qur'anic usage, a pre-Islamic monotheist (3:64–67). In its earliest form, Islam was probably much more positive toward both Christianity and Judaism than it later came to be. Evidence of this openness can be found in the crosses on the early Arab coinage and caliphs' inscriptions, and also in the indications from adversarial literature that the Arabian prophet was making common cause with the Jews. An early Islam that counted Jews and Christians as within the fold could help account for the Qur'an passage promising salvation to various groups: "Lo! Those who believe, and those who are Jews, and Christians, and Sabaeans—whoever believes in Allah and the Last Day and does right—surely their reward is with their Lord, and there shall no fear come upon them neither shall they grieve" (2:62).[6]

## From Monotheism to Muhammad

This Abrahamic monotheism, conceiving of Christ as the servant of Allah and his messenger, probably reached its apotheosis in 691 in Abd al-Malik's Dome of the Rock inscriptions, which could well refer to Jesus. During the same period, the nascent religion began to take shape as an entity in its own right—a forthrightly, even defiantly, Arabic one. The specific features that emerged revolved around the person of the "praised one," *Muhammad,* an Arabian prophet who may have lived decades before and whose words and works were already shrouded in the mists of history.

The historical data about this Muhammad was sparse and contradictory, but there were certain raw materials around which a legend could be constructed. There was the mysterious Arabian prophet to whom the *Doctrina Jacobi* refers, whose words and deeds somewhat resemble those of the prophet of Islam and differ sharply from them in important ways. There was the *Mhmt* to whom Thomas the Christian priest refers in the 640s, whose *Taiyaye* were doing battle with the Byzantines. There was the Muhammad of the cross-bearing coins struck in the early years of the Arab conquests. Did this "Muhammad" refer to an actual person bearing that name, whose deeds are lost, or was it a title for Jesus, or did it refer to someone or something else altogether? The answer to that is not known.

Whatever the case, the records make clear that toward the end of the seventh century and the beginning of the eighth, the Umayyads began to speak much more specifically about Islam, its prophet, and eventually its book. The Dome of the Rock's insistent assertion that the "praised one" was only Allah's messenger and not divine lent itself well to the creation of a whole new figure distinct from Jesus: a human prophet who came with the definitive message from the supreme God.

Muhammad, if he did not exist, or if his actual deeds were not known, would certainly have been politically useful to the new Arab Empire as a legendary hero. The empire was growing quickly, soon rivaling the Byzantine and Persian Empires in size and power. It needed a common religion—a political theology that would provide the foundation for the empire's unity and would secure allegiance to the state.

This new prophet needed to be an Arab, living deep within Arabia. If he had come from anywhere else within the new empire's territory, that place could have made claims to special status and pushed to gain political power on that basis. Muhammad, significantly, is said to have come from the empire's central region, not from borderlands.

He had to be a warrior prophet, for the new empire was aggressively expansionistic. To give those conquests a theological justification—as Muhammad's teachings and example do—would place them beyond criticism.

This prophet would also need a sacred scripture to lend him authority. Much of the Qur'an shows signs of having been borrowed from the Jewish and Christian traditions, suggesting that the founders of Islam fashioned its scripture from existing material. As Arabians, the conquerors wanted to establish their empire with Arabic elements at its center: an Arabian prophet and an Arabic revelation. The new scripture thus needed to be in Arabic in order to serve as the foundation for an Arabic Empire. But it did not have an extensive Arabic literary tradition to draw on. Abd al-Malik and his fellow Umayyad caliphs were not even centered in Arabia at that point; their conquest had brought them to Damascus. It is perhaps no coincidence that the Qur'an betrays many Syriac influences. This Arabic scripture contains numerous non-Arabic elements and outright incoherencies.

## Demonizing the Umayyads

Although the Qur'an issues furious warnings of judgment and divine exhortations to warfare and martyrdom that would have been useful for an expanding empire, it leaves the figure of Muhammad, the "praised one," sketchy at best. By investing Muhammad with prophetic status and holding him up as the "excellent example" of conduct for the Muslims (33:21), the Qur'an sparked a hunger to know what he actually said and did. Thus a larger body of traditions painting the picture of this prophet would have been necessary, not only as a matter of pious interest but also to formulate Islamic law.

The real proliferation of material about Muhammad's words and deeds apparently began in the late Umayyad period but reached its apex during the Abbasid caliphate. The Abbasids replaced the Umayyads in 750; the great canonical Hadith collections were all compiled early in the ninth century.

Hadiths about Muhammad, as we have seen, were minted by the dozen in order to support one political position or another. The Umayyads created hadiths of Muhammad saying negative things about the Abbasids; the Abbasids developed hadiths in which Muhammad said exactly the opposite. The Shiites wrote hadiths of their own to support their champion, Ali ibn Abi Talib.

The Abbasids emerged as the dominant party, and not surprisingly the bulk of the traditions that survive to the present day reflect favorably on them. Many hadiths denounce the Umayyads for their irreligion. But the desire to portray their rivals in a bad light would not have been the only motivation for the Abbasids. They also needed to convince the people that these stories about the prophet of Islam and his new religion were actually not new at all. How to explain the sudden appearance of accounts of what had supposedly taken place in Arabia well over a century earlier? How to explain the fact that fathers and fathers' fathers had not passed down the stories of this great warrior prophet and his wondrous divine book?

The answer was to blame the Umayyads. They were impious. They were irreligious. Although they were the sons and immediate heirs of those who had known Muhammad, they were indifferent to this legacy and let the great message of the Seal of the Prophets fall by the wayside. Now the Abbasids had come along and—Muhammad emerged! His teachings would be taught throughout the empire. His Qur'an would sound from every mosque. His faithful would be called to prayer from every minaret.

The late appearance of the biographical material about Muhammad, the fact that no one had heard of or spoken of Muhammad for decades after the Arab conquests began, the changes in the religion of the Arab Empire, the inconsistencies in the Qur'an—all of this needed to be explained. The hadiths pinning blame on the Umayyads helped, but other explanations would have been necessary, too. A common justification emerged in the hadiths: It was all part of the divine plan. Allah caused even Muhammad to forget portions of the Qur'an. He left the collection of that divine book up to people who lost parts of it—hence its late editing and the existence of variants. It was all in his plan and thus should not disturb the faith of the pious.

### Explaining a Political Religion

This reconstruction of events has a good deal to recommend it. It explains the curious silence of the early Arab conquerors, and of those whom they conquered, about Muhammad and the Qur'an. It explains why the earliest extant records of an Arab prophet speak of a figure who displayed some kinship with both Judaism and Christianity, contrary to the portrayal of Muhammad in the canonical Islamic texts. It explains why Islamic tradition speaks of the Qur'an as the perfect and eternal book of Allah while simultaneously depicting the almost casual loss of significant portions of the holy book. It explains why Islam, the supposed impetus for the Arab conquests, is such a late arrival on the scene.

This scenario also explains why Islam developed as such a profoundly political religion. By its nature, Islam is a political faith: The divine kingdom is very much of this world, with God's wrath and judgment to be expected not only in the next life but also in this one, to be delivered by believers. In considering its adherents as the instruments of divine justice on earth, Islam departs from its Abrahamic forerunners. This departure could reflect the circumstances of Islam's origins: Whereas Christianity began as a primarily spiritual construct and gained worldly power only much later (forcing its adherents to grapple with the relationship between the spiritual and temporal realms), Islam was unapologetically worldly and political from the beginning.

Allah says in the Qur'an: "As for those disbelieving infidels, I will punish them with a terrible agony in this world and the next. They have no one to help or save them" (3:56). Allah also exhorts Muslims to wage war against those infidels, apostates, and polytheists (2:191, 4:89, 9:5, 9:29). In the Qur'an Allah even commands the Islamic faithful to expand the domains of the believers by waging war against and subjugating those outside the fold (9:29), including those among the "People of the Book" who "disbelieve" (98.6)—in other words, the other monotheists who dare to reject the Qur'an's claims. These various teachings could, and did, coalesce easily in Islamic history: They put vengeance against Allah's enemies into the hands of the faithful.

Compare the perspective on display in such Qur'anic verses with the attitude encapsulated by the lapidary phrase "Vengeance is mine, says the Lord, I will repay" (Deuteronomy 32:35; Romans 12:19). However much Christians at various points in history may have departed from both the letter and the spirit of that directive, the sharp contrast between the two sets of teachings underscores an important difference between the faiths. In one, believers are told, "love your enemies, and pray for those who persecute you" (Matthew 5:44). In the other, they are told, "Muhammad is the Messenger of God, and those who are with him are hard against the unbelievers, merciful one to another" (Qur'an 48:29).

The political, and indeed the martial and imperial, components are intrinsic to the Islamic faith, and they are evident from the earliest records. Did the political arise from the spiritual imperatives of the faith, or was it the other way around? The alternative scenario we have considered explains the uniquely political nature of Islam by suggesting that the empire came first and the theology came later. In this reconstruction, the spiritual propositions that Islam offers were elaborated in order to justify and perpetuate the political entity that generated them.

## Did Muhammad Exist?

Did Muhammad exist? As a prophet of the Arabs who taught a vaguely defined monotheism, he may have existed. But beyond that, his life story is lost in the mists of legend, like those of Robin Hood and Macbeth. As the prophet of Islam, who received (or even claimed to receive) the perfect copy of the perfect eternal book from the supreme God, Muhammad almost certainly did not exist. There are too many gaps, too many silences, too many aspects of the historical record that simply do not accord, and cannot be made to accord, with the traditional account of the Arabian prophet teaching his Qur'an, energizing his followers to such an extent that they went out and conquered a good part of the world.

A careful investigation makes at least one thing clear: The details of Muhammad's life that have been handed down as canonical—that he unified Arabia by the force of arms, concluded alliances, married wives, legislated for his community, and did so much else—are a creation of political ferments dating from long after the time he is supposed to have lived. Similarly, the records strongly indicate that the Qur'an did not exist until long after it was supposed to have been delivered to the prophet of Islam.

In light of this evidence, there is compelling reason to conclude that Muhammad the messenger of Allah came into existence only after the Arab Empire was firmly entrenched and casting about for a political theology to anchor and unify it. Muhammad and the Qur'an cemented the power of the Umayyad caliphate and then that of the Abbasid caliphate. That is the most persuasive explanation for why they were created at all. And once legends about Muhammad began to be elaborated, his story took on a life of its own: One legend begat another, as people hungered to know what their prophet said and did regarding issues that vexed them. Once Muhammad was summoned, he could not be sent away. One pious legend fabricated for political purposes would lead to another, and then another, to fill in holes and address anomalies in the first; then those new stories would lead in turn to still newer ones, until finally the faithful Muslims were able to fill wheelbarrows with volumes of hadiths, as is the case today.

As long as the oddities, inconsistencies, and lacunae exist in the traditional Islamic narratives and the records of early Islam, there will arise people with the courage to seek answers to the questions we have considered here. Up to now, however, those brave scholars have been relatively few in number. This is both unusual and unfortunate. It is unusual in that the world's other major religions have undergone thorough historical investigation; the "quest for the historical Jesus," a parallel to inquiries into the historical Muhammad, has been a prominent field of scholarship for two centuries. It is unfortunate in that the lack of interest in examining Islam's origins, among Muslim and non-Muslim scholars alike, robs everyone of access to the truth.

To be sure, many fervent believers in Islam resist such historical investigation. Even raising the question of whether Muhammad existed challenges the very premise of their belief system. No

Muslim authorities have encouraged such scholarship, and those who have pursued this line of inquiry often labor under threat of death. But scholarly examinations of the origins of Christianity and Judaism have gone forward even as some Christians and Jews, including high religious authorities, condemned these historical inquiries as attempts to undermine their faith. Of course, other authorities have actually approved and even welcomed the inquiries. Islam, however, has remained largely exempt from such scrutiny.

For some fourteen hundred years, Islam has profoundly shaped the history and culture not only of the Near East but also of the entire world. At one point, the Islamic Empire stretched as far west as Spain and as far east as India, as far south as Sudan and as far north as the Caucasus. Over the centuries Islamic forces have repeatedly clashed with Western powers, whether it was in the initial wave of conquests that created the Islamic Empire, the clashes with the Crusaders of the Byzantine Empire over Christian holy lands, or the Ottoman Empire's fierce efforts to control the Mediterranean in the sixteenth century. More recently, of course, the nature of the conflict has changed: No longer are traditional powers facing off on the battlefield; instead, Islamic jihadists are terrorizing unbelievers and seeking in various ways, including nonviolent subversion and the electoral process, to impose sharia law.

This long history of conflict demonstrates that there are pronounced differences between the Islamic tradition and the Judeo-Christian tradition of the West. And yet despite those differences, few have bothered to investigate how the Islamic tradition emerged and what those origins might tell us about the "clash of civilizations" that has been a defining feature of world history for well over a millennium.

Did Muhammad exist? The full truth of whether a prophet named Muhammad lived in seventh-century Arabia, and if he did, what sort of a man he was, may never be known. But it would be intellectually irresponsible not to ask the question or consider the implications of the provocative evidence that pioneering scholars have assembled.

Contrary to the common assumption, Islam and its supposed prophet did not emerge in the "full light of history." Now, more than ever before, historical investigators have the opportunity—in fact, the responsibility—to usher Islam's origins out of the shadows and into the light. Were they not to discharge that responsibility fully or properly, we would all be the poorer.

# Notes

## Introduction: The Full Light of History?

1   Michael H. Hart, *The 100: A Ranking of the Most Influential Persons in History* (New York: Hart Publishing, 1978), 33.

2   W. Montgomery Watt, *Muhammad at Mecca* (Oxford: Oxford University Press, 1953); *Muhammad at Medina* (Oxford: Oxford University Press, 1956).

3   For an illuminating discussion of the effect of higher criticism on the various Christian confessions, see Jaroslav Pelikan, *Christian Doctrine and Modern Culture (since 1700)* (Chicago: University of Chicago Press, 1989).

4   Robert Spencer, *The Truth about Muhammad* (Washington, DC: Regnery, 2006), 9, 31.

5   Gustav Weil, *Geschichte der Chalifen*, vol. 2 (Mannheim, 1846–51), 290, trans. William Muir, *The Life of Mahomet*, one-volume edition (London, 1894), xli–xlii (quoted in Ibn Warraq, ed., *The Quest for the Historical Muhammad* [Amherst, NY: Prometheus, 2000], 44).

6   Quoted in Ibn Warraq, *The Quest for the Historical Muhammad*, 16.

7   Muir, *The Life of Mahomet*, xli–xlii (quoted in Ibn Warraq, *The Quest for the Historical Muhammad*, 44).

8   The word *hadith*'s Arabic plural is *ahadith*, and this is found in much English-language Muslim literature. But to avoid confusing English-speaking readers, I have used the English plural form "hadiths."

9   Quoted in Raphel Patai, *Ignaz Goldziher and His Oriental Diary* (Detroit: Wayne State University Press, 1987), 28 (quoted in Martin Kramer, "Introduction," in *The Jewish Discovery of Islam: Studies in Honor of Bernard Lewis*, ed. Martin Kramer [Syracuse: Syracuse University Press, 1999], 1–48, republished online at http://www.martinkramer.org/sandbox/reader/archives/the-jewish-discovery-of-islam/#n38).

10  Quoted in Ibn Warraq, *The Quest for the Historical Muhammad*, 46.

11  Henri Lammens, "The Age of Muhammad and the Chronology of the Sira," in Ibn Warraq, *The Quest for the Historical Muhammad*, 206.

12  Joseph Schacht, *The Origins of Muhammadan Jurisprudence* (Oxford: Oxford University Press, 1950), 4–5.

13  Patricia Crone and Michael Cook, *Hagarism: The Making of the Islamic World* (Cambridge: Cambridge University Press, 1977), vii.

14  Patricia Crone, "What Do We Actually Know About Muhammad?," *Open Democracy*, August 31, 2006, http://www.opendemocracy.net/faith-europe_islam/mohammed_3866.jsp.

15  For an example of the nature of such responses, see Amaal Muhammad Al-Roubi, *A Response to Patricia Crone's Book ("Meccan Trade and the Rise of Islam")*, www.sultan.org/books/Patricia_crone_english_reply.pdf.

16  Ahmad Ali Al-Imam, *Variant Readings of the Qur'an: A Critical Study of Their Historical and Linguistic Origins* (Washington, DC: International Institute of Islamic Thought, 2006), 112.

17  Andrew Higgins, "Professor Hired for Outreach to Muslims Delivers a Jolt," *Wall Street Journal*, November 15, 2008.

18  "Islam Scientist Kalisch No Longer Muslim," *Politically Incorrect*, April 22, 2010, http://www.pi-news.org/2010/04/islam-scientist-kalisch-no-longer-muslim/.

19  Khaled Abou El Fadl, "On Revising Bigotry," *Scholar of the House*, n.d., http://www.scholarofthehouse.org/onrebi.html.

## Chapter 1: The Man Who Wasn't There

1  Yehuda D. Nevo and Judith Koren, *Crossroads to Islam* (Amherst, NY: Prometheus, 2003), 265.

2  Ibid., 265–66.

3  Quotations from the Qur'an are taken, except where noted, from A. J. Arberry, *The Koran Interpreted* (New York: George Allen & Unwin, Ltd., 1955).

4  *Doctrina Jacobi* vol. 16, 209 (quoted in Robert G. Hoyland, *Seeing Islam as Others Saw It: A Survey and Evaluation of Christian, Jewish, and Zoroastrian Writings on Early Islam* [Princeton: Darwin Press, 1997], 57).

5  Historian Robert G. Hoyland notes that the first editor of this text suggested that it had begun as a continuation of Eusebius's ecclesiastical history and was then updated a century after it was first written: "A mid-seventh century Jacobite author had written a continuation of Eusebius and . . . this had been revised almost a century later when the lists of synods and caliphs and so on were added" (Hoyland, *Seeing Islam*, 119).

6  Thomas the Presbyter, *Chronicle*, 147–48 (quoted in Hoyland, *Seeing Islam*, 120).

7  Nevo and Koren, *Crossroads to Islam*, 264.

8  John Moschus, *Pratum spirituale*, 100–102, Georgian translation, Gérard

Garitte, trans., " 'Histoires édificantes' géorgiennes," *Byzantion* 36 (1966): 414–16 (quoted in Hoyland, *Seeing Islam*, 63).

9   *Homily on the Child Saints of Babylon*, §36 (tr. de Vis, 99–100) (quoted in Hoyland, *Seeing Islam*, 121).

10  Sophronius, *Ep. Synodica, Patrologia Greca* 87, 3197D–3200A (quoted in Hoyland, *Seeing Islam*, 69).

11  Sophronius, *Christmas Sermon*, 506 (quoted in Hoyland, *Seeing Islam*, 70).

12  Sophronius, *Holy Baptism*, 162 (quoted in Hoyland, *Seeing Islam*, 72–73).

13  Steven Runciman, *A History of the Crusades*, vol. 1 (Cambridge: Cambridge University Press, 1951), 3.

14  Ibid., 1:4.

15  On the Pact of Umar, see Mark Cohen, "What Was the Pact of Umar? A Literary-Historical Study," *Jerusalem Studies in Arabic and Islam* 23 (1999), 100–158.

16  Muhammad ibn Jarir at-Tabari, *The History of al-Tabari*, vol. XII, "The Battle of al-Qadisiyyah and the Conquest of Syria and Palestine," trans. Yohanan Friedmann (Albany: State University of New York Press, 1992), 191–92.

17  Quoted in J. B. Chabot, trans. and ed., *Synodicon Orientale*, 3 vols. (Paris: Imprimerie Nationale, 1902), Syriac text, 1:224, French translation, 2:488 (quoted in Nevo and Koren, *Crossroads to Islam*, 218).

18  Quoted in Chabot, *Synodicon Orientale*, Syriac text, vol. 1, 224, French translation, 2:488, Nestorian Synod, 676 C.E., Canon 16 (quoted in Nevo and Koren, *Crossroads to Islam*, 219).

19  Quoted in F. M. Nau, "Littérature Canonique Syriaque Inéditée," *Revue de l'Orient Chrétien* 14 (1909): 128–30 (quoted in Nevo and Koren, *Crossroads to Islam*, 217).

20  Quoted in Nau, "Littérature Canonique Syriaque Inéditée," 128–30 (quoted in Nevo and Koren, *Crossroads to Islam*, 217–18).

21  For more on this from a different perspective, see Fred M. Donner, *Muhammad and the Believers: At the Origins of Islam* (Cambridge, MA: The Belknap Press of Harvard University Press, 2010).

22  Patriarch John–Arab Emir, *Colloquy*, trans. Francois Nau, "Un colloque de patriarche Jean avec l'émir des Agareens et fait divers des années 712 a 716," *Journal Asiatique* 11/5 (1915): 225–79 (quoted in Hoyland, *Seeing Islam*, 459).

23  Alphonse Mingana, "The Transmission of the Koran," in Ibn Warraq, ed., *The Origins of the Koran* (Amherst, NY: Prometheus, 1998), 105.

24  Duval, ed., *Corp. Script. Christ. Orient*, tomus LXIV, 97 (quoted in Mingana, "The Transmission of the Koran," 106).

25  Sebeos, *Histoire d'Héraclius par l'Evêque Sebêos*, trans. Frederic Macler (Paris: 1904), 94–96 (quoted in Patricia Crone and Michael Cook, *Hagarism: The Making of the Islamic World* [Cambridge: Cambridge University Press, 1977], 6–7).

26  See Donner, *Muhammad and the Believers*.

27  Quoted in Sebeos, *Histoire*, 139–40 (translated into English and quoted in Nevo and Koren, *Crossroads to Islam*, 229).

28 *Chronica Minora,* tomus IV, 30, 38, in Duval, ed., *Corp. Script. Christ. Orient* (quoted in Mingana, "The Transmission of the Koran," 106–7).

29 Quoted in Alphonse Mingana, *Sources Syriaques,* vol. 1, pt. 2, 146ff. (quoted in Mingana, "The Transmission of the Koran," 107).

30 *The Chronicle of John (c. 690 A.D.) Coptic Bishop of Nikiu,* trans. and ed. Robert H. Church (London: 1916; reprinted Philo Press), ch. 121, pp. 10–11, 201 (quoted in Nevo and Koren, *Crossroads to Islam,* 233).

31 Nevo and Koren, *Crossroads to Islam,* 234.

32 F. Nau, "Lettre de Jacques d'Edesse sur la généalogie de la sainte Vierge," *Revue de l'Orient Chrétien* (1901): 518–23 (quoted in Nevo and Koren, *Crossroads to Islam,* 235).

33 John of Damascus, *De haeresibus* C/CI, 60–61 (= *Patrologia Greca* 94, 764A–765A) (quoted in Hoyland, *Seeing Islam,* 486).

34 Ibid., 63–64 (= *Patrologia Greca* 94, 765C–769B) (quoted in Hoyland, *Seeing Islam,* 486–87).

35 Ibid., 64–67 (= *Patrologia Greca* 94, 769B–772D) (quoted in Hoyland, *Seeing Islam,* 487).

36 Ibid., 61 (= *Patrologia Greca* 94, 765A–B) (quoted in Hoyland, *Seeing Islam,* 488–89).

## Chapter 2: Jesus, the Muhammad

1 *X* represents the Arabic letter ﺥ, a guttural *kh* sound.

2 Quoted in Nevo and Koren, *Crossroads to Islam,* 409.

3 Contrast this with an inscription on a mosque in Medina, dating from the year 752 (quoted in Nevo and Koren, *Crossroads to Islam,* 421):

> In the name of Allah, the Merciful, the Compassionate! There is no God but Allah alone, He has no *sarik* [companion in worship].
> Muhammad is the servant of Allah and His messenger.
> He it is who sent His messenger with the Guidance and the religion of Truth, to make it victorious over every other religion, even in the face of the *musrikun*'s [polytheists'] dislike and hatred!
> The Servant of God, Commander of the Faithful, has ordered to fear Allah and to obey Him which is to act according to Allah's kitab [book] and the sunnah [accepted practice] of the Prophet . . .

4 Quoted in Nevo and Koren, *Crossroads to Islam,* 411.

5 Nevo and Koren, *Crossroads to Islam,* 250.

6 Clive Foss, *Arab-Byzantine Coins: An Introduction, with a Catalogue of the Dumbarton Oaks Collection* (Washington, DC: Dumbarton Oaks Research Library and Collection, 2008), 34.

7   Ibid.

8   A hadith narrated by Abu Huraira tells us: "Allah's Apostle said, 'By Him in Whose Hands my soul is, surely the son of Maryam (Mary) Iesa (Jesus) will shortly descend amongst you people (Muslims) and will judge mankind justly by the Law of the Qur'an (as a just ruler) and will break the cross and kill the pig and abolish the *Jizya* (a tax taken from the non-Muslims, who are in the protection of the Muslim government). This Jizya tax will not be accepted by Iesa (Jesus). Then there will be abundance of money and nobody will accept charitable gifts.'" Quoted in Muhammad Ibn Ismail al-Bukhari, *Sahih al-Bukhari: The Translation of the Meanings*, trans. Muhammad M. Khan (Riyadh: Darussalam, 1997), vol. 3, book 34, no. 2222.

9   Ahmed ibn Naqib al-Misri, *Reliance of the Traveller ('Umdat as-Salik): A Classic Manual of Islamic Sacred Law*, trans. Nuh Ha Mim Keller (Beltsville, MD: Amana Publications, 1999), 011.5(6).

10  For more on this from a different perspective, see Donner, *Muhammad and the Believers.*

11  Volker Popp, "The Early History of Islam, Following Inscriptional and Numismatic Testimony," in Karl-Heinz Ohlig and Gerd-R. Puin, eds., *The Hidden Origins of Islam* (Amherst, NY: Prometheus, 2010), 55.

12  Popp, "The Early History of Islam," 113.

13  Ibid., 55, 56.

14  Ibid., 55.

15  Nevo and Koren, *Crossroads to Islam,* 265 66. The translation of the Qur'anic texts here is that of Nevo and Koren.

16  Ibn Ishaq, *The Life of Muhammad: A Translation of Ibn Ishaq's Sirat Rasul Allah*, trans. Alfred Guillaume (Oxford: Oxford University Press, 1955), 104; Ibn Warraq, *Virgins? What Virgins? And Other Essays* (Amherst, NY: Prometheus, 2010), 50.

17  Alfred Guillaume, "The Version of the Gospels Used in Medina Circa 700 A.D.," *Al-Andalus* 15 (1950): 289–96 (quoted in Ibn Warraq, *Virgins?*, 50).

18  Foss, *Arab-Byzantine Coins*, 34.

19  Ibid., 47.

20  See Donner, *Muhammad and the Believers.*

21  Popp, "The Early History of Islam," 34–36.

22  Foss, *Arab-Byzantine Coins*, 118.

23  Quoted in Nevo and Koren, *Crossroads to Islam*, 377.

24  Nevo and Koren, *Crossroads to Islam*, 383.

25  Yazid was famous as a falconer, and the ruler on this coin is depicted with a bird on his wrist. Foss, *Arab-Byzantine Coins*, 48.

26  See Christoph Luxenberg, "A New Interpretation of the Arabic Inscription in Jerusalem's Dome of the Rock," in Ohlig and Puin, *The Hidden Origins of Islam.*

27  Estelle Whelan, "Forgotten Witness: Evidence for the Early Codification of the Qur'an," *Journal of the American Oriental Society*, 118 (1998): 1–14, reprinted at

http://www.islamic-awareness.org/History/Islam/Dome_Of_The_Rock/Estwitness. html. The bracketed material is in the translation of the inscription as Whelan published it and has not been added by the present author. For more on the Dome of the Rock inscription, see Oleg Grabar, *The Dome of the Rock* (Cambridge, MA: Harvard University Press, 2006), and Donner, *Muhammad and the Believers*. The Qur'an quotations are as in Whelan's translation.

28  Whelan, "Forgotten Witness," reprinted at http://www.islamic-awareness.org/ History/Islam/Dome_Of_The_Rock/Estwitness.html.

29  Luxenberg, "A New Interpretation," 130.

30  Ibid., 128–29.

31  See Karl-Heinz Ohlig, "Syrian and Arabian Christianity and the Qur'an," in Ohlig and Puin, *The Hidden Origins of Islam*, 361–402.

32  Quoted in Nevo and Koren, *Crossroads to Islam*, 411.

33  Foss, *Arab-Byzantine Coins*, 59.

34  Ibid., 110.

35  Hoyland, *Seeing Islam*, 553.

36  Foss, *Arab-Byzantine Coins*, 60.

37  Hoyland, *Seeing Islam*, 551.

38  John bar Penkaye, *Ktaba d-rish melle*, 155/183, in Sebastian P. Brock, trans., "North Mesopotamia in the Late Seventh Century: Book XV of John bar Penkaye's *Ris Melle*," *Jerusalem Studies in Arabic and Islam* 9 (1987), 64 (quoted in Hoyland, *Seeing Islam*, 552).

39  Nevo and Koren, *Crossroads to Islam*, 250–51.

40  Foss, *Arab-Byzantine Coins*, 63, 65.

41  Mingana, "The Transmission of the Koran," 102–3.

42  Fred M. Donner, "The Qur'an in Recent Scholarship," in Gabriel Said Reynolds, ed., *The Qur'an in Its Historical Context* (New York: Routledge, 2008), 35–36.

43  Ali al-Samhudi, *Wafa al-Wafa bi-akhbar dar al-Mustafa*, ed. Muhammad Muhyi I-Din Abd al-Hamid (Cairo, 1955; repr. Beyrouth: Dar al-Kutub al-Ilmiyya, 1984), 4 parts in 3 vols. (quoted in Alfred-Louis de Prémare, "'Abd al-Malik b. Marwan and the Process of the Qur'an's Composition," in Ohlig and Puin, *The Hidden Origins of Islam*, 205).

44  Ibn Hajar, *Tahdhib*, 2:185n388 (quoted in Prémare, "Abd al-Malik b. Marwan," 199).

45  Quoted in Nevo and Koren, *Crossroads to Islam*, 387, 389.

46  Quoted in Nevo and Koren, *Crossroads to Islam*, 397.

## Chapter 3: Inventing Muhammad

1  Muhammad Ibn Ismail al-Bukhari, *Sahih al-Bukhari: The Translation of the Meanings*, trans. Muhammad M. Khan (Riyadh: Darussalam, 1997), vol. 6, book 65, no. 4584.

2 *Asbab Al-Nuzul by Al-Wahidi*, trans. Mokrane Guezzou, on Qur'an 2:44, http://www.altafsir.com/AsbabAlnuzol.asp?SoraName=2&Ayah=44&search =yes&img=A.

3 *Al-Wahidi*, on Qur'an 5:67.

4 Abu Dawud, 2:31 (quoted in Ignaz Goldziher, *Muslim Studies*, trans. C. R. Barber and S. M. Stern, vol. 2 [New York: George Allen & Unwin Ltd., 1971], 130).

5 Muqtedar Khan, "The Legacy of Prophet Muhammad and the Issues of Pedophilia and Polygamy," *Ijtihad*, June 9, 2003.

6 Al-Qastellani, X, 342 (quoted in Goldziher, *Muslim Studies*, 34).

7 An-Nasa'i, 1:143 (quoted in Goldziher, *Muslim Studies*, 34–35).

8 *Kitab al-Kharaj*, 43, 10; Muslim, 5:287; ad-Darimi, 70; an-Nasa'i, 1:229; Ibn Maja, 18 (quoted in Goldziher, *Muslim Studies*, 37).

9 Nabia Abbott, *Studies in Arabic Literary Papyri, Volume II: Qur'anic Commentary and Tradition* (Chicago: University of Chicago Press, 1967), 7–11. On the controversy over writing down hadiths, see Michael Cook, "The Opponents of the Writing of Traditions in Early Islam," *Arabica* 44 (1977): 437–530.

10 Patricia Crone and Martin Hinds, *God's Caliph: Religious Authority in the First Centuries of Islam* (Cambridge: Cambridge University Press, 1986), 62.

11 Al-Ya'qubi, 2:264 (quoted in Goldziher, *Muslim Studies*, 38).

12 Safwat, *Rasa'il*, 2:177 (quoted in Crone and Hinds, *God's Caliph*, 62).

13 Crone and Hinds, *God's Caliph*, 64.

14 Ibid.

15 Abu Dawud, book 14, no. 2744; cf. Goldziher, *Muslim Studies*, 42.

16 Al-Khatib al-Baghdadi, fol. 84b, ed. Hyderabad, 309 (quoted in Goldziher, *Muslim Studies*, 204–5).

17 Al-Khatib, *Taqyid*, 107 (quoted in Goldziher, *Muslim Studies*, 47).

18 As-Suyuti, *Ta'rikh*, 106, 22; 109, 17 (quoted in Goldziher, *Muslim Studies*, 106).

19 Ibn Ishaq, *The Life of Muhammad*, 452; Tabari, *The History of al-Tabari*, trans. Michael Fishbein (Albany: State University of New York Press, 1997), vol. 8, 11.

20 Ibn Ishaq, *The Life of Muhammad*, 452.

21 Tabari, *The History of al-Tabari*, vol. 8, 12.

22 Yaqut, 3:242f (quoted in Goldziher, *Muslim Studies*, 122).

23 Ibn Maja, 102 (quoted in Goldziher, *Muslim Studies*, 45). On the value of a prayer in Mecca, Medina, and Jerusalem, see M. J. Kister, "You Shall Set Out for Three Mosques: A Study of an Early Tradition," *Le Muséon* 82 (1969): 173–96.

24 At-Tabari, vol. 2, 112 (quoted in Goldziher, *Muslim Studies*, 44).

25 *Manaqib al-Ansar*, no. 40; *Riqaq*, no. 51; Muslim, *Iman*, no. 360; *Musnad Ahmad*, vol. 3, 9, 50, 55 (quoted in Goldziher, *Muslim Studies*, 105).

26 Ibn Hajar, 1:59 (quoted in Goldziher, *Muslim Studies*, 110).

27 Quoted in Goldziher, *Muslim Studies*, 113.

28 Ad-Damiri, vol. 2, 400 (quoted in Goldziher, *Muslim Studies*, 114).

29  Bukhari, *Sahih al-Bukhari*, vol. 4, book 55, no. 2741; cf. Goldziher, *Muslim Studies*, 114.

30  Bukhari, *Sahih al-Bukhari*, vol. 5, book 62, no. 3675.

31  Ibid., no. 3677.

32  *Agh.*, VII, 13 (quoted in Goldziher, *Muslim Studies*, 118).

33  Bukhari, *Sahih al-Bukhari*, vol. 5, book 62, no. 3699.

34  Ibn Ishaq, *The Life of Muhammad*, 514; cf. Goldziher, *Muslim Studies*, 120.

35  *Agh.*, 19:54; Yaqut, 4:93 (quoted in Goldziher, *Muslim Studies*, 53–54).

36  *Fragm. hist. arab.*, 198 (quoted in Goldziher, *Muslim Studies*, 107).

37  Goldziher, *Muslim Studies*, 108.

38  Bukhari, *Sahih al-Bukhari*, vol. 1, book 4, no. 157.

39  Ibid., book 19, no. 158.

40  Ibid., no. 159.

41  Muslim ibn al-Hajjaj, *Sahih Muslim*, trans. Abdul Hamid Siddiqi (New Delhi: Kitab Bhavan, 2000), book 23, no. 5017.

42  Ibid., no. 5023.

43  Ibid., book 19, no. 4320.

44  Ibid., no. 4321.

45  Al-Khatib al-Baghdadi, fol. 25b, ed. Hyderabad, 84 (quoted in Goldziher, *Muslim Studies*, 55).

46  *Agh.*, 9:45, 20 (quoted in Goldziher, *Muslim Studies*, 63).

47  Sulaiman bin Al-Aash'ath Al-Azdi as-Sijistani, *Sunan Abu Dawud, English Translation with Explanatory Notes*, trans. Ahmad Hasan (New Delhi: Kitab Bhavan, 1990), v.

48  Muhammad Muhsin Khan, introduction to Bukhari, *Sahih al-Bukhari*, 18–19.

49  "Hadith & Sunnah," www.islamonline.net.

50  Goldziher, *Muslim Studies*, 126–27.

51  Al-Jahiz, *Bayan*, fol. 114b (quoted in Goldziher, *Muslim Studies*, 56).

52  Quoted in Goldziher, *Muslim Studies*, 127.

53  Al-Jahiz, *Bayan*, fol. 114b (quoted in Goldziher, *Muslim Studies*, 56).

54  Ad-Darimi, 77 (quoted in Goldziher, *Muslim Studies*, 133).

55  *Al-Amali: The Dictations of Sheikh Al-Mufid*, trans. Mulla Asgharali M. M. Jaffer (Middlesex, UK: World Federation of Khoja Shia Ithna-Asheri Muslim Communities, n.d.), 7.

56  Abu Abdullah Muhammad b. Yazid Ibn-i-Maja al-Qazwini, *Sunan ibn-i-Majah*, trans. Muhammad Tufail Ansari (Lahore: Kazi Publications, 1996), vol. 5, no. 4067.

57  Goldziher, *Muslim Studies*, 140–41.

58  Schacht, *Origins of Muhammadan Jurisprudence*, 166.

59  Ibid., 164.

60  Mohammad Mustafa Azami, *Studies in Early Hadith Literature: With a Critical Edition of Some Early Texts*, third edition (Oak Brook, IL: American Trust Publications, 1992).

61   Harald Motzki, "The *Musannaf* of 'Abd al-Razzaq al-San'ani as a Source of
     Authentic *ahadith* of the First Century A.H.," *Journal of Near Eastern Studies*
     50 (1991): 16–20 (quoted in Herbert Berg, *The Development of Exegesis in Early
     Islam* [London: Routledge, 2000], 37).
62   Motzki, "The *Musannaf*," 2 (quoted in Berg, *Development of Exegesis*, 36).
63   Quoted in G. H. A. Juynboll, trans., "Muslim's Introduction to His Sahih Trans-
     lated and Annotated with an Excursus on the Chronology of *fitna* and *bid'a*,"
     *Jerusalem Studies in Arabic and Islam* 5 (1984): 277 (quoted in Berg, *Develop-
     ment of Exegesis*, 7).
64   Berg, *Development of Exegesis*, 28.
65   For an excellent discussion of this, see Ibn Warraq's delightful imagined dia-
     logue in *The Quest for the Historical Muhammad*, 38–43.
66   Bukhari, *Sahih al-Bukhari*, vol. 6, book 66, no. 5032.
67   Goldziher, *Muslim Studies*, 62.
68   Ibn Ishaq, *The Life of Muhammad*, 547.

## Chapter 4: Switching On the Full Light of History

1    Alfred Guillaume, "Ibn Hisham's Notes," in Ibn Ishaq, *The Life of Muhammad*,
     691.
2    Ibn Ishaq, *The Life of Muhammad*, xxxvi.
3    Ibid.
4    Ibid., xxxvii.
5    Ibid., xxxvii.
6    Ibid., xxxv.
7    Arthur Jeffery, "The Quest of the Historical Muhammad," in Ibn Warraq, *The
     Quest for the Historical Muhammad*, 340.
8    Ibn Ishaq, *The Life of Muhammad*, 515.
9    Ehteshaam Gulam, "The Problems with Ibn Ishaq's Sirat Rasoul Allah (Arabic for
     The Life of Messenger of Allah) and Other Early Sources of Islam and Prophet
     Muhammad (2009)," Answering Christian Claims, http://www.answering-
     christian-claims.com/The-Problems-With-Ibn-Ishaq.html. The Arabic for "mercy
     for all the worlds" is more properly transliterated as *Rahmatan lil Alamin*.
10   Jeffery, "The Quest of the Historical Muhammad," 340.
11   Ibn Warraq, "Studies on Muhammad and the Rise of Islam: A Critical Survey,"
     in Ibn Warraq, *The Quest for the Historical Muhammad*, 25.
12   Johannes J. G. Jansen, "The Gospel According to Ibn Ishaq (d. 773)," paper for
     the "Skepticism and Scripture" Conference, Center for Inquiry, Davis, Califor-
     nia, January 2007.
13   Patricia Crone, *Meccan Trade and the Rise of Islam* (Princeton: Princeton Uni-
     versity Press, 1987), 223.
14   Ibid., 224.

15  For a related phenomenon, see Daniel Pipes, *Slave Soldiers and Islam* (New Haven: Yale University Press, 1981), 205–14. Note how the origins of military slavery, a secular event that took place two hundred years after Muhammad's supposed life, is variously handled in forty-four different Arabic and Persian sources. In this case, new information kept turning up many centuries after the events took place—about a political event in the early ninth century. How much more easily, then, could such a process unfold regarding religious events in the seventh century that were far more central to the lives of the believers?

16  Gregor Schoeler, *The Biography of Muhammad: Nature and Authenticity* (New York: Routledge, 2010), 16.

17  Ibn Ishaq, *The Life of Muhammad*, 452. I am indebted to Jansen's "Gospel According to Ibn Ishaq" for this discussion.

18  Ibid. 381.

19  Ibid., 501, 605.

20  Ibid., 81.

21  Johannes J. G. Jansen, "The Historicity of Muhammad, Aisha and Who Knows Who Else," Tidsskriftet Sappho, May 16, 2011, http://www.sappho.dk/blog/335/The-historicity-of-Muhammad-Aisha-and-who-knows-who-else.htm.

22  Ibn Ishaq, *The Life of Muhammad*, 106.

23  Jansen, "The Gospel According to Ibn Ishaq (d. 773)."

24  Crone, *Meccan Trade*, 220.

25  W. Montgomery Watt, *Muhammad at Medina* (Oxford: Oxford University Press, 1956), 35–36.

26  Jansen, "The Gospel According to Ibn Ishaq."

27  The Sunni-Shiite conflict has in many instances evolved into a conflict between Arabs and non-Arabs: Sunni Arabs versus Shiite Persians (although there are, to be sure, many Shiite Arabs). This came to a head in modern times in the violence between Shiite Iranian pilgrims and Sunni Saudi security forces in Mecca during the hajj in 1987.

28  Quoted in Crone, *Meccan Trade*, 7.

29  Ibn Kathir, *Tafsir Ibn Kathir* (abridged), vol. 9 (Riyadh: Darussalam, 2000), 153–54.

30  Crone, *Meccan Trade*, 134.

31  Crone disputes the identification by pointing out that the two words actually have quite different roots and that the location Ptolemy gives for Macoraba does not correspond to the site of Mecca. (See Crone, *Meccan Trade*, 135–36.)

32  Crone, *Meccan Trade*, 137.

33  Ibid., 134.

34  Ibid., 137.

35  Richard W. Bulliet, *The Camel and the Wheel* (Cambridge, MA: Harvard University Press, 1975), 105 (quoted in Crone, *Meccan Trade*, 6).

36  Crone notes that according to the medieval Islamic historian al-Azraqi (d. 1072), trade was conducted in pre-Islamic Arabic at "pilgrim stations" includ-

ing Mina, Arafa, Ukaz, Majanna, and Dhul-Majaz. "That Mecca itself is supposed to have been a pilgrim station," Crone observes, "is here totally forgotten"
(Crone, *Meccan Trade*, 175).

37  Crone, *Meccan Trade*, 174.

38  See Ibid., 172–76. She notes that Mecca was "added by way of afterthought only"
in al-Azraqi's account of pilgrimages in pre-Islamic Arabia. She declares, "It
is thus reasonable to conclude with [biblical scholar Julius] Wellhausen that
Mecca was not an object of pilgrimage in pre-Islamic times" (Crone, *Meccan
Trade*, 176).

## Chapter 5: The Embarrassment of Muhammad

1  Bukhari, *Sahih al-Bukhari*, vol. 6, book 65, no. 4480.

2  Jalalu'd-din al-Mahalli and Jalalu'd-din as-Suyuti, *Tafsir al-Jalalayn*, trans.
Aisha Bewley (London: Dar al-Taqwa, 2007), 904.

3  Bukhari, *Sahih al-Bukhari*, vol. 9, book 97, no. 7420.

4  Ibid., vol. 6, book 60, no. 311.

5  Ibid., vol. 7, book 67, no. 5134.

6  Ibid., vol. 5, book 63, no. 3894.

7  Ibid., vol. 4, book 56, no. 2977.

8  Ibid., vol. 7, book 76, no. 5727; cf. online edition, vol. 8, book 82, nos. 794–97.

9  Ibn Sa'd, *Kitab Al-Tabaqat Al-Kabir*, trans. S. Moinul Haq and H. K. Ghazanfar
(New Delhi: Kitab Bhavan, n.d.), vol. I, 439.

10  Bukhari, *Sahih al-Bukhari*, vol. 1, book 4, no. 229. Parenthetical material was
added by the translator, not by the present author.

11  Ibid., vol. 4, book 59, no. 3295.

12  Ibid., no. 3292.

13  Ibid., no. 3289.

14  Ibid., no. 3303.

15  Ibid., no. 3320.

16  Muslim, *Sahih Muslim*, book 23, no. 5113.

17  David S. Powers, *Muhammad Is Not the Father of Any of Your Men: The Making
of the Last Prophet* (Philadelphia: University of Pennsylvania Press, 2009), 9, 25.

18  Ibid., 72.

19  Ibid.

20  Ibid., 73.

21  Ibid., 91.

22  Bukhari, *Sahih al-Bukhari*, vol. 5, book 64, no. 4468.

23  Muhammad ibn Jarir at-Tabari, *The History of al-Tabari*, vol. 10, "The Conquest
of Arabia," trans. Fred M. Donner (Albany: State University of New York Press,
1993), 16–17.

24  *The Chronicle of Theophanes Confessor: Byzantine and Near Eastern History,*

A.D. *284–813*, trans. Cyril Mango and Roger Scott (Oxford: Clarendon Press, 1997), 466–67 (quoted in Powers, *Muhammad Is Not the Father*, 82–83).

25  Ibn Ishaq, *The Life of Muhammad*, 532.

26  Ibid., 532–35.

27  Powers, *Muhammad Is Not the Father*, 84.

28  Ibid., 78.

29  Ibid., 78–79.

30  Bukhari, *Sahih al-Bukhari*, vol. 8, book 78, no. 6063.

31  Ibid., vol. 7, book 76, no. 5765.

32  Ibid.

## Chapter 6: The Unchanging Qur'an Changes

1  Abdullah Yusuf Ali, *The Meaning of the Holy Qur'an*, 11th ed. (Beltsville, MD: Amana Publications, 2009).

2  M. Fethullah Gülen, *Questions This Modern Age Puts to Islam* (Izmir: Kaynak, 1993), 58.

3  Alphonse Mingana, "Three Ancient Korans," in Ibn Warraq, *The Origins of the Koran*, 86.

4  Quoted in Ibn Warraq, *Virgins?*, 218.

5  Ibn Warraq, *Virgins?*, 234–39.

6  Bukhari, *Sahih al-Bukhari*, vol. 6, book 65, no. 4592.

7  "Malik's *Muwatta*," trans. 'A'isha 'Abdarahman at-Tarjumana and Ya'qub Johnson, book 15, no. 15.4.9, Center for Muslim-Jewish Engagement, http://www.cmje.org/religious-texts/hadith/muwatta/.

8  Ibn al-Athîr, *Usûd Ulghâbah fî Ma'rifat Is-Sahâbah* (Beirut: Dâr al-Fikr, 1995), vol. 3, 154, http://www.islamic-awareness.org/Quran/Sources/Sarh/.

9  Mingana, "Three Ancient Korans," 102.

10  Muhammad Ghoniem and M. S. M. Saifullah, "Abdullah Ibn Sad Ibn Abi Sarh: Where Is the Truth?" Islamic Awareness, http://www.islamic-awareness.org/Quran/Sources/Sarh/.

11  Bukhari, *Sahih al-Bukhari*, vol. 6, book 66, no. 5038.

12  Ibid., no. 5032.

13  Ali, *The Meaning of the Holy Qur'an*.

14  Muslim, *Sahih Muslim*, book 4, no. 1787.

15  Bukhari, *Sahih al-Bukhari*, vol. 6, book 66, no. 4992.

16  Ibid., no. 4991.

17  Ibn Abi Dawud, *Kitab al-Masahif*, 23, in John Gilchrist, *Jam' Al-Qur'an, The Codification of the Qur'an Text: A Comprehensive Study of the Original Collection of the Qur'an Text and the Early Surviving Qur'an Manuscripts* (Mondeor, South Africa: MERCSA, 1989), http://www.answering-islam.org/Gilchrist/Jam/index.html.

18  As-Suyuti, *Al-Itqan fi Ulum al-Qur'an*, 525, in Gilchrist, *Jam' Al-Qur'an*.

19  Muhammad Ibn Ismail al-Bukhari, "Translation of Sahih Bukhari," trans. M. Muhsin Khan, vol. 8, book 82, no. 816, http://www.cmje.org/religious-texts/hadith/bukhari/082-sbt.php.

20  Arthur Jeffery, "Abu 'Ubaid on the Verses Missing from the Koran," in Ibn Warraq, *The Origins of the Koran*, 153.

21  As-Suyuti, *Al-Itqan fi Ulum al-Qur'an*, 524, in Gilchrist, *Jam' Al-Qur'an*.

22  Muslim, *Sahih Muslim*, 2:501, in Gilchrist, *Jam' Al-Qur'an*.

23  Ibid.; As-Suyuti, *Al-Itqan fi Ulum al-Qur'an*, 526, in Gilchrist, *Jam' Al-Qur'an*. The *Musabihat* are suras of the Qur'an that start with the words *Sabbaha* (or *_yusabbihu) lil-lahi ma fi-samawati wal-ard*, which means "All that is in the heavens and on earth magnifies God; He is the All-mighty, the All-wise." They include suras 57, 59, 61, 62, and 64.

24  Claude Gilliot, "Reconsidering the Authorship of the Qur'an," in Reynolds, *The Qur'an in Its Historical Context*, 92.

25  Bukhari, *Sahih al-Bukhari*, vol. 6, book 65, no. 4679.

26  Ibn Abi Dawud, *Kitab al-Masahif*, 11, in Gilchrist, *Jam' Al-Qur'an*.

27  As-Suyuti, *Al-Itqan fi Ulum al-Qur'an*, 524, in Gilchrist, *Jam' Al-Qur'an*.

28  "Malik's *Muwatta*," book 30, no. 30.3.17.

29  Muslim, book 8, no. 3422.

30  "Malik's *Muwatta*," book 8, no. 8.8.26.

31  Richard Bell, "From *Introduction to the Qur'an*," in Ibn Warraq, ed., *What the Koran Really Says* (Amherst, NY: Prometheus, 2002), 547.

32  Muhammad M. Pickthall, *The Meaning of the Glorious Koran* (Elmhurst, NY: Tahrike Tarsile Qur'an, 1999). Language modernized.

33  Bell, "From *Introduction to the Qur'an*," 547.

34  For another perspective on this passage, see Joseph Witztum, "Q 4:24 Revisited," *Islamic Law and Society* 16, no. 1 (2009): 1–34.

35  An intriguing consideration of various aspects of the context of Qur'an passages can be found in Angelika Neuwirth, "Structural, Linguistic, and Literary Features," in Jane Dammen McAuliffe, ed., *The Cambridge Companion to the Qur'an* (Cambridge: Cambridge University Press, 2006), 97–115.

## Chapter 7: The Non-Arabic Arabic Qur'an

1  Pickthall, *The Meaning of the Glorious Koran*, iii.

2  Ali, *The Meaning of the Holy Qur'an*. Language modernized.

3  Ibid.

4  Ibid.

5  Ibid.

6  Quoted in Arthur Jeffery, *The Foreign Vocabulary of the Qur'an* (Vadodara, India: Oriental Institute Baroda, 1938), http://www.answering-islam.org/Books/Jeffery/Vocabulary/intro.htm.

7   Ibn Kathir, *Tafsir Ibn Kathir*, 5:134–35.

8   John Henry Cardinal Newman, *An Essay on the Development of Christian Doctrine*, sixth edition (Notre Dame, IN: University of Notre Dame Press, 1989), 151.

9   Ali, *The Meaning of the Holy Qur'an*.

10  Ibn Ishaq, *The Life of Muhammad*, 180; cf. Gilliot, "Reconsidering the Authorship of the Qur'an," 90.

11  Muqatil b. Sulayman, *Tafsir al-Qur'an*, 2:487 (quoted in Gilliot, "Reconsidering the Authorship of the Qur'an," 90).

12  Ibid.

13  Ibid.

14  Bukhari, *Sahih al-Bukhari*, vol. 1, book 1, no. 3.

15  Tabari (i.e., Bal'ami), *Muhammad, sceau des prophètes*, trans. H. Zotenberg (Paris: Sindbad, 1980), 67 (quoted in Gilliot, "Reconsidering the Authorship of the Qur'an," 91).

16  Louis Ginzberg, "Book of Adam," *The Jewish Encyclopedia*, http://www.jewish-encyclopedia.com/view.jsp?artid=759&letter=A.

17  Quoted in William St. Clair Tisdall, *Sources of the Quran*, chapter 3, http://www.truthnet.org/islam/src-chp3.htm. For another perspective on the Cain and Abel story, see Michael Pregill, "Isra'iliyat, Myth, and Pseudepigraphy: Wahb b. Munabbih and the Early Islamic Versions of the Fall of Adam and Eve," *Jerusalem Studies in Arabic and Islam* 34 (2008): 215–83.

18  Tisdall, *Sources of the Quran*, chapter 3. See also Jacob Lassner, *Demonizing the Queen of Sheba* (Chicago: University of Chicago Press, 1993).

19  "Gospel of Thomas Greek Text A," from *The Apocryphal New Testament*, trans. M. R. James (Oxford: Clarendon Press, 1924), http://wesley.nnu.edu/sermons-essays-books/noncanonical-literature/noncanonical-literature-gospels/gospel-of-thomas-greek-text-a/.

20  Quoted in Toby Lester, "What Is the Koran?," *Atlantic Monthly*, January 1999.

21  Theodor Nöldeke, "The Qur'an," *Sketches from Eastern History*, trans. J. S. Black (London: Adam and Charles Black, 1892).

22  Ibn Warraq, "Introduction," in Ibn Warraq, *What the Koran Really Says*, 48.

23  See David S. Powers, *Studies in Qur'an and Hadith: The Formation of the Islamic Law of Inheritance* (Berkeley: University of California Press, 1986), ch. 1; cf. Ibn Warraq, "Introduction," 47–48.

24  Judah Benzion Segal, "The Sabian Mysteries: The Planet Cult of Ancient Harran," in Edward Bacon, ed., *Vanished Civilizations of the Ancient World* (London: Thames and Hudson, 1963).

25  Ibn Warraq, "Introduction," 43.

26  Ibid., 46–47.

27  Ibid., 47.

28  Jeffery, *Foreign Vocabulary*.

29  Ibn Kathir, *Tafsir Ibn Kathir*, vol. 6, 506–7.

30  Jeffery, *Foreign Vocabulary*.

31  Franz Rosenthal, "Some Minor Problems in the Qur'an," in Ibn Warraq, *What the Koran Really Says*, 332–34.

32  Rosenthal, "Some Minor Problems," 337.

33  Al-Mahalli and as-Suyuti, *Tafsir al-Jalalayn*, 1357.

34  Gilliot, "Reconsidering the Authorship of the Qur'an," 98.

35  Ali, *The Meaning of the Holy Qur'an*. Language modernized.

36  "The Contradictions of the Qur'an," *Behind the Veil*, ch. 11, http://www. answering-islam.org/BehindVeil/btv11.html.

37  Christoph Luxenberg, *The Syro-Aramaic Reading of the Koran: A Contribution to the Decoding of the Language of the Koran* (Berlin: Verlag Hans Schiler, 2000), 9.

38  Alphonse Mingana, "Syriac Influence on the Style of the Koran," in Ibn Warraq, *What the Koran Really Says*, 175.

39  Ibid., 176, 180.

40  Ibid., 178.

41  Ibid., 178–79.

42  Ibid., 188.

43  Ibid., 181–82.

44  Ibid., 184–86.

45  Pickthall, *The Meaning of the Glorious Koran*.

46  Mingana, "Syriac Influence," 187.

47  Jeffery, *Foreign Vocabulary*.

48  Ibid.

49  Ali, *The Meaning of the Holy Qur'an*.

50  Al-Misri, *Reliance of the Traveller*, 011.3, 5.

51  Jeffery, *Foreign Vocabulary*.

52  Ibn Warraq, "Introduction to Sura IX.29," in Ibn Warraq, *What the Koran Really Says*, 319.

53  Rosenthal, "Some Minor Problems," 324.

54  Uri Rubin, "Koran and Tafsir: The Case of 'an Yadin,'" in Ibn Warraq, *What the Koran Really Says*, 372–80.

## Chapter 8: What the Qur'an May Have Been

1  Pickthall, *The Meaning of the Glorious Koran*. Language modernized.

2  *Tafsir al-Jalalayn*, 770.

3  For more on *furqan*, see Fred M. Donner, "On Qur'anic Furqan," *Journal of Semitic Studies* 52 (2007): 279–300.

4  C. Heger, "Koran XXV.1: Al-Furqan and the 'Warner,'" in Ibn Warraq, *What the Koran Really Says*, 387–89.

5  M. Abul Quasem, trans. and ed., *The Recitation and Interpretation of the Qur'an: Al-Ghazali's Theory* (Kuala Lumpur: University of Malaya Press, 1979), 40–41

(quoted in Abdullah David and M. S. M. Saifullah, "Concise List of Arabic Manuscripts of the Qur'an Attributable to the First Century Hijra," Islamic Awareness, June 14, 2008, http://www.islamic-awareness.org/Quran/Text/Mss/hijazi.html).

6   Keith E. Small, *Textual Criticism and Qur'an Manuscripts* (Lanham, MD: Lexington Books, 2011), 69–72.

7   David Margoliouth, "Textual Variations of the Koran," in Ibn Warraq, *The Origins of the Koran*, 158.

8   Mingana, "Syriac Influence," 181–82.

9   Ibn Warraq. *Virgins?*, 50.

10  Quoted in Gabriel Said Reynolds, "Introduction: Qur'anic Studies and Its Controversies," in Reynolds, *Historical Context*, 17.

11  Luxenberg, *Syro-Aramaic*, 71.

12  Günter Lüling, *A Challenge to Islam for Reformation* (Delhi: Motilal Banarsidass Publishers, 2003), 1.

13  Christoph Luxenberg, "Christmas in the Koran," trans. Ibn Warraq. An abridged version of this article was first published in German in *Imprimatur* 1 (March 2003): 13–17.

14  Luxenberg, *Syro-Aramaic*, 104.

15  Ibid., 105–6.

16  Luxenberg, "Christmas in the Koran."

17  Luxenberg, *Syro-Aramaic*, 142.

18  Ibid., 256.

19  Ibid., 254.

20  Ibid., 259.

21  Ibid., 288.

22  Ibid., 291.

23  Johannes J. G. Jansen, "Rawwahnahum," www.arabistjansen.nl/rawwahnaahum.pdf, June 16, 2008.

24  Ibn Rawandi, "On Pre-Islamic Christian Strophic Poetical Texts in the Koran: A Critical Look at the Work of Günther Lüling," in Ibn Warraq, *What the Koran Really Says*, 671.

25  Ibid., 673.

26  Ibid., 670.

27  Lüling, *A Challenge to Islam*, 31.

28  Ibn Rawandi, "Pre-Islamic Christian Strophic Poetical Texts," 672–73.

29  Ibid., 671–72.

30  Luxenberg, "Christmas in the Koran."

31  Ibid.

32  Ibid.

33  Samir Khalil Samir, "The Theological Christian Influence on the Qur'an," in Reynolds, *Historical Context*, 149.

34  Samir, "Theological Christian Influence," 149.

35 Luxenberg, "Christmas in the Koran."

36 Samir, "Theological Christian Influence," 149–50.

37 Luxenberg, "Christmas in the Koran."

38 Lüling, *A Challenge to Islam*, 476.

39 Ibn Kathir, *Tafsir Ibn Kathir*, 10:251.

40 Lüling, *A Challenge to Islam*, 440–50.

41 For more on the Christological controversies, see J. N. D. Kelly, *Early Christian Doctrines*, rev. ed. (San Francisco: Harper San Francisco, 1978).

42 See Adolph Harnack, *History of Dogma*, trans. Neil Buchanan, vol. 1 (Boston: Little, Brown, 1901), 291n407.

43 Pseudo-Clementine Homilies, 16.15, http://www.compassionatespirit.com/Homilies/Book-16.htm.

44 Lüling, *A Challenge to Islam*, 476ff.; see also Ibn Rawandi, "Pre-Islamic Christian Strophic Poetical Texts," 680ff.

45 Lüling, *A Challenge to Islam*, 476n66.

46 Ibid., 476.

47 Ibid.

48 Ibn Rawandi, "Pre-Islamic Christian Strophic Poetical Texts," 680–81.

49 Nevo and Koren, *Crossroads to Islam*, 214.

50 Luxenberg, "Christmas in the Koran."

51 Ibid.

52 Ibid.

53 Ibid.

54 Reynolds, "Introduction," 17.

55 Luxenberg, "Christmas in the Koran."

56 Ibid.

57 Ibid.

## Chapter 9: Who Collected the Qur'an?

1 Bukhari, *Sahih al-Bukhari*, vol. 6, book 66, no. 4987.

2 Ibid., book 65, no. 4784.

3 Powers, *Muhammad Is Not the Father*, 159.

4 Muhammad ibn Jarir at-Tabari, *The History of al-Tabari*, vol. 17, "The First Civil War," trans. G. R. Hawting (Albany: State University of New York Press, 1996), 29.

5 Ibid., 34.

6 Ibid., 37.

7 Ibid., 78.

8 Ibid., 79.

9 Ibid., 79.

10 Ibid., 81.

11 Ibid., 82.

12 Ibid., 85–86.

13 See Small, *Textual Criticism*, 15–27, for useful summary descriptions of some of the principal early Qur'anic manuscripts.

14 Lester, "What Is the Koran?"

15 Gilchrist, *Jam' Al-Qur'an*.

16 François Déroche, *La transmission écrite du Coran dans les débuts de l'islam: Le codex Parisino-petropolitanus* (Leiden: Brill, 2009), is a fascinating study of an early Qur'anic manuscript, Bibliothèque nationale de France (BNF) Arabe 328, which he combines with other manuscripts that he establishes came from the same original, consisting of sections of suras 2 through 72. Déroche contends that this manuscript, which does not contain most diacritical marks, dates from between 670 and 720. The scholar Andrew Rippin, in reviewing Déroche's book, notes: "To Déroche, the evidence of the manuscript suggests that the account of the 'Uthmanic collection and production of a master set of manuscripts to be distributed across the new empire simply cannot be historically accurate. The purported goal of 'Uthman could not have been accomplished, given the realities of the orthography available at the time; the variants found in this copy of the text suggest that a unified text was also not achieved that early." See Andrew Rippin's book review, "La Transmission écrite du Coran dans les débuts de l'islam: Le Codex Parisino-petropolitanus (Book review)," *Journal of the American Oriental Society* 129:4 (2009), 706(3). See also Small, *Textual Criticism*, 21.

17 Arthur Jeffery, "A Variant Text of the Fatiha," in Ibn Warraq, *The Origins of the Koran*, 145–46.

18 Jeffery, "Variant Text," 146–47.

19 Ibn Warraq, *Virgins?*, 221.

20 Ibid., 222.

21 Ibid., 223.

22 Ibid., 219.

23 Ibid., 220.

24 Ibid., 223.

25 Monk of Beth Hale, *Disputation*, fol. 4b (quoted in Hoyland, *Seeing Islam*, 471). There were two monasteries of Beth Hale, one in northern Iraq and the other in Arabia; it is not known in which one this monk lived.

26 Prémare, "'Abd al-Malik b. Marwan," 207.

27 Mingana, "The Transmission of the Koran," 102–3.

28 Ibn Hajar al-Asqalani, *Tahdhib al-Tahdhib*, vol. 4 (Beyrouth: Dar al-Fikr, 1984–85), 195–97n386 (quoted in Prémare, "'Abd al-Malik b. Marwan," 206).

29 Ali Ibn Asakir, *Tarikh madinat Dimashq*, ed. Muhibb al-Din Umar al-Amrawi, vol. 12 (Beyrouth: Dar al-Fikr, 1995–2000), 116; Ibn Hajar, *Tahdhib al-Tahdhib*, 5:303–5n600 (quoted in Prémare, "'Abd al-Malik b. Marwan," 209).

30 Powers, *Muhammad Is Not the Father*, 160.

31  Ahmad Al-Baladhuri, *Ansab al-ashraf*, ed. Muhammad al-Yalawi, vol. 7 (Beyrouth: Biblioteca Islamica, 2002), 2, 300–301; Ibn Asakir, *Tarikh madinat Dimashq*, 12:159–60 (quoted in Prémare, "'Abd al-Malik b. Marwan," 208).

32  Ibn Asakir, *Tarikh madinat Dimashq*, 12:160 (quoted in Prémare, "'Abd al-Malik b. Marwan," 209).

33  Crone and Hinds, *God's Caliph*, 28.

34  Ali Al-Samhudi, *Wafa al-Wafa bi-akhbar dar al-Mustafa*, ed. Muhammad Muhyi I-Din Abd al-Hamid, vol. 2 (Cairo, 1955; reprinted Beyrouth: Dar al-Kutub al-Ilmiyya, 1984), 667–69 (quoted in Prémare, "'Abd al-Malik b. Marwan," 205).

35  Umar Ibn Shabba, *Tarikh al-Madina al-munawwara*, ed. Fahim Muhammad Shaltut, vol. 1 (Mecca, 1979), 7 (quoted in Prémare, "'Abd al-Malik b. Marwan," 204).

36  Abu Bakr Ibn Abi Da'ud al-Sijistani, *Kitab al-masahif*, ed. Arthur Jeffery (Cairo: al-Matbaa al-Rahmaniyya, 1936), 35:18–19, 49–50 (quoted in Powers, *Muhammad Is Not the Father*, 161).

37  Prémare, "'Abd al-Malik b. Marwan," 204.

38  Hoyland, *Seeing Islam*, 490–91.

39  Leo-Umar, *Letter* (Armenian), 292, 297–98, from Arthur Jeffery, "Ghevond's Text of the Correspondence between Umar II and Leo III," *Harvard Theological Review* 37 (1944): 269–322 (quoted in Hoyland, *Seeing Islam*, 500–501).

40  Mingana, "The Transmission of the Koran," 109.

41  *The Apology of al-Kindy Written at the Court of al-Mamun, circa* A.D. *830* (quoted in Mingana, "The Transmission of the Koran," 109).

42  Ibid.


## Chapter 10: Making Sense of It All

1  See Crone and Cook, *Hagarism*; Donner, *Muhammad and the Believers*.

2  See Philip K. Hitti, *The Arabs: A Short History* (Princeton: Princeton University Press, 1943; revised edition Washington, DC: Regnery, 1970), 57–58. Hitti reflects commonly held views that the Byzantines and Persians had exhausted themselves fighting each other and that the people in the Byzantine domains that the Arabs conquered welcomed the invaders, because the tribute they charged was lower. See also Nevo and Koren, *Crossroads to Islam*, 93–94.

3  It appears the Arabs did encounter considerable resistance from the captive peoples. Recall the testimony of the Patriarch Sophronius to the brutality of the conquerors and the misery of the conquered, recounted in chapter 1 of this book. Also, the pioneering historian Bat Ye'or notes a hadith in which the caliph Umar asked one of his subordinates, "Do you think that these vast countries, Syria, Mesopotamia, Kufa, Basra, Misr [Egypt] do not have to be covered with troops who must be well paid?" This statement could be a surviving testimony

to an occupation that was not as placid as it is often made out to have been. See Abu Yusuf Ya'qub, *Le Livre de l'impôt foncier (Kitâb el-Kharâdj)*, trans. Edmond Fagnan (Paris: Paul Guethner, 1921) (quoted in Bat Ye'or, *The Decline of Eastern Christianity Under Islam: From Jihad to Dhimmitude* [Madison, NJ: Fairleigh Dickinson University Press, 1996], 274).

4   Popp, "The Early History of Islam," 18–19.

5   For more on this, see the pioneering study by Crone and Cook, *Hagarism*.

6   See Donner, *Muhammad and the Believers*.

# Further Reading

There is a great deal more that can be said, and has been said, about the origins of Islam and the Qur'an, and the historicity of Muhammad. In writing this book I have relied chiefly on these sources, and they in turn can lead the interested reader to numerous fruitful new avenues of inquiry.

Bell, Richard. *Introduction to the Qur'an*. Edinburgh: University Press, 1958.

Berg, Herbert. *The Development of Exegesis in Early Islam: The Authenticity of Muslim Literature from the Formative Period*. London: Routledge, 2000.

Berkey, Jonathan P. *The Formation of Islam: Religion and Society in the Near East, 600–1800*. New York: Cambridge University Press, 2003.

Burton, John. *The Collection of the Qur'an*. Cambridge: Cambridge University Press, 1977.

Crone, Patricia. *Meccan Trade and the Rise of Islam*. Princeton: Princeton University Press, 1987.

Crone, Patricia, and Michael Cook. *Hagarism: The Making of the Islamic World*. Cambridge: Cambridge University Press, 1977.

Crone, Patricia, and Martin Hinds. *God's Caliph: Religious Authority in the First Centuries of Islam*. Cambridge: Cambridge University Press, 1986.

Donner, Fred M. *Muhammad and the Believers: At the Origins of Islam*. Cambridge, MA: The Belknap Press of Harvard University Press, 2010.

Foss, Clive. *Arab-Byzantine Coins: An Introduction, with a Catalogue of the Dumbarton Oaks Collection*. Washington, DC: Dumbarton Oaks Research Library and Collection, 2008.

Gilchrist, John. *Jam' Al-Qur'an, The Codification of the Qur'an Text: A Comprehensive Study of the Original Collection of the Qur'an Text and the Early Surviving Qur'an Manuscripts*. Mondeor, South Africa: MERCSA, 1989.

Goldziher, Ignaz. *Muslim Studies*. Volume II. Translated by C. R. Barber and S. M. Stern. New York: George Allen & Unwin Ltd., 1971.

Grohmann, Adolf. "The Problem of Dating Early Qur'ans," *Islam* 33 (1958).

Hawting, G. R. *The First Dynasty of Islam: The Umayyad Caliphate* A.D. *661–750*. Second edition. London: Routledge, 1999.

———. *The Idea of Idolatry and the Emergence of Islam: From Polemic to History*. Cambridge: Cambridge University Press, 1999.

Hoyland, Robert G. *Seeing Islam as Others Saw It: A Survey and Evaluation of Christian, Jewish, and Zoroastrian Writings on Early Islam*. Princeton: Darwin Press, 1997.

Ibn Warraq, ed. *The Origins of the Koran*. Amherst, NY: Prometheus, 1998.

———, ed. *The Quest for the Historical Muhammad*. Amherst, NY: Prometheus, 2000.

———. *Virgins? What Virgins? And Other Essays*. Amherst, NY: Prometheus, 2010.

———, ed. *What the Koran Really Says: Language, Text, and Commentary*. Amherst, NY: Prometheus, 2002.

Jansen, Hans (Johannes J. G.). *Mohammed: Eine Biographie*. München: Beck, 2008.

Lüling, Günter. *A Challenge to Islam for Reformation*. Delhi: Motilal Banarsidass Publishers, 2003.

Luxenberg, Christoph. *The Syro-Aramaic Reading of the Koran: A Contribution to the Decoding of the Language of the Koran*. Berlin: Verlag Hans Schiler, 2000.

Margoliouth, David S. *The Early Development of Mohammedanism*. New York: Scribner's Sons, 1914. Reprint, Simon Harbor, FL: Simon Publications, 2003.

Nevo, Yehuda D., and Judith Koren. *Crossroads to Islam: The Origins of the Arab Religion and the Arab State*. Amherst, NY: Prometheus, 2003.

Ohlig, Karl-Heinz, and Gerd-R. Puin, eds. *The Hidden Origins of Islam*. Amherst, NY: Prometheus, 2010.

Powers, David S. *Muhammad Is Not the Father of Any of Your Men: The Making of the Last Prophet*. Philadelphia: University of Pennsylvania Press, 2009.

Reynolds, Gabriel Said. *The Qur'an and Its Biblical Subtext*. London: Routledge, 2010.

———, ed. *The Qur'an in Its Historical Context*. New York: Routledge, 2008.

Sawma, Gabriel. *The Qur'an: Misinterpreted, Mistranslated, and Misread*. Plainsboro, NJ: Adi Books, 2006.

Schacht, Joseph. *The Origins of Muhammadan Jurisprudence*. Oxford: Clarendon Press, 1950.

Small, Keith E. *Textual Criticism and Qur'an Manuscripts*. Lanham, MD: Lexington Books, 2011.

At-Tabari, Muhammad ibn Jarir. *The History of al-Tabari*. Volume XVII, "The First Civil War." Translated by G. R. Hawting. Albany: State University of New York Press, 1996.

Wansbrough, John E. *Quranic Studies: Sources and Methods of Scriptural Interpretation*. Foreword, translations, and expanded notes by Andrew Rippin. Amherst, NY: Prometheus, 2004.

———. *The Sectarian Milieu: Content and Composition of Islamic Salvation History*. Foreword, translations, and expanded notes by Gerald Hawting. Amherst, NY: Prometheus, 2006.

# Acknowledgments

I could not have written this book at all without the extraordinarily generous and kind assistance of Ibn Warraq, an indefatigable and innovative scholar whose collections on the Qur'an and the historical Muhammad are essential reading for anyone who has more than a passing interest in the origins of Islam. His recommendations for reading and research have given this book any merit it may have—and in this case, the hoary cliché of author's acknowledgments that "what is good in the book is all his, and its errors and failures are all mine" couldn't be truer.

Indeed, were it not for a memorable conversation that Ibn Warraq and I once had in The Hague, during which he elucidated for me in a particularly compelling way the weakness of Islam's historical foundations, and a subsequent dinner conversation on the same subject with Hans Jansen (to whom also much thanks for his keen eye in spotting errors and other problems in this manuscript), I would never even have thought to write this book. Nor would this book have been possible without the assistance of Daniel Pipes and the Middle East Forum Educational Fund, to whom I remain grateful.

I am indebted to my colleague, partner, and friend Pamela Geller for her aid in sharpening the focus and structure of this book. Her eye for conceptual imprecision, stylistic infelicities, and logical consistency has immensely improved this presentation.

Thanks also to my friend Roland Shirk for his invaluable help in finding a home for this manuscript, and for his many helpful suggestions on matters of content and presentation.

I am deeply grateful to Jed Donahue as well. He has been a superb editor, deeply attentive to large and small questions raised by the manuscript, and full of extraordinary guidance on how to smooth it out stylistically, tie up loose ends, answer questions left unanswered, and strengthen the book's argument in innumerable ways.

There are, as always, many others who have offered advice, support, and searching questions as I have wrestled with the facts and concepts I have tried to outline here. Most would, given the volatile nature of the subject matter, prefer not to be named, but my gratitude to them is not for that any dimmer.

# Index

Aaron, 61, 115

Abbas (uncle of Muhammad), xvi, xvii, 196–97

Abbasids, 60, 64, 78, 85, 86, 198, 206, 211, 212, 215

Abbott, Nabia, 69

Abd al-Malik, 60, 72, 83, 206, 210–11; caliphate of, xiv; coinage of, 58–59; Dome of the Rock inscription and, 50, 197, 209; Islam, introduction of and, 58–59; Muhammad, example of and, 69, 70; Qur'an, collection of and, 197–99, 206

Abd al-Muttalib (grandfather of Muhammad), xvi, xvii, 99

Abd ar-Rahman, 42

Abd ar-Razzaq, 83

Abdullah (father of Muhammad), xvi, xvii

Abdullah bin Salam, 107–8, 109

Abdur Rahman bin Harith bin Hisham, 188

Abel, 148

Abou El Fadl, Khaled, 14–15

Abraham, xiv, 12, 21, 30, 31, 32, 34, 134, 165, 194, 207

Abu Bakr, 92, 111, 118; caliphate of, xiii, xvii; death of, 73; Khaybar, siege of and, 76; Muhammad and, 74; Qur'an, collection of and, 187, 188

Abu Dawud as-Sijistani, 78

Abu Fukayha Yasar, 146, 147

Abu Muslim, 85

Abu Nasr Yahya ibn Abi Kathir al-Yamami, 163

Abu Sufyan, 86

Abu Talib (uncle of Muhammad), xvi, 73

Abu Ubaida, 144, 172

Abu Zura, 89

Adam, 54, 136, 148, 168

adoption, 110, 111, 117

adultery, 65, 74, 135

Ahmad, 21–22

Aisha (wife of Muhammad), 65, 73–74, 82, 91, 94, 135; Muhammad bewitched and, 121–22; Qur'an, collection of and, 137–38; Zaynab, Muhammad's marriage to and, 110, 111–12, 117

Alexander the Great, 157

Ali, Abdullah Yusuf, 154, 159, 165, 166

243

Ali ibn Abi Talib, xvi, xvii, 153; Battle of Siffin and, 189–92; caliphate of, xiv; chain of transmitters (*isnad*) and, 81; death of, 85; factionalism and Hadith and, 76; Muhammad as Seal of the Prophets and, 116; Qur'an and, 65, 73–74, 199–200; Shiite Islam and, 117, 211

Allah: Arabic and, 145; Islam as political and, 213; Jesus and, 38; obedience to, 204; Qur'an and, xiii, 17, 18, 125, 150. *See also* God

Amina (mother of Muhammad), xvi, xvii

Amr bin Umm Maktum, 129, 136

Amr ibn al-As, 30, 190

Anas bin Malik, 103

Andrae, Tor, 166

Antichrist, 21

Antioch, 29

apostasy, 113

Apostles, 29, 30

Arabian conquest, 207; brutality of, xv, 25, 26–27, 35; Christianity and, 25–28; coins and inscriptions of, 42–43, 205; Islam and, 205; Muhammad and, 2, 7, 24–28, 41, 48, 191, 205; Muslims and, 205; Qur'an and, 41, 48. *See also* Arabian Empire

Arabian Empire: Arabian conquerors and, 7; cultural influence of, 2; growth of, 2, 71; Islam and, 12, 28, 100–106; paganism and, 28–30, 158, 182; political theology of, 207–9; polytheism and, 28; unification of, 6, 20, 28, 46, 204, 214. *See also* Arabian conquest

Arabic, 36–37, 171, 206; Allah and, 145; alphabet of, xi, 162, 185; Islam and, 100–106; Qur'an and, 143–60, 162, 185, 210

Arabic calendar, 98

Arabs, 13; as Hagarians, 30–31; monotheism and, ix; monotheism in, 57; as Muslims, 30–35; paganism and, ix, 28–30

Aramaic, 14

Arberry, A. J., 151

archaeology: Arabian conquest and, 7; early Islam and, ix; Muhammad, historicity of and, ix

Arius, 179

Armenia, xiii, 204

Ar-Ridwan pledge of allegiance, 75

*Asbab an-Nuzul* (al-Wahidi), 65

Ash'ath, Al-, 190

Asim an-Nabil, 78

Athanasius II, 29, 30

Azami, Muhammad Mustafa, 82–83

Baha'is, 18

Bahira, 95–96

Bal'ami, 147

baptism, 26, 35, 152

bar Penkaye, John, xv, 35

Bashear, Suliman, 9

Battle of Badr, 75, 194

Battle of the Camel, 65

Battle of Hunayn, 196

Battle of Karbala, xvii

Battle of Muta, 117, 119–21

Battle of Siffin, 189–92

Battle of Tours, xv

Battle of the Trench, 93

Battle of Yamama, xiii, 134, 187

Baydawi, Abdullah al-, 130, 159

believers, 17, 18, 45, 64, 69, 78, 81, 110, 123, 146, 204, 213–15

Bell, Richard, 138–42, 183–84

Bible, 31, 148, 182
bin Hudhafa bin Qais bin Adi,
Abdullah, 64
bin Yahya as-Saji, Zakariya, 78
bin Yazid al-Asari, Tabit, 48, 49
bin Zaid, Abdullah, 77
*Book of History and Campaigns* (al-
Waqidi), 92
Bukhari, Muhammad Ibn Ismail al-,
77, 79–82, 110–12
Bulliet, Richard, 105
Bultmann, Rudolf, 4
Byzantine Empire, 20, 179, 204, 207,
210, 216
Byzantines, xiii, 20, 27–28, 207

Caesarea, 20
Caetani, Prince Leone, 11
Cain, 148
Catholic Church, 5
Center for the Study of Islam and
Democracy, 67
chain of transmitters (*isnad*), xvii,
81–82, 82–84, 90
child marriage, 112
Chosroes, Emperor, 207
Christianity, 35; Arabian conquerors
and, 25–28; cross and, 47; dhimmitude and, 158–59; Dome of the
Rock inscription and, 55; Eucharist and, 37–38; historical scrutiny
and, 3–5, 9; *jizya* (poll tax) and,
27–28; monotheism of, 182, 207;
origins of, 216; Qur'an and, 145;
salvation and, 152; Trinitarian,
53, 179, 181, 207. *See also* Christian tradition
Christian theology, 56
Christian tradition, 22; Islamic theology and, 14; Islamic tradition and,

216; Qur'an and, 3, 13–14, 149,
166–67, 170–75, 175–81, 183–85,
195. *See also* Christianity
Christmas, 183–85
Christology: Christian, 56; of the
ecumenical councils, 207–8;
Qur'an and, 179–80, 181; Trinitarian, 179
Church of Constantinople, 56, 179,
180
Church of the Holy Sepulchre, 27
Clement of Rome, St., 179
coinage, 206, 209; Abd al-Malik and,
58–59; absence of image of sovereign on, xv; of Arabian conquerors, 42–43, 205; cross and, 44–45,
46–47; Islam, introduction of
and, 58–59; Islamic confession of
faith (*shahada*) on, xv; Muawiya
and, xiv; *muhammad* and, 41–46;
Muhammad and, xiv; Yazid I
and, xiv
confession of faith (*shahada*), xv, 19,
51, 52, 58
Constantine, Emperor, xiv, 33–34,
179, 207
Constantinople, xiv, 104, 204, 207
Cook, Michael, 9, 12
Council of Nicaea, 179
Crone, Patricia, 9, 12, 13, 14, 69–70,
92, 99, 105
cross, 206; coinage and inscriptions
and, xiv, 44–45, 46–47; Islamic
disdain for, 25–26, 37, 47, 49–50;
Qur'an and, 25
Cyprus, xiv, 204

*Das Leben Jesu, kritisch bearbeitet*
(*The Life of Jesus, Critically Examined*) (Strauss), 4

David, 115, 152
death penalty, 113
dhimmitude, 27–28, 158–59
Dhul-Qarnayn, 157
diacritical marks, xv, 162–66, 167,
  170, 185
*Divino Afflante Spiritu* (Pius XII), 5
divorce, 109, 112
*Doctrina Jacobi*, 20–23, 31, 209
Dome of the Rock inscription,
  50–57, 69, 197; Jesus and, xv,
  209–10; Muhammad and, xv,
  52–53; *Muslim*, use of term
  and, 36; Qur'an and, xv, 50–57,
  200–201
*Dual Nature of Islamic Fundamental-
  ism, The* (Jansen), xi

Ebonites, 179
ecumenical councils, 207–8
Edict of Milan, 179
Egypt, xiii, 32, 204
Eid ul-Adha, 30
Elias, 115
Elisha, 115
*Encyclopedia Britannica*, 1
Ephraem the Syrian, St., 169–70
Episcopalians, 5
Eucharist, 37–38, 170–75
Europe, xv
Eve, 148, 168

Fatima (daughter of Muhammad),
  xvi, xvii, 116
Fihri, Maslama al-, 70
*Foreign Vocabulary of the Qur'an, The*
  (Jeffery), 153
Foss, Clive, 43
fundamentalism, 5

Gabriel (angel), xiii, 3, 97, 101, 108,
  113, 125, 127, 133, 134, 147, 157,
  170–71, 183, 203
Gadara bathhouse inscription, xiv,
  47–48, 50–51
Gaza, xiii
Gilchrist, John, 192
Gilliot, Claude, 146
God, of Abraham, xiv, 31, 32, 34;
  Christ as Son of, 37; Christ as
  Word of, 38; Jesus as Son of, 47,
  55, 181; monotheism and, ix. *See
  also* Allah
Goldziher, Ignaz, 9, 10–11, 14, 80, 85
Gospels, 4
Gräf, Erwin, 166
Greater Syria, ix
Greek, 20, 21, 24, 36, 46, 91, 104, 145,
  155, 206
Guillaume, Alfred, 165
Gulam, Ehteshaam, 90
Gülen, Fethullah, 126, 127, 193

Hadith, xv; Arabian conquest and,
  12; authority of, 63; centrality
  of, 66–68; chain of transmitters
  (*isnad*) and, xvii, 81–82, 82–84;
  collecting and codifying of, 78–79;
  contradictions in, 77–78; dating
  of, 66; fabrication of, xi, 12, 71–72,
  211; factionalism and, 72–76;
  historical reliability of, 10–12, 63,
  82–84, 85–86; Islamic law and, 10,
  11, 19, 63; Islamic practice and,
  10, 11, 63, 77–78; Islamic theology
  and, 67; Islamic tradition and, 19,
  64, 79, 83; Muhammad, embarrassment of and, 107; Muhammad, example of and, 68–72;
  Muhammad, historicity of and, xi;

Muhammad, words and deeds of and, xv, 10, 19, 63, 68–72, 85–86; occasions of revelation and, 64–66; polygamy and, 113–14; proliferation of forgeries of, 80–82, 118; Qur'an and, 19, 63–66, 69, 80–81, 128, 131–36, 138, 147, 187, 199. *See also* Islamic tradition; Qur'an

Hafsa (wife of Muhammad), 82, 187–88, 189

Hagar, 12, 30

Hagarians, 12, 30–31, 33, 36, 59, 195, 205

Hagarism, 207

*Hagarism: The Making of the Islamic World* (Crone and Cook), 12

Hajjaj ibn Yusuf, xv, 58, 59, 60, 69, 83, 197–200, 206

Hamza, 164

*hanifs*, 182, 208

Hart, Michael H., 1

Hasan (grandson), xvi, xvii

Hasan, al-, 65, 144

Hebrew, 155–56, 161, 162, 172

Hell, 68, 73, 139, 171, 172, 178, 180, 204

heresy, 35, 37, 56, 68, 89, 126

Hijra, 48–49, 73, 92, 93, 204, 222

Hinds, Martin, 69–70

Hisham bin Hakim, 132–33

historical scrutiny, 3–6

Hoyland, Robert G., 23, 58

Hudhaifa bin al-Yaman, 187

Husayn (grandson of Muhammad), xvi, xvii, 73

hypocrisy, 64, 122, 145

Iberian Peninsula, 2

Ibn Abbas, xvi, xvii, 66, 74, 77, 80, 86, 153

Ibn al-Arabi, 79

Ibn al-Athir, 129

Ibn an-Naqib, 154

Ibn Hajar, 60

Ibn Hanbal, 82, 88

Ibn Hisham, 10, 19, 87, 88

Ibn Ishaq, 165; Battle of Muta and, 119, 121; criticism of, 88–90; defense of, 88–90; dependence on, 99–100; historical embroidery and, 92–93; historical reliability of, ix, 88–90, 90–91, 97–98, 98–99; Islamic law and, 88; Jesus as the Muhammad and, 45–46; Muhammad, biographical material about and, ix, xv, 19, 46, 87–106

ibn Jariyah at-Tamimi, Ziyad, 70

Ibn Kathir, 103, 144, 153, 178

ibn Maja, Muhammad, 78, 81, 82

ibn Masud, Abdullah, 193, 198

Ibn Muallim, 81

ibn Numayr, Abdallah, 88

Ibn Rawandi, 9, 171

Ibn Sa'd, 91, 129

ibn Shuayb an-Nasai, Ahmad, 78

ibn Sirin, Muhammad, 83

ibn Sulayman, Muqatil, 115, 146

ibn Umar, Abdullah, 74–76

Ibn Warraq, 9, 14–15, 151

ibn Az-Zubair, Abdullah, xiv, 58–59, 188

Imam, Ahmad Ali al-, 14

Imran, 115

India, 2, 6

infidels, 23, 213

innovation (*bida*), 67–68

*Interpretation of the Koran in Modern Egypt, The* (Jansen), xi

Iran, xiv

Iraq, xiv, 196

Isaac, 34, 115, 155, 165

Isaiah, 21

Ishmael, 12, 30, 115, 155, 207

Ishmaelites, 31, 36, 59, 195, 205

Ishoyahb III, 31

Islam: absence of mention of, 30, 31, 33, 34, 41, 42, 63, 205; Arabian setting of, 13, 100–106; canonical account of, ix, 3–8, 22, 41, 68, 83, 101, 107, 120, 125–26, 162, 203–5; chronology of, xii–xiv; cross and, 25, 47, 49–50; evolution of, 128; first mention of, 206; historical scrutiny and, 3–6, 8–15; literature of, 2, 6, 13; marriage and, 140–41; monotheism of, 182; Muhammad, centrality of and, 67; Muhammad as founder of, ix, 2, 6; oral traditions of, 9, 38, 203; origins of, 1, 2, 3–15, 22, 101, 162; paganism and, ix; as political religion, 208–9, 212–14; polygamy and, 29; practice of, 10, 11, 63, 68, 70, 77–78; prayer and, 33; Shiite, xvii, 65, 73, 116, 211; Sunni, xvii, 116; tolerance and, 47; violence and, 85–86; warfare and, 77. *See also* Hadith; Islamic law; Islamic theology; Islamic tradition; Qur'an

Islamic calendar, 48–49, 204

Islamic law, 6, 211; adoption and, 110; cross and, 47; dhimmitude and, 158–59; Hadith and, 10, 11, 19, 63; Ibn Ishaq and, 88; inheritance and, 152; Muhammad and, 67, 68, 71, 88; punishments in, 113; Shafii school of, 193; treaties between Muslims and non-Muslims and, 94. *See also* Islam; Islamic theology; Islamic tradition

Islamic theology, 6; Christian tradition and, 14; Dome of the Rock inscription and, 50–57; Hadith and, 67; John of Damascus and, xv; Muhammad and, 18, 67; Qur'an, Arabic character of and, 145. *See also* Islam; Islamic law; Islamic tradition

Islamic tradition: Arabia and, ix; Battle of Yamama and, xiii; Christian tradition and, 216; Hadith and, 19, 64, 79, 83; Jews and, 96; Muhammad and, ix, xvi, 10, 21, 22, 67, 117; Qur'an and, xiii. *See also* Hadith; Islam; Islamic law; Islamic theology

*isnad. See* chain of transmitters (*isnad*)

Israel, 32; Children of, 21, 54, 148; tribes of, 34

*Ivanhoe* (Scott), 8

Jacob, 34, 115, 155, 168

Jacob of Edessa, 36

Jansen, Johannes J. G., xi, 91, 99

Jeffery, Arthur, 153–54, 157–58, 193

Jerusalem, 24–26

Jesus, 162; Allah and, 38; of Christianity, 21; Christianity and, 25; crucifixion of, 25, 34, 47, 53; death of, 4, 47; divinity of, 26, 30, 31, 36, 49, 54, 56, 57, 162, 207; Dome of the Rock inscription and, xv, 209–10; existence of, 4; Gospels and, 4; historical scrutiny and, 4–5; Jews and, 20–21, 25; keys of paradise and, 22; as messenger of God, xv, 209; as Messiah, xv, 167, 179; Muawiya's letter to Constantine and, xiv, 34; as the

Muhammad, 41–62; Muhammad, coming of and, 38, 54; nature of, 56, 179–80; in Qur'an, 36, 38–39, 45, 167; Qur'an and, 21; Resurrection of, 5; as Son of God, 37, 47, 55, 179–81; as "the praised one," 45, 46; Virgin Birth of, 5, 167, 184; as Word of God, 38. *See also* Christology
jihad, 46, 61, 100, 128–29, 135, 204
*jizya* (poll tax), 27–28, 158–59
Job, 115
John, 115
John I of Antioch, 30
John of Damascus, xv, 36–39, 196
John of Nikiou, xv, 36–37
Jonah, 115
Jordan, 46, 60
Joseph, 115, 151
*Journal of the American Oriental Society*, 54
Judaism, 22, 31, 35, 216; Christ, coming of and, 20–21; development of, 128; dhimmitude and, 158–59; Dome of the Rock inscription and, 55; historical scrutiny and, 3–5, 9; Islam, development of and, 12–13; Islamic tradition and, 96; of Medina, 64; monotheism of, 182, 207; Muhammad, alliance with of, 33; Muhammad bewitched and, 122; Muhammad kinship with, 31, 49, 118, 209, 212; Muslim antagonism toward, 33–34; Palestine, Arabian conquest of and, xiv; Qur'an and, 122, 145; Reform, 5; salvation and, 152

Ka'ba, 34, 37, 101, 106, 204
Kalisch, Muhammad Sven, 14

Khadija (wife of Muhammad), xvi, xvii, 99, 147
Khan, Muhammad Muhsin, 79
Khan, Muqtedar, 67
Kharrar, raid on, 92, 94
Khudri, Abu Said al-, 65
Khuzaima, 137, 188
Kinana bin ar-Rabi, 90
Kindi, al-, 182, 200
King Fahd Complex for the Printing of the Holy Qur'an, 194
Koran. *See* Qur'an
Koren, Judith, 9

Lammens, Henri, 9, 11
Last Supper, 170–75
Leo III the Isaurian, 199
Leo XIII, Pope, 5
Lewis, Bernard, 12
libertinism, 113
*Life of Mahomet and History of Islam to the Era of Hegira, A* (Muir), 10
*Lisan al-Arab (The Language of the Arabs)*, 185
literalism, 5
Lot, 115
Lüling, Günter, 9, 13–14, 166, 172–73, 177, 179, 180–82
Luxenberg, Christoph, 9, 14, 54, 55, 155, 165–70, 173–75, 183, 184

Macbeth, King of Scotland, 7, 214
Mahdi, al-, 71
Mahdi, Muhammad ibn Mansur al-, 78
*Mahgrayé*, 36
Mahmet, 31–32, 34
Makhul, 70
Malik ibn Anas, xv, 59, 71, 82, 88, 198–99

Mamun, al-, 164

Mansur, al-, 71

Margoliouth, David S., 9, 89, 90

marriage, 109–17, 140–41

martyrdom, 14, 120, 168, 211

Marwan ibn Abi Hafsa, 78

Marwan ibn al-Hakam, 189

Mary (mother of Jesus), xv, 18, 45, 51,
    115, 156, 167

Matthew, Gospel of, 22, 97

Maududi, Syed Abul Ala, 127

Mecca, 13, 30, 33, 34, 48, 72, 94, 101,
    102, 103, 104–5

*Meccan Trade and the Rise of Islam*
    (Crone), 13

Medina, 48, 64, 65, 71, 73, 76, 93, 95,
    99, 101, 102, 106, 120, 147, 204

Messenger of God, 17–18

Messiah, xv, 18, 20, 21, 36, 45, 51, 167,
    179

Methodists, 5

*Mhmt*, 23

Middle East, 6, 13, 63, 195

Mingana, Alphonse, 9, 155–56

miracles, 4, 94–95

*Mohammed der prophet, sein Leben
    und sein Lehre* (*Muhammad the
    Prophet, His Life and His Teach-
    ing*) (Weil), 9

monotheism, 47, 207; Abrahamic,
    209; Arab, ix, 34, 57; Muawiya
    and, 33–34, 49, 57; Muhammad
    and, 102, 106, 203

Monothelitism, 56

Moses, 17, 31, 34, 49, 54, 61, 115

Mother of the Book (*umm al-kitab*),
    126

Motzki, Harald, 83

Muawiya, 206; Battle of Siffin and,
    189–92; caliphate of, xiv, xvii, 41;

coinage and inscriptions and, xiv,
    41–42, 46, 47–48, 49, 50; Con-
    stantine, letter to of, xiv, 33–34,
    207; factionalism and Hadith and,
    72–73; monotheism and, 49, 57;
    Qur'an, standardization of and,
    85–86

Mufid, Sheikh al-, 81

Mughira, al-, 73

Muhajirun, 33, 36, 59, 92, 195, 205

Muhammad, 46–47; absence of men-
    tion of, 17–39, 41, 42, 49, 63, 205;
    Arabian conquest and, 2, 7, 24–28,
    41, 48, 191; as Arab prophet, 100–
    106; archaeological evidence of, ix;
    authority of, xv, 35, 210; canonical
    account of, ix, 6–7, 22, 109, 205–7,
    212–13; coinage and inscriptions
    and, xiv, xv, 42–46, 46–47, 52–53;
    death of, xiii, 2, 21, 22, 205; *Doc-
    trina Jacobi* and, 22–23; embar-
    rassment of, 107–24; example of,
    6, 67–72; existence of, ix–xi, 1–3,
    6–8, 214–17; family of, xvi, xvii;
    first mention of, 206; forgetfulness
    of, 131–34, 212; Hadith and, xi, xv,
    10, 11, 19, 68–72; Hijra of, 48–49,
    73, 92, 93, 147, 204, 222; historical
    impact of, 1–2, 7; historical scru-
    tiny and, 6–8; historicity of, ix–xi,
    1–3, 9–10, 109–14; Ibn Ishaq's
    biography of, ix, xv, 19, 46, 87–106;
    inventing, 63–86; Islam, founding
    of and, ix, 2, 6; Islamic law and,
    67, 68, 71, 88; Islamic practice and,
    68, 70; Islamic theology and, 67;
    Islamic tradition and, ix, 10, 67,
    117; legend and, 2, 6–8, 19, 210–11;
    magic and, 121–23; as Messenger
    of God, xv, 18–19, 21, 52–53, 56,

58, 98, 114, 213; monotheism and, 102, 106, 203; non-Arabic sources of information on, 146–47; non-Muslim sources of information about, 31–34, 41; personality of, 6, 90–91, 123–24; political theology of, 208–9; polygamy of, xvi, 109–17; revelations of Qur'an to, xiii, 3, 18, 125, 127, 128–30, 131–34, 157; satanic verses and, 89–90; as Seal of the Prophets, 18, 114–17, 212; as teacher, 6; Zaynab, marriage to and, 109–19

"Muhammad and the Origins of Islam" (Renan), 1

*Muhammad at Mecca* (Watt), 2, 99

*Muhammad at Medina* (Watt), 2, 99

Muir, William, 10, 126–27

Muslim ibn al-Hajjaj al-Qushayri, 77

Muslims: absence of mention of, 30, 31, 33, 205; Arabian conquest and, 205; in Europe, xv; first mention of, xv, 35–36; historical scrutiny and, 3; Jews and, 33–34; Muhammad and, ix, 6; paganism and, 29; Quraysh and, 102–3; Spain, conquest of by, xv; Treaty of Hudaibiya and, 75; Wars of Apostasy (632–633) and, 28

*Muwatta*, 71, 82

Nativity, 183–85

Nestorian synod, 28, 29

Nevo, Yehuda, 9

Newman, John Henry Cardinal, 145

New Testament, 4, 9, 37, 45, 54, 145, 166

Night of Power, *al-Qadr*, 183–84

Nixon, Richard, ix, xi

Noah, 115, 156

Nöldeke, Theodor, 9, 150–51

non-Muslims: dhimmitude and, 27–28; Muhammad, existence of and, 6; as source of information about Muhammad, 31–34, 41

North Africa, xiv, 6, 63, 195, 196, 204

obedience, 18, 69–70, 204

Old Testament, 37, 166

*100: A Ranking of the Most Influential Persons in History, The* (Hart), 1

*On the Heresies* (John of Damascus), 36

Ottoman Empire, 216

Pact of Umar, 27–28

paganism, 158; animal sacrifice and, 29, 30; Arab, ix, 28–30, 182; Greco-Roman, 207; Islam and, ix; Muslims and, 29

Palestine, xiii, xiv, 21, 46, 47–48

Paradise, 14, 21, 22, 108, 126, 148, 168–70, 183

Paret, Rudi, 171

party of Ali, 73

People of the Book, 51, 55, 140, 158, 159, 213. *See also* Christianity; Judaism

Persia, xiv, 6

Persian Empire, 20, 210

Persians, xiv, 20, 34, 207

Peshitta, 182

Peter, St., 22, 183

Pharaoh, 17, 54, 155

Pickthall, Muhammad Marmaduke, 143, 151, 154, 161

pilgrimage, 30, 72, 86, 94, 101–6, 206

Pipes, Daniel, 17

Pius XII, Pope, 5

*Poem of El Cid, The*, 7

political theology, 207–9
poll tax (*jizya*), 27–28, 158–59
polygamy, 29, 109–14, 114–17
polytheism, 28, 203
Pontifical Biblical Commission, 5
Popp, Volker, 9, 14, 45, 47
Powers, David S., 9, 14, 115
Presbyterians, 5
Procopius of Caesarea, 104
*Prolegomena zur Geschichte Israels*
    (*Prolegomena to the History of
    Israel*) (Wellhausen), 4
Protestantism, 5
*Providentissimus Deus* (Leo XIII), 5
Psalms, 152, 172
Pseudo-Clementine Homilies, 179
Puin, Gerd-R., 149, 165

Qadiani Ahmadis, 18
Qasri, Khalid al-, 76
Qasr Kharana inscription, 60–61
Qastallani, al-, 67
Qatada ibn Diama, 196, 197
Qur'an: absence of mention of, 30,
    31, 34, 41, 42, 63, 195–97, 205;
    Allah and, 17, 125; alterations to,
    128–30; Arabian conquest and,
    41, 48; Arabic character of, xi,
    143–60, 162–66, 171, 185, 210;
    authorship of, 125–27; Battle
    of Siffin and, 189–92; Battle of
    Yamama and, xiii; burning of
    variants of, xiv, xv, 193, 201;
    Christian tradition and, 3, 13–14,
    149, 166–67, 170–81, 183–85, 195;
    Christmas in, 183–85; Christol-
    ogy of, 179–81; collection of, xiii,
    xiv, xv, 126, 134–38, 185, 187–201,
    206; cross in, 25; cultural vocabu-
    lary of, 157–60; dating of, 192–93;
    diacritical marks and, xv, 162–66,
    167, 170, 185; distribution of, xiv,
    xv, 185, 201, 205; Dome of the
    Rock inscription and, xv, 50–57,
    197, 200–201; evolution of, 128;
    first mention of, 195–97; Hadith
    and, 63–66, 69, 80–81; Hafs tradi-
    tion of, 194–95; Islam and, 12,
    78–79; Jesus and, 21, 36, 38–39,
    45, 167; Jewish tradition and, 3;
    Jews in, 33, 122; Judaism and,
    145; lack of clarity in, 14, 149–51,
    152–55; Last Supper in, 170–75;
    Muhammad, example of and,
    67; Muhammad, forgetfulness of
    and, 131–34, 212; Muhammad,
    historicity of and, x–xi; Muham-
    mad and, 13, 45, 125–27, 210;
    non-Arabic sources of, 146–47,
    148–49; nonce words in, 152–55;
    occasions of revelation and,
    64–66; origins of, 161–62, 187,
    195; political theology of, 208–9;
    revelations to Muhammad of, xiii,
    3, 18, 125, 127, 128–30, 131–34,
    157; signs of alteration of, 138–42;
    as source of information about
    Muhammad, ix–x, 17–19; stan-
    dardization of, xiv, xv, 85, 126,
    188, 193, 201, 206; Syriac substra-
    tum and, 14, 155–57, 173, 174, 182,
    183, 195, 211; text of the Camel
    of God in, 37, 39, 196; text of the
    Cow in, 38, 39, 196–97; text of the
    Table in, 37; text of the Woman
    in, 39, 196; variants of, xiv, xv,
    125–42, 192–93, 194–95, 201;
    Warsh tradition of, 194; Zaynab,
    Muhammad's marriage to and,
    114. *See also* Hadith; Islam

Quraysh, 65, 71, 75, 86, 89, 93–94, 96, 97, 101–3, 104, 105–6, 188, 203–4
Qurtubi, al-, 154

Reform Judaism, 5
Renan, Ernest, 1, 3, 4, 9, 19
Resurrection, 5
Rhodes, xiv
Robin Hood, 8, 214
Romans, 23, 207
Rosenthal, Franz, 154
Ruqayya (daughter of Muhammad), xvi, xvii
Russell, Bertrand, ix

Sabians, 152
Said ibn al-As, 188
Salman the Persian, 146, 199
salvation, 152, 209
Samir, Samir Khalil, 174
Saracens, 20, 21, 24, 25, 26, 33, 36, 59, 195, 205
Satan, 54, 89–90, 113, 120, 148
Savians, 152
Schacht, Joseph, 9, 11–12, 82
Schoeler, Gregor, 94
Scott, Sir Walter, 7–8
Seal of the Prophets, 18, 114, 115, 177, 121
Sebeos, Armenian bishop, xiv, 31–32
September 11, 168
Shafii, ash-, 12, 82, 89, 155
shahada (Islamic confession of faith), xv, 19, 51, 52, 58
Shakespeare, William, 7
Shiite Islam, xvii, 65, 73, 116, 211
Sira, 19, 98
Sirat Rasul Allah (Biography of the Messenger of Allah) (Ibn Ishaq), 87

skepticism, 4, 5
Solomon, 115, 148, 155
Song of Roland, The, 7
Sophronius, 24–28
Spain, xv, 6
Sprenger, Aloys, 9, 10, 166
Strange Matters of Hadith (Gharib al-Hadith) (Abu Ubaida), 172
Strauss, David Friedrich, 4
Sunni Islam, xvii, 116
Surat Al-Ahzab, 188
Surat Al-Furqan, 132–33
Suyuti, as-, 59
Syria, ix, xiii, 196, 204
Syriac, 14, 23, 146, 155–57, 165, 166, 173, 174, 182, 183, 195, 206

Tabari, Muhammad ibn Jarir at-, 27–28, 87, 91, 152, 153, 154, 191
Tafsir al-Jalalayn, 109, 161
Taiyaye, 23, 33, 209
Targum of Esther, 148–49
tayyaye d-Mhmt, xiii, 23
Temple Mount, 33, 50
Theophanes the Confessor, 119, 120
Thomas, Christian priest, xiii, 23, 209
Tirmidhi, Abu Isa Muhammad At-, 78
Tisdall, W. St. Clair, 148
Torah, 4, 54, 158, 196
Treaty of Hudaibiya, 75, 93–94, 103
Truth about Muhammad, The (Spencer), 6–7

Umar, 73, 74, 76, 129; caliphate of, xvii, 69; Jerusalem, conquest of and, 26–27; Qur'an, collection of and, 134, 135, 187; Qur'anic revelations and, 132–33
Umar II, 199

Umayyads, 41, 47, 58, 60, 62, 198, 210;
    demonizing of, 211–12; Hadith,
    fabrication of and, 211; Hadith
    and, 73–74, 76, 86; impiety of, 85,
    206, 211; Muhammad and, 215;
    Qur'an and, 215
Umm Ayman, 198
unbelievers, 17, 94–95, 100, 103, 125,
    145, 147, 260
Usama bin Zayd bin Muhammad,
    116, 117–19
Uthman, 69, 73, 74, 195, 196; Ar-
    Ridwan pledge of allegiance and,
    75; caliphate of, xiv, xvii; death
    of, 83; factionalism and Hadith
    and, 73–76; fleeing from battle
    of, 74–75; Muhammad, family of
    and, xvi, xvii; Qur'an, burning of
    variants of by, xiv, 193; Qur'an,
    collection of and, xiv, 126, 134,
    135, 185, 187–88, 189, 193, 201,
    206; Qur'an, distribution of by,
    xiv, 185; Qur'an, standardization
    of and, xiv, 192
Urwa ibn Az-Zubair ibn al-Awwam,
    91, 93
Uzza, al-, 182

Vie de Jésus (The Life of Jesus)
    (Renan), 4
Virgin Birth, 5, 167
virgins of Paradise, 168–70

Wahidi, al-, 65–66
Walid I, 60, 76
Walid II, 76
Wansbrough, John, 9, 12, 13
Waqidi, al-, 92, 94, 99, 119–21, 130
Waraqa bin Naufal, 147
warfare, 211
War of Austrian Succession, 191
Wars of Apostasy (632–633), xiii, 28
Watt, W. Montgomery, 2, 98–99,
    103–4, 105
Weil, Gustav, 9
Wellhausen, Julius, 4, 9, 10
Whelan, Estelle, 50, 54
Wittgenstein, Ludwig, ix

Yazid I, xiv, 50

Zachariah, 115, 156
Zayd bin Haritha, 109, 116, 198; death
    of, 119–21; as historical figure,
    117–19
Zayd bin Muhammad (adopted son
    of Muhammad). See Zayd bin
    Haritha
Zayd ibn Thabit, 128–29, 136–37, 187,
    188, 195, 196
Zaynab bint Jahsh (wife of Muham-
    mad), 109–19
Zoroastrians, 207
Zuhri, Muhammad ibn Shihab az-,
    71, 72